The Hidden Wealth of Cities:
Policy and Productivity Methods
for American Local Governments

CONTEMPORARY STUDIES IN SOCIOLOGY, VOLUME 8

Editor: Thomas Hood, Department of Sociology, University of Tennessee

CONTEMPORARY STUDIES IN SOCIOLOGY
Theoretical and Empirical Monographs

Editor: **Thomas C. Hood**
Department of Sociology, University of Tennessee

For Robert Cary Hayes
The best there is

The Hidden Wealth of Cities:
Policy and Productivity Methods
for American Local Governments

Edited by: EDWARD C. HAYES
Metro Associates
San Diego

 JAI PRESS INC.

Greenwich, Connecticut   *London, England*

The Hidden wealth of cities : policy and productivity methods for
   American local governments / edited by Edward C. Hayes, II.
      p.   cm. — (Contemporary studies in sociology : v. 8)
   Bibliography: p.
   Includes index.
   ISBN 0-89232-989-0
   1. Municipal finance—United States.   2. Federal-city relations—
United States.   3. Intergovernmental fiscal relations—United
States.   4. Local government—United States—Labor productivity.
I. Hayes, Edward C. (Edward Cary), 1937–   .   II. Series.
HJ9145.H47   1989
336'.01473—dc20

Copyright © 1989 JAI PRESS INC.
55 Old Post Road – No. 2
Greenwich, Connecticut 06836

JAI PRESS LTD.
3 Henrietta Street
London WC2E 8LU
England

ISBN: 0-89232-989-0
Library of Congress Catalog Card Number: 89-11019
Manufactured in the United States of America

CONTENTS

LIST OF CONTRIBUTORS

Alan Beals

Executive Director
National League of Cities
Washington, D.C.

Russell C. Brannen

National Director
State and Municipal Programs
American Society of Value Engineers
(SAVE)
Northbrook (Chicago), Illinois

Paul D. Epstein

Principal
Epstein and Fass
New York City

Suzanne Fass

Principal
Epstein and Fass
New York City

Philip E. Fixler, Jr.

Director
Local Government Center
Santa Monica, CA

Ted A. Gaebler

President
The Gaebler Group
San Rafael, CA

Edward C. Hayes

President
Metro Associates
San Diego, CA

Roger L. Kemp

City Manager
Clifton, New Jersey

Thomas W. Wenz

County Administrator
Hamilton County
Cincinnati, Ohio

PREFACE

When the wood slat and canvas machine flew at Kitty Hawk in December 1903 the Wright brothers were both elated and confident. With this success they knew, with certainty, something that even the skeptics now had to consider: having gone 100 feet in the air, man-made machines could go far, far beyond. Orville lived to work on planes that could fly inter-city mail; to help develop the automatic pilot; and to co-found the company whose engine powered Lindbergh nonstop across the Atlantic.

It is now 1989 and cities are debating how and whether to get along with less federal aid. In the midst of this debate the fact stands out that, like the short burst at Kitty Hawk, our cities have already flown: they have taken deep cuts, both in the loss of whole federal grants programs and in the erosion of buying power of programs that remain, *and they are in better fiscal health and are providing roughly as many services as ever in their history.*

Therefore, the question must now be entertained, by even the staunchest skeptic: Is it possible for cities to go a long, long way beyond, finding methods to meet their service responsibilities with less and less help from the federal sovereign?

Every bold idea seems foolish at its inception. And the boldest idea to occur to observers of federalism in this last decade of the twentieth century, is the idea that cities not only can live with less federal money, but can finally, by fully addressing the question of *productivity*, reverse the flow of dollars from Washington, and begin helping in the reduction of an enormous standing federal deficit. In the twenty-first century, the cities could become the life support of the federal government if they would first find ways to finance themselves.

That is, admittedly, a wild and foolish hope to pin on twelve letters of the English alphabet, whether those letters spell productivity or anything else. Yet is it any wilder than what we have already seen? Is it any more unlikely than the fact that Americans, who began this century in the horse and cart, are now riding in turbocharged steel beauties, all in the lifetime of one person? Productivity—the advance of technology and production methods—is a golden key. It has opened the door in the private economy to wealth and to new ways of thinking and living which have far surpassed any generation's ability to predict. Fully accepted and applied, it can transform the structure and functioning of government.

It is one thing to recognize productivity in industry and the march of progress in space, and quite another thing to believe that the federal government shall someday receive aid from the cities. But this is 1989. In 1903, it was insane to believe that man could raise himself ten feet off the ground with a motorized vehicle, yet some of the skeptics of that year lived to fly at close to the speed of sound, and to see an American flag placed by human hands in the dust of the moon itself.

Welcome to this book, an extended examination of a foolish idea. The cities are already off the ground. What we are looking for now is a pathway to the stars.

Edward C. Hayes
Editor

PART I

FEDERAL AID: HOW MUCH IS NECESSARY?

Chapter 1

FEDERAL GRANTS IN AID: AN OUTLINE HISTORY

Edward C. Hayes

SUMMARY. Federal grants to state and local government began to grow just after passage of the Sixteenth Amendment, legalizing federal income tax, in 1913. They grew to $1 billion once during the New Deal, and in the post-World War II period became institutionalized. Grants to state and local government soared from $6.8 billion in 1949 to $80 billion in 1979, the period of "The Three Decades" that gave the federal grants budget its present broad configuration. Yet since President Carter's reforms in 1979, federal grants have been in steady decline as a percent of state and local revenue; and in real dollars, grants have dropped over 30% since 1980, making the present period a "post grants era."

THE RISE OF GRANTS IN AID

The history of significant federal grants to state and local governments begins, not with Lyndon Johnson's War on Poverty, but with the passage of the Sixteenth Amendment to the United States Constitution, which allowed the federal government to levy a small amount against the incomes of the wealthiest ten percent of the population.[1] This gave the federal government access to a large new source of revenue; as a result federal aid to states and localities increased a thousand fold between 1914 and 1917. From 1929 to 1939, a period which included Franklin Roosevelt's New Deal, federal grants increased another ten fold (see Table 1).

Table 1. Federal Grants to State and Local Governments, 1929–1985
(in billions of dollars)

Year	Total Federal Aid	Federal Aid as Percentage of State and Local Revenue	Federal Aid as Percentage of GNP	Federal Aid as Percentage of Local Government Revenue
1929	0.1	1.3	0.1	0.9
1939	1.0	12.5	1.1	6.5
1949	2.2	12.7	0.9	3.9
1954	2.9	11.1	0.8	3.2
1959	6.8	17.1	1.4	5.3
1964	10.4	17.5	1.6	6.0
1969	20.3	20.3	2.2	6.8
1974	43.9	26.2	3.1	9.6
1978	77.3	30.8	3.6	11.3
1980	88.7	29.8	3.4	10.6
1981	87.9	26.4	3.0	9.2
1982	83.9	23.4	2.7	8.6
1983	86.3	22.0	2.6	8.4
1984	92.9	21.5	2.5	8.2
1985	99.3	21.3	2.6	na

Sources: U.S. Advisory Commission on Intergovernmental Relations (ACIR), *Significant Features of Fiscal Federalism 1984* (Washington, D.C., ACIR 1985), p. 12, Table 3; and author's computations. For 1985 estimates: ACIR, *Significant Features of Fiscal Federalism 1985–1986* (Washington, D.C.: ACIR, February 1986), p. 10, Table 3.

Whereas the $1 billion in aid during 1939 (the high water mark for aid during the New Deal) seems miniscule by present day standards it was actually many times that amount in current dollars, and represented a percent of local government revenues not again equalled until the late 1960s (see Figure 1, last column).

From 1965 to the end of the 1970s the United States entered an era of federal grants to state and local government that was unique in several ways. In terms of total dollars sent out from Washington it exceeded every previous period; moreover, this money was being focused on the problems of the poor at a time when there was no national depression. And it was unique, especially in the 1960s, in its rhetoric and optimism. Public officials talked easily about *solving* poverty and creating a "Marshall Plan for the Cities."

The rhetoric was matched by dollars. Between 1965, the start of Lyndon Johnson's "War on Poverty," and 1980, when grants first declined as a percent of state-local revenue, federal grants to state and local government equalled no less than 679.3 in adjusted 1988 dollars, an amount more than one-quarter the total standing federal debt in 1988

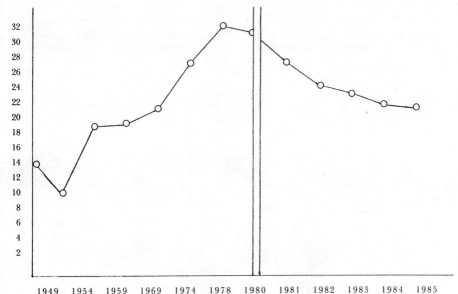

Figure 1.   Federal Grants as a Percentage of
Pre-Grant Combined State and Local Revenues

Sources: U.S. Advisory Commission on Intergovernmental Relations (ACIR), *Significant Features of Fiscal Federalism 1985–1986* (Washington, D.C.: ACIR, 1986), p. 10, Table 3; and author's computations.

($2.67 trillion), and 48 times greater than the real Marshall Plan for Europe, which cost Americans a relatively modest $13 billion over its lifetime.[2]

The last column in Figure 1 gives a clear picture of the growth history of aid. Using the twenty years 1949–1969 as the base period, federal grants almost doubled *as a percent of local government revenue.* But it only took 10 years, half as long as the base period, for grants to almost double again by 1978, while population in America in the same period grew by only 10.8%.[3] Had grants continued to grow at the same rate in the decade 1978–1988, the United States would have been spending $144 billion in 1988, roughly $36 billion more than the current projection.[4]

The importance of "The Three Decades" is shown in Table 2. While the biggest decennial jump (after 1914–1917) occurred during the New Deal, the third greatest jump occurred in the decade 1949–1959, the first of "The Three Decades" of postwar grants growth, and several years before the War on Poverty. If we look at 5-year changes in federal aid, the largest jump in aid between 1949 and 1984 occurred in the period 1960–1964, just prior to the Great Society programs.[5]

Table 2. Decennial Growth in Federal Grants to State and Local Governments: Dollar Amount and Percentage of GNP, 1929–1984

Aid as Percentage of GNP (percentage increase)	Years	Aid in Unadjusted Dollars (percentage increase)
110	1929–1939	1000
(18)	1939–1949	120
55	1949–1959	300
275	1959–1969	298
154	1969–1979	436
(23)	1979–1984	(18)

Sources: Author's computations based on U.S. Advisory Commission on Intergovernmental Relations (ACIR), *Significant Features of Fiscal Federalism 1984* (Washington, D.C., 1985), p. 12, Table 3; and U.S. Bureau of the Census, *Governmental Finances in 1983–84* (Washington, D.C.: U.S. Bureau of the Census, October 1985), p. 4, Table 3.

A TYPOLOGY OF FEDERAL GRANTS

The explosive growth of grants after World War II has led to hundreds of grants programs. Yet all of them can be grouped under three basic headings.

Entitlements

"Entitlements" are income transfer payments from government to low-income individuals who presumably are entitled to them. These programs include Aid to Families with Dependent Children (AFDC), Medicaid, and Food Stamps. AFDC is the basic "local" welfare program in America. In 1982 the Reagan administration agreed to pay half the total costs, including half the costs of state program administration.[6]

In those states which have a cost-of-living adjustment for welfare programs, the amount of money pushed out to the states and counties from Washington has risen sharply in the past five years, giving the appearance, when aid is increasing, of a great deal of money going to states and local governments; and when aid is contracting, of a great deal being taken away. Allowance levels are generous. A family of ten with an income of $25,000 can qualify for AFDC in states with Cost of Living Allowances (COLAs).[7] Yet in fact these *entitlement programs constitute an administrative and financial drain on state and local governments.* The federal money goes to the poor, but half the costs of administering the programs must be born by the state and local levels. Local governments do not generally consider foodstamps, senior centers, or child health care grants as "their" programs; they were added to their agenda by fiat from Washington. Yet state and local governments pick up half the cost of administration. "Losing" all of these programs would mean, in fact, a net financial gain for local administrators.

Operating Grants

Operating grants are used to run ongoing local programs. Law Enforcement Assistance Administration (LEAA) money has been used extensively by police departments to pay salaries and other operating expenses. Other operating grants go to run bus systems, pay school teachers, hire neighborhood organizers and "advocates" and train the unemployed. General Revenue Sharing (GRS), discontinued in 1987, was used any way the local government desired, including but not limited to operations. Operating grants go to the heart of basic city administration, and have been the chief source of urban "dependency" on federal grants. This is discussed at length in Chapter 2.

Capital Grants

Capital grants go for construction of capital facilities: water and wastewater plants, sewers, heavy equipment (including buses), and roads. Urban Development Action Grants (UDAGs), authorized but unfunded in 1989, paid part of the cost of private commercial developments. In capital grants, cities and states have grown heavily dependent on federal assistance over the past twenty-five years.

Exactly what are the titles of these grants and block grants? Table 3 shows a typology, with program titles as they appeared after the Reagan administration consolidated over fifty individual programs into seven new block grants. The CETA programs listed have been retitled as Job Training Partnership Act (JTPA), and focus on placement with the private for-profit sector. Both California and Massachusetts have new programs, using some JTPA funds, which puts *all* AFDC recipients into job prep and training.

How much grant money to states becomes a "pass through" to cities? The Advisory Commission on Intergovernmental Relations (ACIR) estimated in 1977 that 40% of "state" money was passed through, including 14% of grants for highways and 66% of grants for criminal justice.[8]

Table 3. A Typology of Federal Grants to State and
Local Government, 1982 (in millions of dollars)*

		Budget Authority	
Program	Type	1982	1988 (est.)
Grants to states for programs administered primarily by states			
Medicaid	Entitlement	17,624	26,864
Food stamps	Entitlement	10,280	NL
Federal aid to highways	Capital	8,279	12,533
Aid to Families with Dependent Children (AFDC)	Entitlement	5,461	9,776
Social services block grant	Operating	2,400	2,697
State employment service	Operating	757	843
Maternal and child health care block grant	Entitlement	374	1,684[a]
Trade adjustment assistance	Entitlement	306	[b]
Preventive health block grant	Operating	82	63
Youth conservation corps	Operating	0	0
Highway safety	Capital, Operating	−73	128
Grants to states primarily distributed to local governments and nonprofit agencies			
Child nutrition	Entitlement	2,847	3,895
Low-income energy assistance block grant	Operating	1,875	[b]
Education block grant	Operating	470	576
Alcohol, drug abuse, and mental health block grant	Operating	432	[b]
Community services block grant	Operating	348	328
Primary care block grant	Operating	248	[b]
Special milk	Operating	28	2
Grant to states and local governments and nonprofit agencies			
Community development block grant	Capital, operating	3,456	3,047
Compensatory education	Operating	2,914	3,946
CETA (JPTA) job training	Operating	3,037	3,209[c]
Economic development	Capital, operating	199	163
Energy conservation	Capital, operating	145	58
CETA public-service employment (Title VI)	Operating	0	0[d]
Grants to local governments or nonprofit agencies			
Assisted housing	Capital, operating	16,367	7,143
Mass transit	Capital, operating	3,495	2,692

(continued)

Table 3.   (Continued)

Program	Type	Budget Authority 1982	Budget Authority 1988 (est.)
Wastewater treatment	Capital	2,400	2,320
Public housing operating subsidy	Operating	1,490	4,489
Urban development action grant	Capital	440	0e
Education impact aid	Operating	437	576
General revenue sharing	Operating	2,475	0d
Housing rehabilitation loan fund	Capital	0	0

*Purely regional grants, grants for military construction, and agricultural grants not included in this Table.
aIncludes Women, Infants, and Children's programs.
bDisbursed among other grants.
cIn 1988, called the Job Partnership Training Act (JPTA).
dAbolished by Reagan.
eStill authorized, but at zero current funding in 1989.
Sources: Office of Management and Budget (OMB), *The Budget of the United States Fiscal Year 1988, Special Analyses* (Washington, D.C.: U.S. Government Printing Office, 1987), Table H–11; and John William Ellwood, ed., *Reductions in U.S. Domestic Spending* (New Brunswick, N.J.: Transaction Books, 1982), Part Two.

A CLOSER LOOK: GRANTS FOR STATE AND LOCAL CAPITAL PROJECTS

Capital grants during The Three Decades grew at a substantially greater rate than grants for program operations. In 1952 state and local governments financed 92% of their capital projects through own-source revenues and 8% through federal grants. By 1980 these percentages had changed to 60% own-source and 40% federal grants,[9] with the fed then paying 100% of the costs of local sewer treatment plants. As of the mid 1980s federal grants pay for 75% of sewer treatment plants, 25% of all state and local roads and 7% of state and local hospital and school construction. Capital grants are the most dramatic illustration of where the grants program can lead.

GRANTS TO MUNICIPALITIES AND FEDERAL BUDGET "SHARES"

Table 4 shows how grants specifically to cities have grown. The bigger the city the larger its increase in aid between 1960 and 1980. Cities over 1 million enjoyed an increase of just over 29 times in this period, where-

Table 4.   Per Capita Federal Aid*
to Municipalities by Population Size, 1960–1984

City Size	1960	1965	1970	1975	1980
Over 1 million	4.93	5.09	17.77	70.34	144.45
500,000–999,000	8.81	14.64	30.42	100.82	192.06
300,000–499,999	7.56	5.31	13.37	64.68	131.45
200,000–299,999	5.24	3.78	13.18	60.96	101.74
100,000–199,999	5.39	4.37	11.09	42.93	79.45
50,000–99,000	2.56	3.76	7.11	33.49	53.14
under 50,000	3.99	2.84	3.04	21.84	34.66
All Cities	3.90	4.79	10.13	43.06	77.13

Note: *Federal aid per capita is total intergovernmental aid minus State intergovernmental aid.
Source: U.S. Bureau of the Census, *City Government Finance* (various years), as reported in *President's National Urban Policy Report 1984* (Washington, D.C.: HUD, 1984).

as cities under 50,000 had an increase of only 8.7 times. Total grants to cities of all sizes increased 19.7 times, far in excess of the growth of the total federal budget during the same period of time.

The Shift In Federal Budget Shares

This rapid increase in grants was paralleled by a similar rapid growth in Social Security. Together these two items have had a pronounced effect on the shape of the federal budget. Between 1959 and 1974, federal grants rose significantly from 7.5 to 10.6% of the total budget, while Social Security rose astronomically from 11.2 to 27.8% of the total budget, the most rapid increase in budget share of any item since the expansion of military procurement during World War II. Something had to give, and it was defense, a category that dropped from 50.1% to 25.2% over the same period. Table 5 gives these shifts in per-capita terms.

WHY DID AID GROW?
FOUR REASONS OUT OF MANY

The first reason for the growth of aid-plus-Social Security is the ratchet of incremental budgeting.[10] Once a spending program begins it creates a constituency; the next year, the "smart" political thing to do is to add to it a little. With all grants programs during the Three Decades, "a little" increasingly came to mean billions of dollars. Food stamps offer an example. This program began with less than $25 million in the 1960s; by

Table 5.   Federal Expenditures, Per Capita, for Defense,
Social Security, and Grants, 1959–1985
(in millions of dollars)

Year	Defense	Social Security (OASDI)	Aid to State and Local Government
1959	397	85	57
1985	448	477	180
Percentage increase 1959–1985	18	461	215

Sources: Department of Commerce, Bureau of Economic Analysis, *National Income and Product Accounts [NIPA], 1929–1976*; and *Survey of Current Business* (July 1984 and October 1985) as reprinted in U.S. Advisory Commission on Intergovernmental Relations (ACIR), *Significant Features of Fiscal Federalism 1985–86* (Washington, D.C.: ACIR, 1985), p. 17, Table 6.

1984 it had grown to $12 *billion*.[11] The growth in Social Security has been alluded to. It is the mushrooming of originally-small programs in all kinds of federal grants that has led the Office of Management and Budget and some think-tanks to call for the total elimination, as opposed to the simple reduction, of federal programs, and the call to put them into the private sector.[12]

A second factor was the Great Society, not so much because of the actual amounts of money which it initially required, but because of its great expansion of the scope of federal projects.Before 1965 federal aid had been concentrated in federal highway, agriculture, and unemployment insurance programs. But with the War on Poverty the variety and sheer numbers of funded programs expanded in a most magical way, going from some 100 programs to over 500 between 1960 and 1970, a phenomenon unique in the nation's history. This variety of programs, and Congress' habit of incremental budgeting, guaranteed significant increases in non-military expenditures.

A third factor in the growth of grants was the redefinition of citizens' economic "rights." Transfer payments—social security, welfare, housing rent supplements—were henceforth to be known as "entitlements," money to which the low-income were entitled by right of citizenship and economic status.[13] In addition, Congress borrowed the idea of cost-of-living allowances from the private sector, where COLAs had been used in United Auto Workers (UAW) contracts since the 1950s, and wrote COLAs into welfare and Social Security programs. Congress has steadily refused to repeal this "indexation of benefits" despite steady cries from a minority of its own members.[14]

The fourth and final factor has been the rapid increase in the numbers of retired and poor people participating in welfare and entitlement programs. Allan Schick points out that there are now five million more people participating in Social Security than ten years ago, adding an additional $30 billion to that program's cost. AFDC rolls in California grew a phenomenal 67% between 1970 and 1985, while the California population grew at a rate of just 27%.[15]

This fourth factor itself requires some explanation. Why should welfare rolls suddenly mushroom? In large part it has been due to a new public attitude toward poverty, one which tends to blame society, not the individual, for poverty. And as part creature and part creator of that attitude is the new welfare worker. The political radicalism of the 1960s brought a new kind of welfare worker into the bureaucracy, one who wanted more relaxed eligibility rules and who positively searched out those who were eligible for assistance. The stigma of welfare disappeared.

COMING DOWN OFF THE WAVE: CARTER AND REAGAN

It was the Carter administration that first put the brakes on grants. Viewing grants as a percentage of combined pre-grant *state and local* revenues, grants peaked at 30.8% in 1978, dropped to 29.8% in 1980, then rose to 21.3% in 1985 as shown in Figure 1. Viewing grants as a percentage of the *federal* budget, grants also peaked in 1978 at 16.8%, and then dropped steadily to 10.3% in 1985.[16]

Cuts in aid will continue through 1988, the tenure of the Reagan administration, and could well continue beyond that year. The public's acceptance of big spending programs has declined, reflected in the fact that the Democrats lost 41 states in the 1988 Presidential election, while the Republicans continue to register gains in all regions and among the youth.[17] The campuses are now famous, not for students who want to turn society on its head, but for students who want to turn a dollar, and a quick one at that. Watergate is again a hotel; the memory of Vietnam is gradually being replaced in the public's thinking by terrorism, hostages, and possible MIAs. Even without a Republican president, grants would be under attack to some degree.

On top of this Congress has been forced to recognize the deficit as a priority issue. The Gramm-Rudman-Hollings act of 1985 requires Congress to reduce the annual deficit to "only" $150 billion by October 1987, and to bring it down to zero by 1991.[18] The requirements of this legisla-

Table 6. Federal Aid to Cities, in Dollars and Constant 1979 Dollars, 1980–1984 (in millions of dollars)

Year	Total Aid in Current Dollars Including GRS	Average Annual Increase in Consumer Price Index	Total Aid in Constant 1979 Dollars
1980	13,000	+13.5	11,245
1981	13,750	+10.4	10,468
1982	13,473	+ 6.1	9,431
1983	13,300	+ 3.2	8,885
1984	12,903	+ 4.3	8,064
1985 est.	13,100	+ 4.0	7,664
Average percentage change:		+ 6.9/yr	− 31%

Sources: For column 1: U.S. Bureau of the Census, *City Government Finances in 1983–1984* and *City Government Finances 1982–83* (Washington, D.C.: U.S. Bureau of the Census); for column 2: U.S. Advisory Commission on Intergovernmental Relations (ACIR), *Significant Features of Fiscal Federalism 1984* (Washington, D.C.), p. 11, Table 2, Col. 3; and author's computations.

tion put grants in the cross hairs by proscribing any cuts from the "safety net" of over $300 billion in Social Security and welfare payments. This leaves only military procurement, $256 in 1985, and grants-in-aid, $106 billion in the same year, as the two big places to cut. The third largest item, interest on the federal debt, amounted to $179 billion in 1985[19] and is unlikely to be reduced. For cities, the handwriting is on the wall.

Before leaving this discussion it is worth examining the value of federal grants after corrections for inflation. Using the Department of Commerce's Consumer Price Index as a deflator, federal aid to cities alone has dropped by some 31% in the five years 1980–85 (see Table 6).

CONCLUSION: THE POST GRANTS ERA

The decline in grants has been with us for a decade. Whereas predictions are risky and must be made conditional, the elements that underlie the decline—a large federal deficit and broad changes in public attitudes—have been with us through all or part of three administrations and three Presidential elections, making it likely that this "era" will not come to an early end.

NOTES AND REFERENCES

1. James Q. Wilson, "The Rise of the Bureaucratic State," *The Public Interest*, 41, 3 (Fall 1975): 91.
2. Charles L. Mee, Jr., *The Marshall Plan In Action* (New York: Simon and Schuster, 1984), p. 258.
3. Between 1968 and 1978 the population of the United States grew from 200,700,000 to 222,600,000; See *Statistical Abstract of the United States* (1984).
4. Source of the 1988 estimate: U.S. Office of Management and Budget, *The Budget of the United States FY 1987*, p. H–17.
5. That the War on Poverty only accelerated a powerful existing trend is further evidenced by the growth of federal aid as a percent of Gross National Product (GNP), viewed at 5-year intervals:

Federal Aid as Percent of GNP: Percent Increases At Five Year Intervals, 1949–1984

Years	Percent
1949–1954	(11.1)
1955–1959	75.0
1960–1964	100.0
1965–1969	37.5
1970–1974	40.9
1975–1979	9.6
1980–1984	(26.4)

The interesting fact about these figures is that aid had its greatest increase as a percentage of GNP in the five years just preceding the War on Poverty. In this century the corresponding figure was higher only during the New Deal and for the five years 1914–1919.
6. A few states have small AFDC programs paid solely by state and local governments, in addition to the federal program. In California, one such state, about 45% of all AFDC money is federal. Source: California Department of Treasury, telephone interview (February 1986).
7. The federal government gives states leeway in determining the basic level of aid, and allows discretion in indexing COLAs. After the state has set these levels, federal standards then mandate a 180% multiplier to determine the maximum amount of eligible income. In California in 1986 these levels were:

Family Size	Maximum Qualifying Income	Maximum Allowable Aid[a]
1	$ 6,220	$ 3,456
3[b]	12,679	7,044
10	26,848	14,916

[a]Graduated scale; only minimum income gets maximum aid.
[b]Average size AFDC family in California, 1985.

To get Column 2, multiply Column 3 by 180%.

8. Advisory Commission on Intergovernmental Relations (ACIR), *The Intergovernmental Grant System As Seen By Local, State, and Federal Officials* (Washington, D.C.: U.S. government Printing Office, 1977). Until the 1930s federal grants were virtually a state monopoly; cities got next to nothing. The federal Housing Act of 1937 was the first federal act to put substantial amounts of money directly into city treasuries. Even as late as 1970 less than 12% of all federal aid went directly to cities and other local governments. James Q. Wilson, "The Rise of the Bureaucratic State," p. 92.

9. U.S. Office of Management and Budget, *The Budget of The United States FY 1986,* Special Analysis H, p. H–20.

10. See Aaron Wildavsky, *The Politics Of The Budgetary Process,* 4th ed. (Boston: Little, Brown, 1984); and Wildavsky, *The Costs of Federalism* (New Brunswick, N.J.: Transaction Books, 1984).

11. Richard P. Nathan and Fred C. Doolittle, "Federal Grants: Giving and Taking Away," *Political Science Quarterly,* 100, 1 (Spring 1985): 61, Table 3.

12. See Eugene Bardache, ed., *Special Issue* on Termination of Policies, Programs, and Organizations, *Policy Sciences,* 7, 2 (1976); Stuart M. Butler, *Privatizing Federal Spending: A Strategy to Eliminate the Deficit* (New York: Universe Books, 1985); and Peter Ferrara, ed., *Social Security: Prospects for Real Reform* (Washington, D.C.: The Cato Institute, 1985).

13. See Allan Shick, *Congress and Money: Budgeting, Spending and Taxing* (Washington, D.C.: The Urban Institute, 1980).

14. See Allan Shick, *Congress In The Budget Process: Exercising Political Choice* (Washington, D.C.: American Enterprise Institute for Public Policy Research, 1986), pp. 22–26.

15. California State Department of Social Services, "Administration and Legislators Reach Accord on Welfare Work Bill" (Sacramento: Department of Social Services, 1986), Appendix.

16. U.S. Advisory Commission on Intergovernmental Relations (ACIR), *Significant Features of Fiscal Federalism 1985–86* (Washington, D.C.), p. 8, Table 2; and author's computations.

17. See David S. Broder, "Realignment in Politics Seen; Political Scientists Note Shift From Democrats to Republicans," *The Washington Post* (September 3, 1985), p. A4; Jack Nelson, "GOP Voters Now Outnumber Democrats, Polls Indicate," *Los Angeles Times* (February 23, 1985), p. 19, section 1; and "Reagan Has Big Margin In Schoolchildren's Poll," *The New York Times* (October 24, 1984), p. 12. See also John Goodman, *Public Opinion During The Reagan Administration* (Washington, D.C.: Urban Institute Press, 1984).

18. The Gramm-Rudman-Hollings act of 1985 required cuts in the annual deficit of $11 billion only in 1986 and $50 billion in FY 1987, by which time the annual deficit would be down to $144 billion. The same legislation required the deficit drop to $108 billion in FY 1988, to $72 billion in FY 1989, $36 billion in FY 1990, and to zero by 1991. In 1986, the Supreme Court found the actual budget-cutting mechanism of the legislation unconstitutional, but left the deficit targets intact. In the fall of 1987, however, after the act had been in effect a little over one year, Congress voted to raise the allowable deficit by $20 billion in 1987, and to postpone deficit elimination until 1992.

19. The interest on the federal deficit will reach $198 billion in 1988, the single largest line item in the budget. Source: Executive Office of the President, *The United States Budget In Brief [The President's Budget] Fiscal Year 1988* (Washington, D.C.: U.S. Government Printing Office, 1987), p. 107, Table 4.

Chapter 2

GRANTS IN AID AND THE FEDERAL BALANCE

Edward C. Hayes

SUMMARY. The growth in federal grants is part of an even larger phenomenon, the growth in size and power of the federal government as against the states and municipalities. The growth in grants has been part cause and part result of this new balance, and of several negative consequences, including an increase in federal deficits, in the bureaucratic factor, and in federal mandates. Cutbacks in federal aid means a reduction of these unwanted consequences. Just under half of all local officials express willingness to accept reductions in federal aid, and the substantial cutbacks of 1982 were less traumatic than expected.

In this century the United States government has drawn closer to the unitary model in which all power emanates from the center. Of course we have not gone that far, either in practice or in Constitutional form; yet the "march of power to Washington," to use Leonard White's phrase, which began at least with the Interstate Commerce Act of 1887, is still in progress.[1] This chapter looks at the reasons for this "march" and the extent of it, and at the unwanted consequences which flow from it. By placing the growth of federal grants in the context of the growth of federal power generally we better understand the grants process, and the difficulty, at least, of controlling or reducing this growth.

17

THE MARCH OF POWER TO WASHINGTON

There have been at least four areas of growth of federal power. The first is growth in the areas of power assigned the federal government by the writers of the Constitution, including defense, treasury, international diplomacy, and general government. If the federal government had never passed through a New Deal or Great Society, the growth of these traditional areas would still make it an enormous power by nineteenth-century standards and local areas would find themselves heavily influenced by federal budgets.

The second area is the growth of regulatory bodies and administrative agencies,[2] and a third is the growth of the federal government as banker, influencing directly or indirectly almost $1 trillion of credit.[3]

The fourth, and largest source, is the growth of social expenditures, the area in which grants per se have played the greatest role. This new purpose of federal power can be seen most clearly in the percent of the federal budget devoted to transfer payments, payments that are not

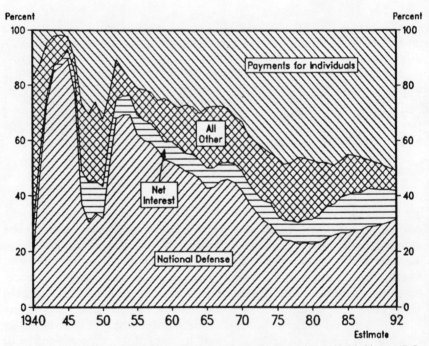

Source: Executive Office of the President, *The United States Budget In Brief FY 1988* (Washington, D.C.: U.S. Government Printing Office, 1987), p. 2.

Figure 1.   Percentage Composition of Federal Government Outlays.

Table 1. Transfer Payments in
The 1988 Federal Budget
(in billions of dollars)

Item	Amount
Social Security	219.4
Veterans Income	15.2
Payments to Farmers	24.5
Medicare	73.0
Income Security*	125.0
Total	457.1
Percentage of Total Budget	49.5

Note: *Includes: Retirement and Disability ($50 billion); Housing and Food Assistance ($30 billion); Unemployment Compensation ($20 billion); Other Income Security ($25 billion).
Source: Executive Office of the President, *The United States Budget In Brief FY 1988*, p. 76.

labor compensatory. The first national budget in 1788 contained a small amount of such payment in the form of retirement pay for revolutionary war officers and soldiers, so transfer payments in themselves are not a new subject. But their size is a new phenomenon. By 1989, transfer payments have come to be almost exactly 50% of the total federal budget. The bulk of these payments are shown in Table 1. Given this new purpose of federal government, the creation of large federal grants for social programs becomes all but inevitable.

CONSEQUENCES OF THE NEW BALANCE

To fully examine all the consequences of this new state of affairs would require an encyclopedia, and we will probably not fully understand the meaning of the present trends until fifty years have passed. There have been certain financial advantages reaped by state and local government, which are presented in the next chapter. The consequences which are negative, or which are alleged to be so, are reviewed here.

Preemption of State Legislation

Preemption of state legislation has been accomplished in at least three areas of legislation: the Clean Air Act, the Occupational Health and Safety Act, and legislation affecting the powers of the Food and Drug

Administration, all passed in the 1970s. In these three areas Congress has given federal agencies power to preempt (nullify) all state legislation in these areas, unless the standards of the states are more stringent than federal legislation. This is a broad opening wedge. But in the case of OSHA, federal legislation has gone further, allowing the agency to ". . . undermine virtually all state provisions that are *more* protective than federal standards, regardless of whether the federal interest in interstate commerce is at stake."[4]

Direct federal control over purely municipal matters has also developed through court cases. Although not the same as preemption, court decisions result in federal precedence in what was formally a purely local matter. The *Garcia* case is an example, in which the Supreme Court has allowed the federal government to legislate the pay scales of strictly local municipal employees.[5]

The phrase that explained and rationalized the growth of federal power in the 1960s was "cooperative federalism," a notion that replaced the established "dual federalism" theory. Writing in the early 1970s political scientist Daniel Elezar noted:

> So well has the idea of cooperative federalism been accepted that federal authorities have been able to use it to advance their notion of concentrated cooperation at the expense of established state prerogatives, raising the rather ironic question of whether the existence of the old theory of dual federalism, inaccurate as it was as a description of empirical reality, was not more functional for the health of the federal system, since it assumed that federal actions had to be constitutionally justified in a way that they do not have to be any more.[6]

In response to cooperative federalism the Nixon and Reagan administrations introduced "New Federalism," which combines the themes of reducing federal aid with returning authority to the state and local level. The Presidents' argument that such turnbacks were necessary to maintain the viability of states and municipalities in the Federal system has met with strong support from the Advisory Commission on Intergovernmental Relations.[7]

Touching the Lives of Citizens

It is worth taking a moment to understand the extent to which federal programs have an impact on the daily lives of "local" citizens. The federal payroll has an impact in every state of the union, from Wyoming, where federal salaries account for $250 million of state incomes, to the District of Columbia, where federal salaries account for over $7 billion.[8] Federal grants now cover such a broad scope of programs that the lives of everyone are touched at some point. Grants pay for free hot lunches

Confederation Articles of Confederation (1777–89)	Federalism U.S. Constitution (1789–Present)			
	Dual Federalism (1789–Civil War)	Cooperative Federalism (Civil War–Present)		Centralized Federalism
	Isolated instances of national government involvement in state affairs	Highly limited national government involvement in state affairs; virtually no involvement in local affairs (Civil War–New Deal)	Fairly extensive national government involvement in state affairs; virtually no involvement in local affairs (New Deal–Mid 60s)	Extensive national government involvement in both state and local affairs (Mid 60s–Present)	State and local governments act as administrative agents of the national government (presently in certain areas, e.g., state prisons, mental health facilities, clean air, OSHA)

Source: Advisory Commission on Intergovernmental Relations (ACIR).

Figure 2. Historical Models of Federalism

in school, and for planning studies of *mixed*-income local housing developments. Medicare pays for the hospital stays of the very wealthy. Mr.
Jones rides on a Jonesville road paid in part by Economic Development
Administration (EDA) grants; he travels from the city to his suburban
home on the federal interstate. He is given a ticket in his middle-class
suburb by an officer whose salary until recently was paid by the federal
Law Enforcement Assistance Administration (LEAA), and whose motor-
cycle and uniform were bought with federal General Revenue Sharing
(GRS) money. GRS money paid for the computer at City Hall where the
ticket was processed. When Mr. Jones leaves his car at home and takes a
local bus line, the bus he rides on and the operating cost of the ride is
largely subsidized by the Urban Mass Transit Administration (UMTA).
When he gets home the water he flushes from the toilet is treated by a
100% federally-funded local sewage treatment plant; indeed, the toilet
itself is located in a home whose mortgage is guaranteed by the Federal
Housing Administration (FHA). When Mr. Jones goes to the swank
shopping center built in the middle of his thriving city he is entering a
project paid in good measure by the Urban Development Action Grant
(UDAG) program. His poor cousin, who meets the federal standard of
poverty by having an income of just under $15,000 for a family of six,
shops in the same center, spending state and federal AFDC pocket money. The commercial developer, the middle-class Mr. Jones, and the poor
cousin are all included in.

Not all of this scenario is problematic, but there are some aspects to it
which should be highlighted. First, a substantial amount of federal economic development money has gone to K-Mart and commercial projects
whose need for federal assistance is not always clear. Second, Mr. Jones
and his cousin are getting used to not paying their own way. The federal
(or state) government is paying it, or helping pay it, or guaranteeing the
loans to pay it. The independence of the middle class, and not just the
poor, is affected by the federal cornacopia of grants and programs.

Third, federal social programs were originally intended to halt or
significantly reduce poverty. If that had happened then the volume of
aid would have achieved its purpose. In fact federal aid has reduced
poverty in one sense: federal programs reduce the percent of people in
poverty in America from 24% to around 12%, and if non-cash benefits
are included, to about 6% only.[9] At the same time the argument has
been made that by paying out enormous amounts of welfare, and
providing food, spending money, and housing to single parents who do
not work, the government has actually encouraged people to stay on
welfare and stay poor.[10]

Whatever the truth of this dispute the fact remains that in 1986, with at least one trillion dollars spent in recent years on poverty and the "safety net," poverty stood at a higher level than it did in the 1960s. In 1967 there were 27.8 million poor; in 1978, the low point in our history, the number had dropped to 22.6 million; but by 1986, there were 33.1 million,[11] despite the billions spent on poverty programs. The new federal balance has not lowered the number of poor, while it has weakened the popular perception of the link between work and income.[12]

The Growth of Bureaucracy

With $100 billion in annual federal aid and billions more in mainline programs comes, inevitably, the growth of federal regulatory control. Regulatory federalism has many manifestations, including federal and state "mandates," which are described in a later section of this chapter. The 1985–86 compilation of *The Code of Federal Regulations*, the complete edition of all rules for all federal programs and grants, occupies a full library shelf and comprises one hundred seventy three volumes.[13] There are ten volumes entitled "Protection of the Environment" on environmental legislation, a total of 7,550 pages. The volume governing the Office of Personnel Management (OPM), whose charge is to reduce bureaucracy and increase federal employee efficiency, is 857 pages. The compilation of Presidential Proclamations and Executive Orders for the one year 1985 is an even 500 pages, signed into law by the anti-bureaucrat, Ronald Reagan.

The U.S. Department of Housing and Urban Development (HUD) prints five volumes of regulations, for a total of 2,652 pages, regulating both its own programs and the actions of state and local officials who receive HUD money. Many of these rules are difficult to understand, and all depend on a list of acronyms which have redefined English. The following rule is from the HUD volumes:

> Nor may a [city] recipient, except for activities reimbursable under 24CFR 570, 200 (h), incur costs before approval of the RROF. If an activity is exempt under para. 58.34, no RROF is required, and therefore the above two statements would not apply.[14]

Or consider the following acronyms from another page of HUD's regulations:

NEPA	EFF	RROF
CEQ	NOI-EIS	SOA
FONSI	ROD	UDAG
RFP	ROF	

HUD STEPS OUT.   Mary and Merrian Snyder in front of the house they now own
in McKeesport, PA, the first such owners under HUD's Tenant Home Ownership
Demonstration Program. By getting out of the business of owning scattered site
housing, HUD could save billions of dollars by reducing staff and the size of needed
grants to local agencies.
Source: Photo by Willilam A. Ross, Staff Photographer. *The Daily News,* McKeesport, PA
          (January 8, 1986). Reprinted with permission.

New federal programs inevitably spell out the proliferation of rules and acronyms such as the above, and require the hiring of thousands of administrators to do nothing more than write and interpret the rules. The result is a new Parkinson's formula, properly called the Entanglement Quotient (EQ), which rises at a rate equal to the square of administrative rules: $EQ = AR^2$.

Smaller cities, less dependent on federal grants, are openly critical of this result, as is shown in the last two sections of this chapter. Big city mayors feel they must have federal aid, but complain loudly about federal mandates, the inevitable concomitant, as is shown in the next few pages. Yet it would be safe to guess that, if the big city mayors could locally finance the federal portion of aid, they would gladly dispense with Washington's rules and be masters of their own house.

Fiscal Dependence for *Basic* Programs

The loss of municipal autonomy can be seen in the way that federal aid has, for many cities, become the chief means for supporting local functions that have always been considered the basic responsibility of local government.

There are degrees of dependency. A city in which receives only 1% of its income from federal grants is clearly less dependent than one getting 15%. "Percent of budget" is one measure of dependency.

Another basic consideration is the distinction between operating and capital expenditures. One-shot capital improvements create less dependency than grants which fund daily expenses of on-going programs. The most serious kind of dependence occurs when cities use grants to run operating programs which are "basic," the programs which cities view as their real and prime responsibility, including public works, planning, and public safety.

Some cities are more dependent than others using either of these considerations. The status of eleven cities in the Richard C. Nathan network project is presented in Table 2.

With the advent of cutbacks in 1978, and the rude shock of 1982 when grants were cut by $6.6 billion, including half of CETA ($3 billion), cities have undertaken to "distance" themselves from grants dependency by diverting grant money to capital programs including one-time improvements. There is no good annual survey to show how well cities have succeeded in this effort, but from talking with city managers across the country the author has found both a widespread effort and considerable success. Cuts in the future will, as a result, hurt a little less.

Table 2.   Federal Support for Basic Services
(Operating Programs) by Financial Condition

	Percentage of Federal Funds Spent on Basic Services	Federal Spending as Percentage of Total Spending for Basic Services
Hard Pressed Cities		
Detroit	49.0	25.5
St Louis	49.0	27.0
Cleveland	46.0	24.0
Rochester	92.4	22.3
New York	55.3	22.7
Boston	39.3	13.0
Average, hard-pressed cities	54.2	21.2
More Prosperous Cities		
Houston	16.5	4.4
Phoenix	30.2	14.7
Tulsa	18.3	11.3
Chicago	28.7	10.9
Los Angeles	10.3	4.5
Average, more prosperous cities	20.5	9.1

Source: James W. Fossett, *Federal Aid To Big Cities. The Politics of Dependence* (Washington, D.C.: The Brookings Institution, 1983), p. 39, Table 6.

The Impact on Local Priorities

Some investigators argue that federal aid has distorted local priorities, and some deny it.[15] Yet the word "distortion" may itself be an under-statement. Had the federal government not offered billions of dollars to cities to undertake job training programs, senior centers, and dozens of other programs, local government would never have dreamed of under-taking them. Federal grants did not distort local priorities so much as *create* them, and on a broader range of subjects than local politicians would have contemplated. Cities that were barely getting by with old sewer treatment plants found themselves buying expensive new systems, paid 100% by the federal Environmental Protection Agency (EPA). When EPA reduced its share to 75% in the mid-1980s and threatened to reduce it still further, these same cities began redesigning their more lavish treatment plants to conform with the new federal funding lev-els.[16] In this case, full federal funding created an agenda, and revised funding created a revised agenda. In the case of Job Corps, nutritional programs for pregnant mothers, rent supplements, and the long list of programs outlined in Chapter one, the federal government held out money to local officials and let human nature take its course. Generally local government was asked to put up less than 20% of the federal program, so that one local dollar brought in five federal dollars, a very sweet deal; but as programs mounted, the "20 percents" of local shares have come to account for an ever rising proportion of "local" budgets.

A Larger Federal Deficit

Until the tax reform act of 1986, local government contributed to the federal deficit in three ways: Direct grants in aid, the subject of the first chapters of this book; deductibility of state and local taxes from federal income tax, a practice which the 1986 tax act eliminated; and the deductibility from federal income tax of interest earned on municipal bonds, and on economic development bonds issued by local authorities. The total cost to the fed of these three sources is shown in Table 3.

In 1985, Congress put a cap on the amount of industrial revenue bonds that local jurisdictions could issue, but in the 1986 tax act it allowed full tax deductibility on municipal bonds, a practice of long standing, and one which cities strongly urged. In 1987, due to the actual workings of the 1986 tax act, the federal government realized a windfall, and the annual deficit for FY 87 was $148 billion although the government spent over $1 trillion for the first time that year. The elimination of deductibility of state and local taxes contributed at least $27 billion to this improved situation.

Table 3. Tax Expenditures and Grants for State and Local Governments; Compared U.S. Deficit, 1982–1986 (in billions of dollars)

	1982	1983	1984	1985	1986(est.)
Deductibility of state and local taxes	27.4	26.0	21.9	24.5	27.4
Exclusion of interest	11.4	20.4	13.7	15.1	17.0
State and local grants in aid	88.2	92.5	97.6	105.9	108.8
Total Outlays/Losses	127.0	139.4	133.2	221.6	202.8
Annual U.S. Deficit	127.9	207.9	185.3	190.1	192.7

Sources: OMB, *The Budget for FY 1982, 1983, 1987*; and *Economic Report of the President* (February 1986), p. 339, Table B–73.

MANDATES

There are several kinds of federal mandates to state and local government. *Direct orders* are regulations that require state and local action under penalty of civil or criminal prosecution. An example is the Equal Employment Opportunity Act of 1972.[17] In addition, there are:

- *crosscutting mandates*—broad requirements imposed on local governments under the threat of losing federal grant money which include bans on discrimination in hiring, environment impact procedures, the Davis Bacon "prevailing [union] wage" rule and many others;
- *crossover sanctions*—under which any failure of state or local government to follow federal requirements in one program results in curtailing aid in another program;
- *conditions of aid*—the method, or vehicle, by which any sanction is imposed.

Before the 1960s there were only two federal acts that included mandates; today there are 36 such federal acts.[18] A university survey done in 1979 showed a total of 1,234 federal mandates and 3,415 state mandates, a total of *over 4,500 commands directing municipal and county governments.*[19] Over 90% of the total budgets of California counties is mandated—and hence outside the control of county officials—by state and federal legislation.[20] Every city in America faces mandates; the larger the city, the more the mandates, governing not only behavior but requiring extensive paperwork in reporting. In the 1979 survey, for example, Milwaukee, Wisconsin had to comply with 613 federal mandates and 594 state mandates, a total of 1,207 mandates on every aspect of city affairs from community development to health.

Besides the eroding effect on municipal self governance, mandates have a number of specific drawbacks. First, they contribute to the Entanglement Quotient. They are ponderous, and once enacted, easily outlive their usefulness. The 55 mph speed limit, and Department of Labor rules against piecework in the home, are two examples.

Second, they aggravate local officials. A survey by the National Association of Counties, released in 1981, identified requirements of the EPA and the Davis Bacon act as creating a "heavy financial burden" for counties, and concluded that mandates in general "confused counties' management process." A survey in late 1980 and 1981 by the National League of Cities, in which 1,601 surveys were mailed and 928 replies received, showed that the League's local officials considered two mandates in particular to be "too costly": EPA's wastewater treatment re-

Table 4. Federal and State Mandates, by Conditions of Aid, Direct Orders, and Applicability

	Federal				State			
	Conditions of Aid		Direct Orders		Conditions of Aid		Direct Orders	
Jurisdiction	Applicable	Non-applicable	Applicable	Non-applicable	Applicable	Non-applicable	Applicable	Non-applicable
Cities								
Milwaukee, WI	498	536	115	100	20	0	574	58
Winston-Salem, NC	527	507	173	42	10	0	223	26
Olympia, WA	254	780	93	122	63	14	340	68
Trenton, NJ	562	472	32	183	7	0	499	25
San Bernardino, CA	601	433	133	82	7	17	528	923
Counties								
Dane County, WI	565	469	126	89	15	5	491	141
Guilford County, NC	455	579	133	82	10	0	174	75
Thurston County, WA	217	817	55	160	66	11	337	71
Somerset County, NJ	414	620	26	189	7	0	515	9
Orange County, CA	647	387	88	127	18	6	1151	300

Source: Catherine H. Lovell et al., *Federal and State Mandating on Local Governments: An Exploration of Issues and Impacts* (Riverside, CA: Graduate School of Administration, University of California, Riverside, 1979), p. 82.

quirements, and the Department of Transportation's design requirements affecting federally assisted purchases of new buses.[21] In this same
survey, 40% of local officials believed that mandated behavior resulted
from the federal government playing an *inappropriate role* (original emphasis); 50% believed the mandated standards were *unrealistic*; and 51%
thought the federal government went *too far* in specifying the means of
achieving mandated objectives.[22]

SOME TYPICAL MANDATES

1. Congress has mandated full Social Security health insurance
   coverage for state and local employees hired after March 1,
   1986. In 1986, this will cost local governments about $3,000 per
   employee through a tax on state and local governments of
   7.15%.
2. On October 1, 1986, a trigger mechanism takes effect "allowing"
   states to "voluntarily" exempt purchases made with food stamps
   from state and local sales tax. If they do not do so voluntarily,
   federal legislation preempts the field. Total cost to local governments is unknown.
3. States must raise the drinking age to 21 or suffer the loss of 5%
   in federal highway funds in 1986 and 10% in 1987 and beyond
   (a "cross-cutting" mandate).
4. In the rush to undo the effects of the *Garcia* decision, cities
   voluntarily gave Congress the right to control the bulk of state
   and local personnel system policies. The implementation of this
   will be gradual, but one-way.

—Randy Hamilton[23]

Third, mandates, together with congressional "preemptive legislation" and Supreme Court decisions throughout this century, have all but
interred the 10th Amendment to the Constitution, which reserves
powers to the States and the people.[24] This creates a Constitutional
dilemma, because the Constitution allows for its own amendment, and
denies local officials the ability to act for themselves.

San Francisco's experience with the Department of Transportation in
the 1980s is typical. Mayor Diane Feinstein complained that the federal
Department of Transportation requirements for wheelchair lifts on all
city buses cost $20,000 per bus and "are frankly not used and are not

Table 5. Ten Burdensome Federal
Mandates Identified by Regulatory Impact
Studies, 1976–1980*

1. Section 504 of the *Rehabilitation Act of 1973* (non-discrimination against handicapped)
2. *Clean Water Act*
3. *Education for All Handicapped Children Act*
4. *Davis-Bacon Act*
5. *National Environmental Policy Act***
6. *Clean Air Act*
7. *Safe Drinking Water Act*
8. *Civil Rights Act of 1964*, Title VII**
9. *Civil Rights Act of 1964*, Title VI**
10. *Bilingual Education Requirements*

Notes: *Ranked in approximation of level of impact, based on the number of different studies identifying a regulation as burdensome and the magnitude of impact indicated.

**Rankings are based on prior evaluations and do not take into account regulatory modifications that may have been adopted subsequently. The regulations marked were subject to reform and simplification under the Carter Administration. Most of the remaining regulations have been modified or are under review by the Reagan Administration.

Source: Advisory Commission on Intergovernmental Relations, *Regulatory Federalism* (Washington, D.C.: ACIR, 1984), p. 184, Figure 5.2.

cost effective." San Francisco pleaded with the federal government to be allowed to use Dial-A-Ride *free* services for the handicapped instead of installing the expensive lifts. The Department of Transportation refused.[25] In Los Angeles, the cost of Dial-A-Ride per ride is $6.22; the cost per bus trip on a lift-equipped bus, for each person in a wheelchair, is $300, according to the Los Angeles Metro Transit Development Board. Yet the requirements for lifts in San Francisco and Los Angeles remain.

Finally, mandates are expensive, and the federal government often fails to provide any money to cover mandated costs. A survey of seven cities by the Joint Economic Committee of the U.S. Congress in 1980 showed that mandates cost $31 *per capita* in Alexandria, Virginia; $6 exact per capita in Burlington, Vermont, and a whopping $51.51 per capita in Newark, New Jersey, largely due to clean water requirements.[26] As an estimate a large state, such as New York, spends over $350 million at the state and local level in satisfying federally mandated requirements.[27]

CUTTING BACK: "NOT THE TRIALS OF JOB"

Would cutbacks in federal grants prove devastating? In 1982 the Reagan administration cut over $6 billion in federal aid, and this experience provides some guide to the cutback experience. While cities in 1982 predicted chaos, the result was relatively benign. George Peterson of the Urban League came to the following conclusion:

> The subsequent financial experience of both the cities and the nonprofit organizations is so at odds with the pessimistic predictions made at the time that it obliges reconsideration of what we know about the response to recession and external (federal cutback) financial pressure.[28]

Among other evidence, Peterson shows that many city officials welcomed cuts in federal grants. Reductions in entitlement programs *saved the cities' money*. Local officials responding to national surveys displayed "complete neutrality" towards federal cuts in public housing support, and almost complete neutrality toward cuts in youth employment programs. A majority of city officials *favored* cuts in CETA Title VI, public service employment.[29]

Similar findings have been made by political scientist Richard Caputo, who surveyed 131 local officials in four Midwestern states in 1983. This survey revealed that 47% of those surveyed preferred President Reagan's federalism to President Nixon's. In only one state, Wisconsin, did local officials anticipate a tax increase as a result of the Reagan cuts. Only 21% of the cities surveyed planned any cut in services.[30]

The most complete, on-going survey of federal grants has been made continually since the 1970s by Professor Richard P. Nathan, whose study has tracked grants to fourteen states and forty cities of all sizes within those states. Nathan found that the $6.6 billion cut in aid in 1982 was buffered by various factors, including a $3 billion emergency jobs program and higher unemployment payments triggered by a relatively high rate of unemployment. His conclusion was that the 1982 cuts were "not really the trials of Job."[31]

CONCLUSION: WILL LOCAL OFFICIALS ACCEPT CUTS?

While the several professional organizations representing local government in Washington strongly protest any aid cuts, including those proposed in FY 1987 and 1988, the response of local officials is more varied. Just under half (47%) show a willingness to accept federal aid cuts under certain conditions (see Table 6). The willingness to accept reductions has

Table 6. Methods Preferred by Local Officials for Reducing The Federal Budget

Method	Percentage Choosing This Method
1. Cut local programs	15
2. Cut local programs no more than other federal programs	32
Total	47
3. First cuts should come from military and entitlements	45
4. No local cuts	6
Total	51
5. Other	2

Source: National League of Cities/Francis Viscount, *City Fiscal Conditions and Outlook for FY 85*, p. 14, Table I-9; and author's computations.

been expressed by many local officials, including Roy Pederson, former city manager of Scottsdale, Arizona, and now of Colorado Springs, Colorado;[32] Ralph Webb, city manager of Baldwin Park, California;[33] Mayor Wilson Goode of Philadelphia; and Mayor William H. Hudnut III of Indianapolis.[34] Given the number of unpleasant consequences of federal aid, and the number of local officials willing under certain circumstances to accept aid reductions, such reductions seem politically viable. The remainder of this volume tries to show how local governments can accommodate any reductions by significant increases in productivity.

NOTES AND REFERENCES

1. Leonard White, *The States and the Nation* (Baton Rouge: Louisiana University Press, 1953). In the Preface, White writes that "the march of power to Washington should be reversed whenever possible [and] the states should strengthen their capacity to take a greater share of the burden of government" (p. 3). For similar views see Edward S. Corwin, *The Commerce Power v. States Rights. Back To The Constitution* (Princeton, NJ: Princeton University Press, 1936); and Corwin, *Constitutional Revolution* (Claremont, CA: Scripps College, 1941). For similar views by contemporary writers see Joseph S. McNamara, Executive Editor, *Still The Law Of The Land? Essays on Changing Interpretations of the Constitution* (Hillsdale, MI: Hillsdale College Press, 1987), especially the Forward by Forrest McDonald.

2. See Dwight Waldo, *The Administrative State* (New York: Holmes & Meier, 1984); Advisory Commission on Intergovernmental Relations (ACIR), *Regulatory Federalism: Policy, Process, Impact, And Reform*, Publication A-95 (Washington, D.C.: ACIR, February 1984).

3. At the end of 1986 the federal government held outstanding loans with a face value of $252 billion, and had guaranteed another $450 billion in loans. Government-sponsored enterprises lent another $453 billion, yielding a total of over $1 trillion in credit. See Executive Office of the President, *The United States Budget In Brief FY 1988* (Washington, D.C.: U.S. Government Printing Office, 1987), p. 42.

4. Susan Bartlett Foote, "Administrative Pre-Emption: An Experiment in Regulatory Federalism," *Virginia Law Review*, 70, 7 (October 1984): 1454. Foote details, among other things, how the Federal Drug Administration (FDA) and the Occupational Safety and Health Administration (OSHA) deliberately exceeded the powers given them by Congress (pp. 1442–1461).

5. See A.E. Dick Howard, "Garcia: Federalism's Principles Forgotten," *Intergovernmental Perspective*, 11(Spring/Summer 1985): 12–14; and Paul J. Hartman and Thomas J. McCoy, "Garcia: The Latest Retreat on the 'States Rights' Front," *Intergovernmental Perspective*, 11(Spring/Summer 1985): 8–11.

6. See Daniel Elazar, *American Federalism: A View From The States* (New York: Crowell, 1966); and Elazar, *Exploring Federalism* (Tuscaloosa: University of Alabama Press, 1987).

7. The Advisory Commission on Intergovernmental Relations, a quasi-official Federal agency charged with monitoring the condition of federalism, said in its 1986 report: "In recent years a consensus has developed, among citizens and public officials alike, that the American system of government has grown too centralized, too complicated, and tends to lack accountability at critical points. One area of special concern has been the elaborate system of federal grants in aid that has developed over the last 30 years." The Report goes on to apply a framework, developed in part by earlier work of the Kestnbaum Commission, the Joint Federal-State Action Committee, and the ACIR itself, for deciding which of 400 federal programs properly belong at the state or local level, and comes up with 177 programs that should be "devolved." No "means tested" (welfare) programs were included on the list, because ACIR was studying these elsewhere.

The Report shows how turnbacks could take place at five different levels of magnitude, from $10 to $22 billion of program responsibility. While this report received a favorable vote from the majority of mayors, state and county legislators, and Congressmen and Senators who comprise it, several minority reports were filed which are discussed in Chapter 3. See Advisory Commission on Intergovernmental Relations (ACIR), *Devolving Federal Program Responsibilities and Revenue Sources to State and Local Governments* (Washington D.C.: ACIR, March 1986).

For an historical view of federalism and New Federalism, see Deil Wright et al. *Federalism and Intergovernmental Relations* (Washington DC: American Society for Public Administration, 1984). For a view supporting ACIR see Robert B. Hawkins, ed., *American Federalism: A New Partnership for the Republic* (San Francisco: Institute for Contemporary Studies, 1982). For views more sympathetic to centralized federalism see Lewis G. Bender and James S. Stever, *Administering the New Federalism* (Boulder, CO: Westview Press, 1986); and Marilyn Gittell, *State Politics and the New Federalism* (White Plains, NY: Longman, 1986). See also Donald F. Kettl, *The Regulation of American Federalism* (Baltimore, MD: The Johns Hopkins Press, 1986). In 1981, the Reagan administration proposed and Congress authorized the states to assume responsibility for the Small Cities Program of the Community Development Block Grant program. For a favorable history of this process see Edward T. Jennings *et al.*, *From Nation To State: The Small Cities Community Development Block Grant Program* (Albany, NY: SUNY Press, 1986).

8. California ranked the highest in federal salaries with $14 billion, followed by Virginia with $8 billion, the District of Columbia with $7 billion, and New York with $5 billion. Thirty states get over $1 billion in federal salaries. See U.S. Bureau of the Census, *Federal Expenditures by State For Fiscal Year 1985* (Washington, D.C.: U.S. Bureau of the Census), p. 16, Table 3.

9.   See Ben Wattenberg, *The Good News Is The Bad News Is Wrong* (New York: Simon & Schuster, 1985), p. 154. Wattenberg shows that, when *non-cash* assistance is included in income statistics, a method which the Census Bureau does not use in calculating poverty in America, the percent of poor was equal to 6.4% in 1979. By ignoring non-cash assistance, poverty was officially reported that year as 11.6% of the population. See also Charles Murray, *Losing Ground* (New York: Basic Books, 1984), pp. 64–65.

10.   *Ibid.* Most of Murray's book leads to this conclusion. For a rebuttal see Juan Williams, "Liberal Thinkers Rally In Defense of 'Great Society'," *The Washington Post* (May 28, 1985), p. A–4.

11.   U.S. Census of the Population, "Population Estimates," Series P–40 (September 1985).

12.   The reform Welfare bill introduced by Democratic Senator Patrick Moynihan, and finally passed in 1988, contains a "workfare" clause requiring AFDC recipients to do some work, or take training for work, as a condition of receiving aid.

13.   *Code of Federal Regulations* (Washington, D.C.: U.S. Government Printing Office, 1985–86).

14.   *Ibid.*, vol. 24, p. 365.

15.   See Terry Nichols Clark and Lorna Crowly Ferguson, *City Money: Political Processes, Fiscal Strain, and Retrenchment* (New York: Columbia University Press, 1983), p. 225.

16.   The author found this happening throughout the state of Michigan in 1985, after EPA cutbacks had been announced.

17.   See Advisory Commission on Intergovernmental Relations (ACIR), *Regulatory Federalism* (1984), pp. 88–91; and Jane Massey and Jeffrey D. Straussman, "Another Look at Mandates" *Public Administration Review,* 45 (March–April 1985): 292–299.

18.   Including the Age Discrimination Act of 1975, Civil Rights Act of 1964 (Title VI), Education Amendments of 1972 (Title IX), Federal Water Pollution Control Act Amendments of 1972, National Environmental Policy Act of 1969, Clean Air Act Amendments of 1970, Occupational Safety and Health Act (1970), and others. Only two acts preceded the 1960s: Davis Bacon Act (1931), and the Hatch Act (1940).

19.   Advisory Commission on Intergovernmental Relations (ACIR), *Regulatory Federalism* (1984), Table 5.2, p. 159.

20.   County Supervisors Association of California (CSAC), *County Fiscal Crisis 1985– 1986* (Sacramento: CSAC, July 17, 1985), chart, p. 5. Data compiled from California State Controller, *Annual Report of County Budget Requirements and Means of Financing* (1985), p. 6.

21.   Clint Page, "NLC surveys Members on Federal Rules," *Nation's Cities Weekly* (April 6, 1981), p. 10.

22.   National League of Cities, "Municipal Policy and Program Survey," unpublished tabulation, 1981; in Advisory Commission on Intergovernmental Relations, *Regulatory Federalism,* p. 175.

23.   Randy Hamilton, "Home Rule is Headed for Extinction Unless. . . . ," *Western City* 62, 10 (October 1986): 5 *et. seq.*

24.   George D. Brown, "The Tenth Amendment Is Dead. Long Live The Eleventh!" Advisory Commission on Intergovernmental Relations *Intergovernmental Perspective* (March 1987), pp. 26–30; see also President's Working Group on Federalism, *The Status of Federalism in America* (Washington, D.C.: Office of the White House, Council on Domestic Policy, 1986).

25.   *The Washington Times* (July 21, 1986).

26.   For a strong defense of mandates, see Chapter 3, pp. 15–16.

27.   Thomas Muller and Michael Fix, "The Impact of Selected Federal Actions on Municipal Outlays," *Government Regulation: Achieving Social and Economic Balance.* Vol. 5: *Special Study on Economic Change,* U.S. Congress, Joint Economic Committee (Washington D.C.: U.S. Government Printing Office, 1980), p. 368.

28.   George E. Peterson and Carol W. Lewis, *Reagan and the Cities* (Washington D.C.: Urban Institute Press, 1986), p. 5.

29.   *Ibid.*, p. 3.

30.   David A. Caputo, "American Cities and Their Future," *Society* (January/February 1985).

31.   Richard P. Nathan and Fred C. Doolittle, "Federal Grants: Giving and Taking Away," *Political Science Quarterly* 100, 1 (Spring 1985): 53–74.

32.   Roy R. Pederson, "Thanks, Howard," in *Managing With Less. A Book of Readings*, ed. Elizabeth Keller (Washington D.C.: International City Management Association, 1979), p. 58.

33.   Ralph H. Webb, "Fiscal Independence," *Public Management* (August 1985): 12, 14.

34.   "Hurting Cities Must Decide Between Tax Increase Or Retreat," *San Diego Union* (December 22, 1985), p. A–21.

Chapter 3

FEDERAL SUPPORT TO CITIES MUST NOT BE REDUCED

Alan Beals

SUMMARY. The federal government should maintain its present level of support to cities for many reasons. Cities *are* the nation; urban problems are national problems. Cities get a relatively small amount of money; balancing the budget by taking these grants away will seriously damage cities and not reduce the deficit as much as a tax reform which closes loopholes. City officials do care about the deficit and have taken steps to become self-financing, but to eliminate programs wholesale, or turn them over to states with no financial support from Washington, is a serious error at a time when unemployment and poverty are at high levels.

American cities have been called "engines of the American economy" and "laboratories of social and economic experimentation." Cities are, in fact, the place where most people work, where most of the jobs are created, where most of the new businesses are born, and where most of the national wealth is created. According to the Census Bureau, in 1984 nearly three-quarters of the U.S. population was living in metropolitan areas, and the population of these areas was increasing at a greater rate than the population in rural areas.[1] Some 85% of personal income is generated in metropolitan areas.

FEDERAL GOVERNMENT AND CITIES:
A SYMBIOTIC RELATIONSHIP

The above mentioned statistics clearly indicate that there is a symbiotic relationship between the nation and its cities. Cities could not separate themselves from federal policies even if they wished to, and Washington cannot extricate itself from the problems of urban America. Because we are an urban nation, federal policy *ipso facto* becomes urban policy as well. The success or failure of our cities to create jobs, provide housing, and maintain the environment is the measure of our success or failure as a nation. Accordingly, it is very much in the national interest for the federal government to assist cities in carrying out broad national policy goals and in their efforts as incubators and sustainers of economic growth.

At the core of federal aid programs toward cities are the following current (or recent) well-designed programs:

* General Revenue Sharing (GRS)[2]
* Community Development Block Grants (CDBGs)
* Urban Development Action Grants (UDAG)[3]
* Housing assistance programs for the low-income, the elderly, and handicapped
* Public Transit and Municipal Wastewater grants
* Job Training (JPTA)
* The use of tax-exempt financing for low-income housing, infrastructure investment, and industrial development

In its legislative advocacy throughout the 1980s it has been the policy of the National League of Cities (NLC) to preserve these programs at their present levels. Because of the cutbacks in Washington the NLC has directed its efforts toward maintainence rather than program expansion. This stance is consistent with the NLC's broad recommendation that expenditures across the entire federal budget be frozen, with the exception of entitlement programs and Social Security.

THE ATTACK ON AID TO CITIES

City finances have been hit hard in the past decade both by occurrences in the economy and by federal cuts. Since 1975 cities have gone through two serious recessions, have been ravaged by a period of inflation that sent prices up 50% in 10 years, and are caught, in 30 states, by local or statewide ordinances limiting local tax revenues.[4]

Within this context federal aid cuts have been more serious than they might otherwise have been. Federal aid as a percentage of state and local budgets peaked in 1979 (see Chapter 1, Figure 1, p. 5) and has been declining ever since. The Law Enforcement Assistance Administration (LEAA) and public-sector job training have disappeared entirely. Other programs, including Urban Development Action Grants (UDAGs), the entire Economic Development Administration (EDA), and General Revenue Sharing (GRS) were all targeted for elimination by the Reagan administration in FY 1987.[5] The first two programs were saved by Congress, at much reduced levels compared to their late 1970s levels; General Revenue Sharing was completely eliminated that year. UDAGs have survived as a shell, authorized as programs, but with a zero appropriation in 1989. Both the EDA and legal services for the poor have already been scaled back, as have the Community Services Block Grant (CSBG), wastewater treatment grants, the Community Development Block Grant (CDBG) down to a $2.6 billion appropriation in 1989), and various health, education and nutrition programs (for details, see Chapter 1, Table 3).

One of the hardest hit programs is federal housing assistance. A research report commissioned by the National League of Cities recently chronicled a decline in reservations for additional low-income units under HUD and Farmers Home programs. Reservations have dropped from 541,534 in 1976 to 395,000 in 1986.[6] The President's proposed budget for FY 87 called for no additional authorizations. Meanwhile, housing starts from previous authorizations fell below 40,000 in 1985, and completion of new or rehabilitated housing from a backlog of previous authorizations was down to 100,000 units.[7]

Federal aid to transit has likewise been closely cropped. Only the passage of a gasoline tax increase maintained urban transportation funding into the mid-1980s, and even those levels represented some reduction for cities. The administration sought and won municipal support for the gas tax increase while offering assurances that one cent of the new five cents per gallon tax would be dedicated to additional funding for public transit. Once the new tax had gone into effect, however, the administration's memory suffered a lapse, and it proposed a new round of cuts in federal transit assistance.[8] In addition, the latest administration initiative is a state-administered transportation block grant that would incorporate both highway and transit functions, at lower combined funding levels and without stipulation as to use.[9]

General Revenue Sharing, before its elimination, had lost half its real dollar value while frozen at the 1976 level of $4.6 billion for local governments. The state share of $2.3 billion fell under the budget axe in 1980.[10]

Some sharp-eyed observers of the federal budget have noted, with dismay, that the fiscal 1987 budget submitted by the administration contained more foreign economic development aid than economic development assistance for the nation's cities. To put this comparison directly, the administration is more prepared to come to the aid of Athens, Greece than Athens, Georgia.

THE FEDERAL DEFICIT: MAKING CITIES THE GOAT

Throughout all its budget cutting, the avowed goal of the administration and congressional leadership has been to restrain the growth of federal spending, to weed out special interest programs and to put the nation's fiscal house in order. This concern for the deficit is shared by the country's municipal officials. A NLC survey of 487 officials from 371 cities and towns, taken at the end of 1985, found that for 66% of these officials, deficit reduction was the foremost concern. Unemployment was a distant second with 18% of the tally.[11]

But when the actual job of budget cutting began the performance of the administration was not as benign as its stated intentions, and it was cities that stood the gaff. In 1980, budget authorization for urban programs totaled $58 billion; the federal deficit was $73 billion. By 1986, annual deficits had exploded to around $200 billion while authorization for urban programs had been cut to $26.3 billion.[12]

Over the same time period tax *advantages* for certain groups actually increased. A NLC analysis of the federal budget has found, for example, that accelerated depreciation for office buildings went from $10 billion in 1984 to $15 billion in 1986, while over the same two years Community Development Block Grants were slated for a 32% reduction. Special capital gains allowances for timber went up by 150% under new tax code provisions, while low income housing was taking a 67% cut. The purchase price of a corporate airplane can be recouped entirely through tax credits and deductions, while public transit funding faced a 62% cut between 1986 and 1987. Corporate tax preferences and subsidies, including entertainment, gifts, and business lunches, cost the Treasury about $120 billion in 1986, the same time that General Revenue Sharing was slated for extinction.[13]

Indeed it is worth dwelling for a moment on so-called "tax expenditures," the tax deductions, tax credits, and other shelters provided for individuals and corporations by the federal code. Between 1982 and 1986, federal tax expenditures for state and local government grew from $38 billion to $47 billion, a 23% increase, while the total for all tax expenditures combined—all the "loopholes" for public and private indi-

Chart 1.   1986 Tax Expenditures
(billions)

Category	Amount	Percentage of Total
Tax-Exempt Go Bonds	14.8	3.5
Other Tax Exempt Bonds	14.5	3.4
Deductibility of State–Local Taxes	35.2	8.3
Mortgage Interest Deduction	27.1	6.4
Investment Tax Credit	35.8	8.4
Accelerated Depreciation	32.9	7.7
Other Tax Expenditures (Individuals)	218.5	51.5
Other Tax Expenditures (Corporations)	45.7	10.8
Total	424.5	100.0

Source: Joint Tax Committee.

viduals and corporations—grew from $200 billion (in 1979) to $439 billion in 1986, a 120% increase.[14] In 1988, reflecting the influence of the 1986 Tax Reform Act, which tried to remedy tax inequities, total tax expenditures fell to $303 billion, still over 33% greater than the 1979 level.[15]

If the federal government wished to solve its deficit crises, it would not have to put itself through the agony of Gramm-Rudman-Hollings legislation. Instead it could simply close off the large "loopholes," or tax expenditures, to an even greater degree than the 1986 Tax Reform Act, which still leaves $303 billion in loopholes in 1988. Yet all of the tax bills introduced in 1986 to foster tax reform, including the successful Tax Reform Act itself, were "revenue neutral"; they closed loopholes to varying degrees, but also reduced taxes on individuals and some business taxes to such a point that tax reform was of no assistance in budget balancing.[16] Without raising revenue, the budget will not be balanced easily, and efforts to balance will make cities pay the price.

OF TAXES, DEFICITS, AND FEDERAL GRANTS: COMMON QUESTIONS AND NLC ANSWERS

In Washington, a city beset with deficit problems, an aversion to tax increases, and Gramm-Rudman deficit reduction requirements, it is difficult in the extreme to maintain the present level of federal aid to cities. Perhaps the best way to defend current levels of aid is to answer common questions about the need of federal aid and the position of the NLC. Mayor Henry G. Cisneros, recent president of the NLC, has done this in an address on city priorities. Cisneros posed the tough questions and gave some clear answers.

Isn't it hypocritical for city officials to express concern about the federal deficit, and then turn around and oppose Gramm-Rudman because it will cut city programs?

No, it's not. The Gramm-Rudman legislation substitutes a nonelected federal official, the chief of the General Accounting Office, to make critical budget cutting decisions, a role which is constitutionally that of the elected Congress and President. It puts a faceless bureaucrat in charge of the country's future,[17] contrary to Constitutional requirements.[18] Moreover, Gramm-Rudman is not really effective, because in its final version it exempted over 50% of the federal budget from any cuts.

Aren't cities really calling for a federal tax increase to save themselves?

No. What cities want is not a tax increase, but a *tax reform* which would provide increased revenues to reduce the deficit. The present federal tax code has hundreds of billions of dollars of loopholes. Simply freezing federal tax expenditures would reduce the deficit by over $36 billion.[19]

Won't a tax increase, or increased revenues through tax reform, cause a recession, as the President insists?

Not necessarily. There is no consensus among experts on that question because a recession depends on so many variables. In our recent history, we had a tax cut in 1981, and the next year had a recession anyway. In 1982 Federal taxes rose but caused no recession; instead we have had steady economic growth.

What will happen to and in cities if Gramm-Rudman operated for five years without a major federal tax increase?

If Gramm-Rudman continues for five years all federal aid to local governments will likely be eliminated. But because such a small portion of the federal budget is subject to Gramm-Rudman, the federal deficit itself will very likely remain. We will have succeeded only in dismantling the intergovernmental system that has been so carefully built up over the past 30 years and more.

How can cities reconcile their call for capping or closing tax expenditures while at the same time vigorously lobbying to retain the deductibility of state and local taxes, and the federal exemption for interest on local bonds?

Tax expenditures are incentives built into the federal tax code to encourage certain types of activities, but the deductibility of state and local taxes, and the exemption of municipal bonds from federal tax, were not put into the code to encourage citizen payment of property taxes. Deductibility and tax exemption for bonds represent a recognition of the federal-local partnership, a most Constitutional relationship. They are not an incentive device as are all the other tax expenditures in the code.

Federal grants are going down and local taxes may go up. Some call that passing the buck, but isn't that really the best way to finance local activities, insuring that they meet the local agenda?

No, it's not the best way. First, federal spending of money coming *from* our cities and towns is going up; only aid going back *to* our municipalities is going down. Second, not all cities and towns have the same capacity to raise their own local taxes. Poorer cities and towns have to impose a disproportionately high tax rate because of a poorer tax base. Some cities are burdened with fiscal responsibility for schools, welfare, and hospitals, thus adding to these municipalities' tax burden. A "trade-off" of program and costs from the federal to the local level will find that some localities can handle it and some cannot.

And finally, any trade-off will force all government to rely less on the progressive federal income tax and more on regressive local taxes and fees.

More than a majority of cities seem to have a satisfactory financial condition. Why be so insistent about the dire effects of Gramm-Rudman and the loss of federal aid? Isn't this exaggerating and painting an unnecessarily bleak picture just in order to rationalize keeping federal grants programs for your constituency?

It is true that cities have made sacrifices, giving up aid and raising taxes, for the past several years. Some are in good shape, but many, especially in regions beset by economic turndown, and across the South where oil revenues have taken a disastrous plunge, are at the end of their ropes or fast getting there. Poverty in America, after dropping to 11.1% of the population in 1973, since 1980 has remained at or above 13%, reaching 15% in 1984. Unemployment, which remained at 4% or less in the 1950s, had risen to 6.9% in 1980 and was 7.2% of the workforce in 1985.[20] Cutting aid now can only make these situations worse.

What is the rationale for General Revenue Sharing when the federal government is so deep in debt and when many of the jurisdictions getting this aid are already very wealthy?

General Revenue Sharing was not introduced to rise or fall with the fiscal fortunes of the federal Treasury. It was created to help defray the costs of city compliance with federal mandates (for added discussion of Mandates, see Chart 2; and Chapter 2, pp. 16–21). Moreover, Revenue Sharing money was apportioned largely on the basis of city need. The poorer cities got the larger allotments. When President Nixon signed General Revenue Sharing into law in 1972 there was a federal deficit; despite this, the bill was enacted.[21]

Chart 2. Recent Federal Mandates on Cities

- Small Quantity Generator Hazardous Waste Regulations
- Stormwater Permit Requirements
- Leaking Underground Storage Tank Regulations
- Fair Labor Standards Act Amendments
- IRS Vehicle Requirements
- Medicare Coverage
- Social Security Coverage
- Reporting Requirements on Property, Personal Property, and Income Taxes

The impact of losing revenue sharing may not be noticed in the more prosperous jurisdictions that receive minimal amounts under the bill's allocation formula. But the impact on communities that benefited the most from it has been devastating. The affluent California community of Walnut Creek, population 55,000 has lost only $231,000, or about 1.7%, of its locally raised revenues. In contrast, for East St. Louis, Illinois, a hard-pressed community of about 55,000, elimination of Revenue Sharing has meant a loss of $1.36 million, or nearly 22% of its locally raised revenues. It is clear from this who has been hurt most.[22]

AS FOR THE FUTURE . . .

There are many reasons for the federal government maintaining a strong support role for cities, and this chapter has touched on many. But there is one overriding reason for continuing this role through this

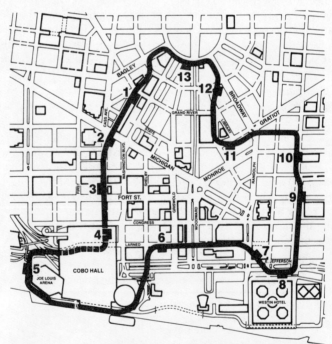

THE PEOPLE MOVER covers a 2.9 mile route through downtown Detroit. Thirteen elevated stations are designed for wheelchair access. Fares: adults, 50¢; seniors, free.

Source: Route map courtesy of Detroit Transportation Corporation. Reprinted, with permission, from Kolon, Bittker & Desmond, Inc., Troy, Michigan.

WHAT FEDERAL AID CAN DO.   The Detroit People Mover, under discussion since 1971, completed 1987. Funded in 1982 for $137 million; final cost $200 million, with $157 million (78%) paid by federal grants. Twelve driverless vehicles are pulled by magnetic traction; computerized control system operates the system.
Source: Courtesy of Detroit Transportation Corporation. Reprinted, by permission, from Kolon, Bittker & Desmond, Inc., Troy, Michigan.

decade and into the 1990s: No other level of government can handle the tasks of the national social agenda as well, and support that agenda at a level which is required.

Consider, first, the question of low-income housing. This is not a state or local problem in essence; it is a national problem, and one in which the federal government has been deeply, and successfully, involved since the Housing Act of 1937. Consider, also, the problems of maintaining the safety and purity of water, ground, and air. None of these substances are respectors of state boundaries; all lie on and across each of the 50 states. Fifty sets of differing regulations would guarantee no regulation at all of these basic national resources.

Consider the fact of federal mandates. The federal government does not set up its own bureaucracy to enforce its regulations; it works through existing state and local public agencies, requiring them to enforce mandates dealing with civil rights, housing, the environment, and many others. These mandates cost money to enforce. Unless the federal

government puts up the money to pay for this enforcement, the result
will be either, that state and local governments do nothing, or they groan
and take the money from their own pocket. Neither result is fair to all
concerned. Federal aid, including the defunct General Revenue Sharing, exists in part to avoid these negative outcomes (see Chart 2).

Consider, too, the fact that federal money is really essential for most
federal social, economic, and environmental programs to operate at all.
If the federal government withdraws, it is very unlikely that state or local
administrations will step in to fill the gap. A report to the Urban Institute in Washington, D.C., titled "Testing The Social Safety Net," closely examined the events in four metropolitan areas between 1981 and
1983 as cuts were made in federal assistance for abused and neglected
children, the chronically mentally ill, and the low-income elderly. The
study found that federal cuts led to parallel or modified reductions in
San Diego, Boston, and Richmond, Virginia. Only Detroit came close to
offsetting the loss, drawing on state and local assistance. Local charities
also helped.[23] In general, studies on the subject show that "substitution"
of local money for lost federal money does not occur. No feds, no
program.

Consider as well the facts of a recent study by the National Alliance of
Business. This study concluded that there will be a significant growth
over the next ten to fifteen years of the "less well-educated segments of
the population that have typically been the least prepared for work."
This growth of the less-educated worker will occur at the same time that
the economy is demanding higher levels of skills in the workforce. Yet,
in the words of the study, anticipated "pervasive mismatches between
workplace needs and workforce capabilities" will require an enormous
amount of general and vocational education money, a strong justification for the continuation of federal job training programs which specialize in exactly that kind of training.

And finally, consider the fact that many of the federal grants programs have gone to help private business, to keep the urban industrial
machine running full speed ahead. The grants in this category include
the now-defunct UDAG and CDBG, the still-functioning Small Business
Administration, and others. If we take seriously the metaphor of cities as
"engines of our economy" then we should also maintain a serious federal
commitment to insure the machine is kept running well, a commitment
that includes exercising federal, legal, regulatory, tax, and financial assistance powers.

CONCLUSION: DEVOLUTION, GOOD AND BAD

In 1982 President Reagan proposed, as a focus of his State of the Union
address, a devolution of federal powers to the state and local levels. The

outline of this proposal was received with initial enthusiasm by city officials. But the enthusiasm waned rapidly when it became apparent that
little, if any, federal financial support would accompany this "shedding"
of federal program responsibilities onto the states. In practice, the devolution anticipated by the administration was a devolution of program
responsibility without devolution of program money.

In a 1985 report by the Advisory Commission on Intergovernmental
Relations the subject of devolution and turnbacks was examined again.
The report drew several lengthy and pointed dissents. In their dissent,
Governor Ted Schwinden of Montana, Mayor Joseph P. Riley Jr. of
Charleston, South Carolina, and Mayor William H. Hudnut III of Indi-
anapolis stated:

> [The Commission's turnback recommendation] would result in a dereliction of
> responsibilities by Washington, particularly toward the nation's cities. This recom-
> mendation is not so much an effort to decongest the federal system as it is a
> philosophical desire by some to have our national government wash its hands of any
> concern for local needs and problems.[24]

In his dissent, Senator David Durenberger (R-Minn.) expressed concern
that the Commissions proposal "would seriously exacerbate fiscal inequities in our federal system, rather than reduce them." Representative
Ted Weiss (D-NY) also dissented without submitting formal
comments.[25]

Can there be a constructive "devolution" proposal which does not
sacrifice the cities? In the current deficit-cutting atmosphere of Washington, it seems unlikely. In the meantime the cities will rely on their
own entrepreneurial spirit and fiscal abilities to promote economic
growth and encourage innovation.

However, over the long haul, the development of cities will also require a strong fiscal presence by the national government, a presence
that will have to include both direct programs of financial assistance and
a judicious use of tax incentives.

NOTES AND REFERENCES

Note: In the following citations, the acronym NLC refers to the National League of Cities.
Nation's Cities Weekly is the official weekly publication of the National League of Cities.

1. Census Bureau Report (Spring 1986).
2. The GRS program, providing unrestricted grant money to local governments, was
terminated in FY 87 (1986).
3. UDAGs were authorized, but at zero funding, in 1989.
4. Advisory Commission on Intergovernmental Relations (ACIR) staff calculations.
5. NLC analysis of Budget of the U.S. Government for Fiscal 1987, as reported in
Nation's Cities Weekly (February 10, 1986).

6.   Reggie Todd, "Federal Housing Policy Is In Disarray," *Nation's Cities Weekly* (special report) (February 24, 1986), p. 3.

7.   Cushing Dolbeare, "Federal Housing Assistance: Who Gets It? Who Needs It?" *NLC Policy Working Paper* (1985), p. 32, Chart.

8.   Barbara Harsha, "Transit Funding Shows DOT Reneged On Gas Tax Promises," *Nation's Cities Weekly* (February 7, 1983), p. 7.

9.   Barbara Harsha, "Transportation Proposal Once Again Would Decimate Transit," *Nation's Cities Weekly* (February 10, 1986), p. 9.

10.   John F. Shirey, "Revenue Sharing Renewed," *Nation's Cities Weekly* (December 22, 1980), p. 1. The reauthorization for GRS deleted the state share for fiscal 1981 and made the 1982 and 1983 state share subject to annual appropriations by Congress.

11.   NLC, "Survey on Economic Conditions and Outlook," findings reported in *Nation's Cities Weekly* (January 13, 1986). For more details on this survey of officials' attitudes, see Chapter 2, p. 23, Table 6.

12.   FY 1980 budget authority, taken from Budget of the United States Government for Fiscal 1981, as reported in *Nation's Cities Weekly* February 4, 1980; and FY 1987 proposed budget authority as taken from Budget of the United States Government for Fiscal 1987, as reported in *Nation's Cities Weekly* February 10, 1986.

13.   Reggie Todd, "The Dismantling of Housing Assistance," *Nation's Cities Weekly* (February 10, 1986), p. 3.

14.   U.S. Congress, Joint Committee on Taxation, "Estimates of Federal Tax Expenditures for Fiscal Years 1986–90" (JCS-8-85) (April 1985).

15.   Office of Management and Budget (OMB), *The Budget of the United States Fiscal Year 1988. Special Analyses*, Table G-1.

16.   Frank Shafroth, special report on tax reform, *Nation's Cities Weekly* (May 12, 1986), p. 5.

17.   Since this was written, the Supreme Court has invalidated that portion of the Gramm-Rudman Act that allowed the GAO to make final budget cutting decisions. The act itself remains in force. For more detail of Gramm-Rudman provisions, see Chapter 1, note 18.

18.   Frank Shafroth, "Gramm-Rudman: Deciphering Reality," *Nation's Cities Weekly* (January 20, 1986), p. 1.

19.   NLC analysis of Budget of the United States Government for Fiscal 1987, as reported in *Nation's Cities Weekly* (February 10, 1986).

20.   Figures from U.S. Bureau of Labor Statistics (BLS).

21.   In a message to NLC, President Nixon stated:

   I look forward to signing this legislation with a very special feeling, for I am convinced that this is potentially one of the most important bills I will ever sign.

And in 1976, when there was a deficit of $66 billion, President Gerald A. Ford signed the revenue sharing reauthorization, declaring, "If there ever was a program that earned its keep, revenue sharing is that program." Even President Reagan, upon signing the 1983 reauthorization declared that "The federal government never spent money more wisely than by devoting it to revenue sharing." The deficit in 1983 was $195 billion.

22.   Figures from a state-by-state analysis on the effect of eliminating revenue sharing for local governments, prepared January 1986, by Fiscal Planning Services, Washington, D.C.; for the National Coalition to Save General Revenue Sharing.

23.   Martha R. Burt and Karen J. Pittman, "Testing the Social Safety Net," a study published by the Urban Institute, Washington, D.C. (April 1986).

24.   Advisory Commission on Intergovernmental Relations (ACIR), "Devolving

Federal Program Responsibilities and Revenue Sources to State and Local Governments"
(Document A–104) (March 1986), p. 5.
  25. For more detail on this ACIR *Report,* see Chapter 2, note 7.

PART II

INCREASING PRODUCTIVITY,
CONTROLLING COSTS

Chapter 4

PROGRAM RANKINGS, REDUCTION LEVELS, AND ALTERNATIVE BUDGETS: A RATIONAL METHOD FOR DECREMENTAL BUDGETING

Roger L. Kemp

SUMMARY. This chapter outlines two devices and a strategy for dealing with revenue cutbacks at the local government level. The first device is to establish a ranking of programs by their value to the community, a *program value heirarchy*. The second is to define four possible *levels of reduction* for any program. The strategy is to prepare and publicize an *alternative budget*. This alternative budget is disseminated *before* anticipated cuts (or revenue losses) are actually imposed to clarify to the public exactly what cuts will mean in terms of possible service loss. This overall approach will make rational, and minimize the pain inherent in, any process of budget reductions.

INTRODUCTION

Much has been written in recent years about techniques for coping with urban austerity.[1] Some have dealt with cutback management in an international perspective.[2] Alongside these useful volumes is the basic literature on public budgeting.[3]

All of these sources have enlarged our knowledge of the budgetary

53

process. But together they lack what this chapter will attempt: a rational, step-by-step process for making budget reductions. Central to this process is the determination of the relative value of each public service. This chapter will show how to define the value of public programs, or at least, will provide a way to think about the value of public programs as a means to establishing a "program value heirarchy." And it will define four different levels of service reduction, from total (or near total) elimination to very limited reduction, and show how to use these rankings and reduction levels to develop an alternative budget.

A considered, or rational, process such as this has been used successfully in various California cities, including Seaside (pop. 36,500) and Placentia (pop 37,300).[4] Adopting such a process by city or county elected officials helps to minimize the pain inevitably associated with budget reductions, and helps to keep the process from becoming a battleground of special interest groups.

DECREMENTAL BUDGETING: THE WRONG WAY

The first step in reducing budgets is to decide the very political question of the relative value of all public services. Any service has some value, certainly to those who utilize it. Elected officials who have tried to reduce public services benefiting only a select segment of the population can attest to this fact. Those benefiting from a service which is under consideration for reduction invariably desire, and succeed, in participating vocally in the deliberation process. By jamming the hall of a public meeting they can apply enormous pressure on decisionmakers. As a result it is often difficult or impossible to reduce public services. This is simply a fact of political life.

Budget reductions done in this political way have unfortunate results. The services that have the smallest public constituency are the first to go. Generally these are staff departments, such as finance, data processing, or productivity programs. There are only limited reductions that can be made in these programs, however; and equally important, their value, such as that of a program in productivity and effectiveness evaluation, are often worth more in annual government savings than their entire annual cost. Savings can most easily be extracted from such programs, but the resulting cuts are not large, the cost may be great, and the whole process avoids the central issue of establishing the relative value of all public services.

WHAT GIVES A PROGRAM "VALUE"?

The procedure recommended for reducing outlays relies on a "value heirarchy" or pyramid that ranks programs by their value. Whereas value is itself a subjective phrase, the program heirarchy is based on the simple assertion that some programs are worth more than others, and the assumption that a specification of their value (or importance) can be made explicit and defended.[5]

"Value" and "importance" are based on two elements: *how widely* a service is used and needed (service diffusion); and whether the service is *vital* (essentiality) to a non-majority of users.

The first element is by far the most important and easiest to agree on. It requires that the public program not be oriented toward "special interests" but is genuinely community-wide, with a vast majority, or totality of the population, either at risk or at need.

The second element recognizes the need for those services which may be used by less than a majority, or by only a few, yet which are absolutely needed by such a non-majority. Ramps for wheelchairs at curbsides and at building entrances are used only by people with a handicap; however, they are so important to the normal existence of the handicapped that such a program has a strong claim on the public purse.[6] Sickle cell anemia, which affects only a non-majority (specifically, blacks), because it is a matter of life and death, has a claim. Additional police patrols in a high crime area is another example. In general, programs that benefit non-majorities strengthen their claim when they heavily impact the health, safety, and security of property of their beneficiaries. Training housing inspectors to identify lead in wall paint is an example. Although it is generally only children in low-income areas who suffer from ingesting leaded wall paint, some city attention to this would be justified, both because it is a matter of life and health, and because training inspectors who will be on the site anyway involves a very small amount of additional resources.

In thinking about programs that benefit majorities or non-majorities, the distinction between programs that are "vital" and those that are simply "important" is crucial. A tree planting program may be important in beautifying a neighborhood. In years when budgets are growing it might be an affordable program. But when budgets must be cut, and the first dollar must be cut either from the emergency ambulance program or from tree planting, it is obvious which has to go. The difference between "important" and "vital" is itself a vital difference.

CREATING A PROGRAM VALUE HEIRARCHY

The first step in a program value heirarchy is to arrange programs according to their value; their required (mandated) character; and their impact on city finances. The spectrum of public services includes programs that cannot under any circumstances be reduced and programs that pander to special interests. The former programs include basic, or essential services and services mandated by higher levels of government. The latter are "nice to have" services that neither promote the overall health, welfare, and safety of the majority nor the vital interests of the minority. The key to successful budget reduction is to take into account this basic dichotomy.

The first step in creating a heirarchy is to divide all public services into four separate categories based on value, mandate, and financial impact. All government programs are categorized, including those that have non-local funding, or are paid from enterprise funds, or that run largely on volunteer labor. The resulting heirarchy is shown in Table 1.

Value Level A

This level of public services encompasses essential public services. These programs, because of their nature, cannot or should not be reduced under any circumstances except loss of population. Minimal levels of police, fire, and public works services fall into this category.[7] Public services that are mandated by federal or state government, those that are necessary to meet debt service obligations, or those whose net cost to government's discretionary funds is zero or negative due to outside funding, fall in this category. Programs that are financed entirely from user fees should be included here, because cutting such programs results in no tax saving.[8]

Value Level B

These programs include those that are highly desirable but not absolutely essential. The public services provided in this category usually fall into four groups. First, the program is strongly supported by local elected officials. Second, the services provided make an important and measurable contribution to the safety, health, and general welfare of the entire community. Third, the service in question results in the receipt of substantial funding from another level of government (state or federal). Fourth, the program generates substantial volunteer services which no-

Table 1.   Program Value Heirarchy

Value Levels	Category
A	Essential Programs
B	Highly Desirable Programs
C	Nice-But-Not Necessary Programs
D	First-To-Go Programs

ticeably contribute to the overall level of service to the whole community. By cutting a program that costs $1 but provides an additional $2 in volunteer services, a local government may be doing itself more harm than good.

Value Level C

This is the "nice but not necessary" category. Programs at this level have significant value but do not provide essential or necessary public services. These programs do not contribute to the overall health, safety, or general welfare of the entire community. Such programs usually benefit only a specific client group for whom the service is not vital, or generate volunteer services which contribute to the level of services provided to only a portion of the community. Such programs generate only a portion of their revenues, or no revenues, through user fees, and receive no outside funding. These services are usually initiated at the request of special interest groups and typically only benefit the group seeking the service.

Value Level D

Services that fall into this level are the "first to go" programs. If funds are restricted for any reason these programs would be the first to be eliminated or reduced. Public services provided by such programs contribute to the health, safety, or general welfare of only a minor portion of the community. They usually augment a preexisting basic level of services, and not funding them would have no great impact on the prevailing service level.

Outdated, impractical, or frivolous programs are in this category. Examples of such programs include recreational fads which come and go; yesterdays popular synchronized swim program may be today's unsupported event. A burglary prevention program that once required house calls by police may now be available on cable TV.

Programs in this service level are often ones that should be eliminated regardless of the fiscal situation.

DEFINING CATEGORIES: A PUBLIC PROCESS

The previously mentioned definitions of four value levels are suggestive only. It would lend greater political legitimacy to the budget-reduction process if the criteria used to rank public services were determined by elected officials in a public forum setting where citizen input could be solicited. Once agreement has been reached on how to place value on different services; or exactly, on how to define each level of value, then an objective framework exists on which to evaluate and classify all government activity. With this step completed, all department programs can be examined, analyzed, and ranked.

The input of the public is needed for several reasons. First, no budget cutting is going to go on *without* vociferous public input; local government officials will have to deal with it sometime. Second, it does help give guidance both to council and administrators as to how the public values each program. Third, and most important, it includes the public "in" in setting up the rules of the budget cutting game; having decided on the rules, public groups cannot so easily complain about how the game is played, or its outcome.

But we are not through yet. Programs usually are not eliminated in their entirety. Another set of criteria is needed for deciding *how much* to cut a program.

REDUCTION LEVELS:
HOW DEEP SHALL THE CUTS BE?

Governments usually increase their annual budgets by varying increments. Occasionally new programs are added, but the majority of additional funds are usually the result of increases in personnel, inflationary increases in operation and maintenance costs, and increases in the level of existing services.[9]

Because budgets increase incrementally, it stands to reason that they should be decreased in the same manner. Moreover it is politically less abrasive to reduce the level of a program than it is to eliminate a program entirely. Reducing the budget in such a way is known as "decremental budgeting." Public services are not eliminated wholesale but are instead reduced, a method that reduces stress on both citizens and officials. Finally, decremental budgeting minimizes the impact of reductions in those programs where vacancies exist. Eliminating a position that is currently vacant has no immediate negative consequences.

Yet sooner or later "real" cuts must be made, and public officials must establish reduction levels to help in this task. These reduction levels are defined in Table 2.

Reduction Level 1

Program reductions at this level would reduce well over half of, or the entire, program. Cuts of this magnitude may occur in basic public ser-

Table 2. Service Reduction Levels

Reduction Level	Extent of Reduction
1	Substantial; or Elimination
2	Major Portion of Program
3	Minor Portion of Program
4	No Impact on Public Services

services, and if so, would affect the health, safety, and general welfare of the citizens of the community.[10]

Reduction Level 2

Program reductions at this level would reduce a sizeable portion of a program. Essential services would not be affected. The impact of this program reduction would definitely be felt by those citizens using the provided service, but the reduction would only marginally influence the health, safety, and general welfare of the community. These cuts could affect special groups—in a certain neighborhood, or the elderly, or the low income—or a segment of the general public. Cuts could be made in any public service outside of police and fire, and could include such acts as phasing out of a recycling program, closing a library or golf course, or ending special transit services.

Reduction Level 3

Reductions at this level would have only a marginal impact on prevailing public services, and would not have more than a marginal impact on service levels, nor substantially affect the safety, health, or welfare of citizens in the community. Most of the cuts in General Revenue Sharing, in those communities where GRS was not supporting essential services, would fit in this category.

Reduction Level 4

Reductions in this grouping would have little or no impact on prevailing public services. They should be implemented regardless of a local government's financial condition. This category includes program reductions resulting from reorganizations, planned economies, or simply reductions in operation and maintenance costs that do not affect the services being provided. Such reductions do not influence the safety, health, or general welfare of citizens in any way.

Once the relative importance of public services has been properly determined and the impact of particular budget reductions categorized, program cuts can be implemented. Governments, regardless of their level, will rarely have to institute cuts at reduction levels 1 or 2. Most budget reductions will fall into levels 3 or 4.

PUTTING IT ALL TOGETHER

Once public services have been arranged by value heirarchy, those programs placed in service level D (first-to-go programs) would be the first to be reduced, commencing with reduction level 4 (no impact on public services). Other programs would then be reduced to levels 4, 3, 2, or 1 as needed to balance the budget.

If the agency's budget is still not reduced to the desired level, this process would then be applied to those programs in Public Service Grouping 3 (nice-but-not-necessary), and so forth, until the budget was in balance. Simple forms may be developed to expedite this process. The forms would be based on the logic contained in Table 3. Prior to eliminating any public services for reasons of economy, consideration should first be given to financing the program on a user-fee basis. The willingness of people to pay the cost of a service demonstrates the existence of citizen demand for the service. Financing a program on a user-fee basis enables government to provide a level of service that meets the demand. All fees should be realistically developed to reimburse government for the full expense of providing the service, including applicable overhead costs.[11] Every effort should be made to preserve equity in the delivery of public services, and consideration should be given to those individuals who may find that a charge for services creates an undue economic hardship. In such cases, exemptions may be granted.

Table 3. The Decremental Budgeting System

Cuts Are Made	Program Value	Level of Reduction by Sequence
First	D	4, 3, 2, 1
Second	C	4, 3, 2, 1
Third	B	4, 3, 2, 1
Last	A	4, 3, 2, 1

USING THE METHOD: CASE HISTORIES

In the City of Oakland, California, the initial process of proposing budget reductions in response to Proposition 13 in the late 1970s was piecemeal. For the most part, department managers were permitted to propose their own budgetary reductions, subject to the scrutiny of the Office of Budget and Management Services, and the approval of the city manager. The *political* process of reviewing these administratively-instigated program reductions can be characterized as controversial. Several alternative budget cut rounds were necessary to reach agreement among the city's elected officials. Subsequent budget balancing efforts reflected the more orderly administrative process described in this chapter. The resulting political process of reviewing proposed cuts and making them was less political. The process of coping with Proposition 13 cuts lasted in Oakland into the early 1980s.

Budget reductons in the City of Seaside, California, where the author was City Manager during this period, employed the process described in this chapter. This process involved the use of priority rankings for public services. All budgetary reductions were initially prepared at the departmental level, and differences of opinion were reconciled through negotiations with the city manager prior to presenting a list of proposed reductions to City Council. This overall process can be characterized as tranquil in comparison to the process initially employed in Oakland.

Both Oakland and Seaside have strong ethnic and political groups. The Program Ranking Process that worked well in such an environment can be expected to work as well or better in more homogeneous communities.

EMPLOYING THE "ALTERNATIVE BUDGET" METHOD: INITIAL STEPS

Complementary with the method of Program Rankings is the use of an Alternative Budget. This is a budget which, prepared before actual cuts are implemented, shows citizens exactly what cuts will (or could) mean in terms of service reductions. It brings home the "real" meaning of anticipated reductions.[12]

Step 1: A "Pre-Cuts" Legal Opinion

If a revenue-reducing measure is under consideration, then top management has the responsibility to obtain an authoritative opinion as to the impact of this potential cut on local government. The city or county attorney's opinion would be desirable because of its authoritative nature.

This "legal opinion" should analyze all provisions of the proposed legislation and set forth the most likely reductions on city operations. Any special features of the proposed legislation, such as mandated deadlines for compliance, should also be analyzed. Alternative legislative scenarious (outcomes) can be developed, together with an examination of the political climate surrounding such legislation, and from this the most likely scenario developed.

Step 2: A Financial Assessment

A financial assessment of the anticipated cuts should then be undertaken. This should look at anticipated direct losses, and at secondary losses such as loss of matching funds, loss of possible property and sales tax dollars due to loss of new construction, and all other possible losses.

Once all possible revenue losses have been properly assessed, the total "most likely" anticipated revenue loss can then be estimated. A "worst case" and "best case" scenario can be included if desired.

Step 3: Operational Impact Assessment

The initial operational impact assessment should examine several factors. If the potential revenue loss affects discretionary funds, such as General Revenue Sharing, most of the public services provided by that government unit will be directly impacted. If nondiscretionary revenue sources are reduced, such as grants targeted at specified uses or user groups, the analysis need only address the impact of revenue loss on these services. If other funds can be diverted to pay for these services, however, the impact of diverting funds away from these other services must be examined. In any event, the operational analysis should be thorough and should assess the anticipated impact of the reduction on both directly and indirectly affected services.

CREATING THE ALTERNATIVE BUDGET

Doing the first three steps, and publicizing the results, educates the council and the public, and leads naturally to the next step, preparing the actual alternative budget. This alternative budget is the hypothetical budget that would result should the most likely legislative scenario come about. It should include cuts that result both directly and indirectly, and where choices exist as to ways to implement cuts, those choices should be highlighted. If a hiring freeze is a likely result, this should be noted.

The leadership for the development of this budget should come from elected councilmen, because they alone are directly responsible to the citizens. When this leadership does not exist, it is up to the appointed administrative officials to propose an overall strategy, based on value rankings, reduction levels, and the alternative budget.

Once the alternative budget is developed by administrative officials, it can be presented to the council and public hearings or meetings can be scheduled and conducted. The purpose of such hearings or meetings is to permit citizens to review the proposed budgetary and service reductions and to provide for proper public input into the political decision-making process. Needless to say, the alternative budget will have to be modified until a consensus is reached by the council as to the desireability of any set of proposed service reductions. Once this has been accomplished, the alternative budget can be finalized and adopted—and implemented, if Congress or the state follows through on proposed reductions.

THE NEXT STEP: PUBLIC NOTIFICATION

As soon as the alternative budget is adopted it should be publicized. Now, instead of the city talking vaguely about possible cuts from Washington, the public can see, in specific service-reduction terms, exactly what possible cuts are going to mean to them. A "public service impact statement" can be prepared and made available to the public, and notices posted in facilities that are facing cuts.

It is at this point that the alternative budget can be used as a political tool to galvanize citizens, who see what projected cuts will really mean, into writing state or federal legislators to oppose the cuts. Yet the purpose of this process is not to campaign against cuts. It is to accomplish two ends, which are accomplished magnificently: (1) to inform citizens of anticipated possible cuts, so that when cuts do come, they are anticipated and are not a wrenching surprise; and (2) to prepare the city for a completely orderly transition to a new, lower level of revenue. Instead of waiting for the axe to fall, and then making cuts in a spirit of acrimony, the necessary adjustments have already been anticipated, planned out, and executed, reducing stress to the minimum possible level.

And, of course, if anticipated cuts do not occur, the council can adopt a budget at full funding levels,[13] although in the present political environment it might be well advised to start now to build up a "rainy day fund," as Indianapolis and other cities have done.

AND IF THE AXE DOES FALL . . .

If Congress or the state does follow through on cuts the city is faced with a new situation. Its alternative budget was based on anticipated cuts; actual cuts will always differ in some degree. In the light of what the real cuts are, the city should revise its financial and operational analyses, and adopt a revised final budget.

It is worth noting that this methodology works as well with legislatively-mandated aid cuts as with voter-approved initiatives. California and Wisconsin are the best known states providing for voter-initiated popular initiatives having the force of law. Even if the state house or Congress acts first to head off a popular tax-control movement, the process previously outlined is perfectly serviceable.

THE FUTURE

Local governments will probably face the threat of revenue reductions, from the "property tax revolt" movements or from federal budget cutters, into the 1990s. The process previously outlined can give local officials the assurance that there is, in fact, a way to accommodate such cuts with a minimum of political and psychological stress.

The process of cutting federal aid levels began under President Carter in 1978. In 1986 General Revenue Sharing was eliminated by a bipartisan Congress. The desire for "less government" seems to have become a bipartisan rallying point. Local government which started out like the Model T, a simple entity providing only the most basic services, became a greatly enlarged, luxury model over the past fifty years. Now the public seems to be saying "Stop." The desire to simplify, as well as the practical need to do something about a federal deficit now between $100 and $200 billion annually, suggests that budget reductions will be with us for a while. A strategy for making such reductions, such as the strategy outlined in this chapter, which is responsible not only to consumers of special services but also to those who "foot the bill," must ultimately prevail.

APPENDIX: THE ALTERNATIVE BUDGET PROCESS USING FLOWCHART SYMBOLS[14]

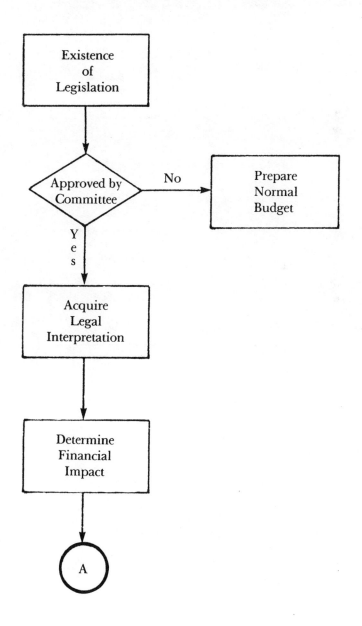

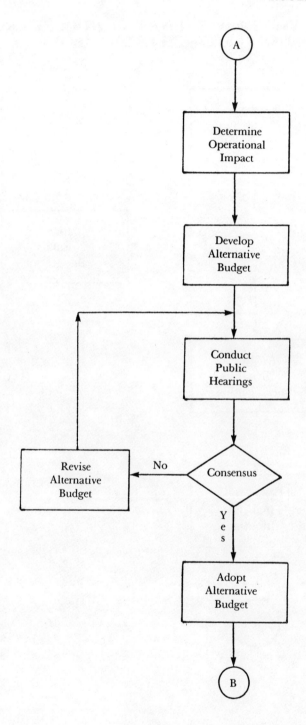

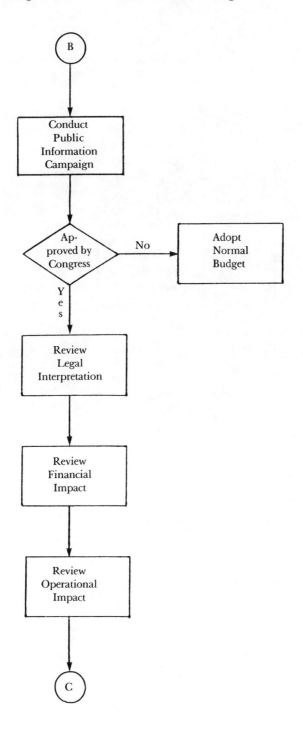

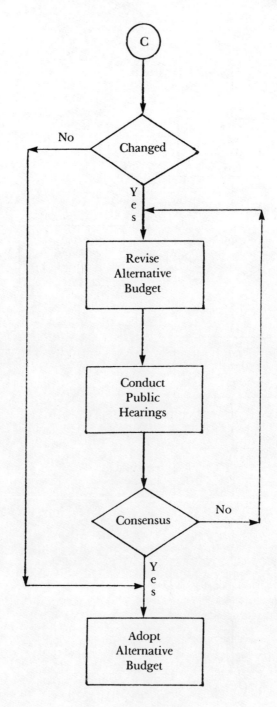

NOTES AND REFERENCES

1.   Terry N. Clark, and Lorna C. Ferguson, *City Money* (New York: Columbia University Press, 1983); Terry N. Clark, *Coping With Urban Austerity* (Greenwich, CT: JAI Press, 1985); Elizabeth K. Kellar, *Managing With Less* (Washington, D.C.: International City Management Association, 1979); Roger L. Kemp, *Coping With Proposition 13* (Lexington, MA: Lexington Books, 1980); Charles H. Levine, *Managing Fiscal Stress* (Chatham, NJ: Chatham House Publishers, 1980); John Matzer, *Practical Financial Management* (Washington, D.C.: International City Management Association, 1984); Jacob B. Ukeles, *Doing More With Less* (New York: AMACOM Press, 1982). See also Terry N. Clark, *Financial Handbook for Mayors and City Managers* (New York: Van Nostrand, 1985).

2.   George G. Wynne, *Learning From Abroad—Cutback Management: A Trinational Perspective* (New Brunswick, NJ: Transaction Books, 1983).

3.   Allen Schick, *Perspectives on Budgeting,* rev. ed. (Washington, D.C.: American Society for Public Administration, 1986); Frederick O'R. Hayes *et al., Linkages. Improving Financial Management In Local Government* (Washington, D.C.: The Urban Institute Press, 1982); Gerard Miller, *The Cutting Edge: Effective Budgetary Presentations* (Washington, D.C.: Municipal Finance Officers Association, 1982).

4.   For a description of the Seaside experience see page 16.

5.   The theory of value is an established field of study in Philosophy. While philosophers often seem to be impractical in what they write, in fact there are philosophers who have made relatively practical examinations of values and the "proof" of values, and who have applied this to social questions. See Herbert Feigl and May Brodbeck, eds., *Readings in the Philosophy of Science* (New York: Appleton-Century-Crofts, 1953); Richard B. Brandt, ed., *Value and Obligation* (New York: Harcourt, Brace, 1961); Richard B. Brandt, with Kenneth Boulding, *Social Justice* (New York: Prentice-Hall, 1962); Alvin Goldman, ed., *Values and Morals: Essays in Honor of Richard Brandt, William Frankena, and Charles Stevenson* (Boston: D. Reidel, 1978); Michael Scriven, *Reasoning* (New York: McGraw-Hill, 1976). It would be of some value for a Master's candidate in Public Administration to apply value theory, as developed by social philosophers, into a method for Program Value Ranking and decremental (or incremental) budgeting.

6.   It is important to note that all claims are relative. A strong claim may or may not justify actual expenditure. How vital a program is to a non-majority will vary according to time and place.

7.   "Minimal levels" can be defined broadly as those levels below which the health and safety of citizens is endangered.

8.   Having defined an essential service or essential service level, local government is not thereby mandated to provide the service itself. Provision can be made under contract to an outside agency. For a cogent discussion of the difference between government's responsibility to ensure service, as opposed to actually providing it, see Ted Kolderie "Let's Not Say Privatization," *Urban Resources,* 2, 4 (Summer 1985): 9–15.

9.   On incremental budgeting, see the several volumes by Aaron Wildavsky, including *The Politics of the Budgetary Process,* 4th ed. (Boston: Little, Brown 1984); and Allen Shick, *Perspectives on Budgeting,* 2nd ed. (Washington D.C.: American Society for Public Administration, 1986).

10.   The easy and tempting way to cut is to simply eliminate positions from programs that have vacancies (unfilled positions). But this would mean that a city's entire budget reduction strategy is driven by the accident of where vacancies exist now. A better way is to first set up a heirarchy of programs, based on value; then, if unfilled positions exist in programs with a high value, the city can retrain present employees from low-value programs into new skills and place them in the program of higher value. The position in the

low-value program is then eliminated. Department directors in Cincinnati in 1986 were asked to "valuerank" their own Departments' programs into such a heirarchy and follow this retrain/replace procedure. See Chapter 8, page 15.

11.   For a useful and highly accurate way to estimate total program costs, including the costs of overhead, see Joseph T. Kelley, *Costing Government Services: A Guide for Decision Making* (Washington DC: Government Finance Research Center, of the Government Finance Officers Association, 1984).

12.   Of course, if such a budget is drawn up and disseminated during a "hot" campaign over a Proposition 13–type measure, the city could be accused of trying to panic the electorate. Here, the use of the Alternative Budget is proposed to concretize anticipated cuts and help the public make cuts that maximize the public's priorities.

13.   Using the language of Target Based Budgeting, the Alternative Budget represents a Service Level 1 budget; the "normal" budget, Service Level 2. See Chapter 8, "Target Based Budgeting," and table on p. 35.

14.   This process was originally developed by the author as a result of research conducted for his Ph.D. dissertation in Public Administration. © 1987, Roger L. Kemp.

Chapter 5

CONTRACTING OUT FOR LOCAL PUBLIC SERVICES

Philip E. Fixler, Jr. and Edward C. Hayes

SUMMARY. Contracting out for local government services has roots in the "economy and efficiency" tradition of public administration, dating from the turn of the century. Contracting today is used for support services by almost every local government in the country. The scope of contracting expanded in the 1970s to include health and human services, and in the 1980s to include "privatized" infrastructure. While there are critics who point to cases of failure, the failures are generally traceable to preventable causes, while the scholarly literature shows that contracting results in significant cost savings. An Appendix lists think tanks and information sources on contracting.

EFFICIENCY IN PUBLIC ADMINISTRATION: THE GENEALOGY OF SERVICE CONTRACTING

The founding writers of American public administration, from the turn of the century at least through the 1940s, were concerned directly or indirectly with the concept and practice of *efficiency*. It is important to remind ourselves of their passion for this idea, and of their enthusiasm for the corporate model which they saw as embodying it to the highest extent, for it is the same idea, and the same corporate vehicle transposed into service deliverer, that motivates the partisans and practitioners of contracting out. Although the founding writers never considered contracting in its modern form, replete with RFPs, RFQs, detailed service

71

specifications, computerized MIS and skilled monitoring—all of this so-
phistication having taken place in recent years—the shared concern for
efficiency of these writers and present day contracting theorists provides
service contracting with an intellectual pedigree which merits special
attention.

Woodrow Wilson and Frank Goodnow[2] are among the earliest of
American writers on public administration. A primary concern for
them, as for all the early writers, was to establish public administration as
a legitimate and distinct field of study, to separate policy *making* from
disinterested *administration*. Goodnow writes extensively on the need for
disentangling political (legislative) influence from lower level administrators, while leaving high level administrative "executives," to use his
word, subject to some policy oversight by Congress. This plea for political non-interference, from Goodnow and his contemporaries, can properly be read as a plea for both policy and administrative efficiency, with
efficiency and political meddling at opposite ends of the spectrum.

Wilson wrote of the need for a "science of administration" which
would "make [government's] business less unbusinesslike." "The field of
administration," he declared, "is a field of business." For the American
W.F. Willoughby, and for the German writer on bureaucracy, Max
Weber, whose impact on American writers was significant, efficiency is
the great value underlying all of their intellectual labors.

In addition there are many American writers whose plea for efficiency
is direct, requiring no explanation; so many, in fact, that it is tempting to
conclude that efficiency was the prime object of public administration
from the beginning. Woodrow Wilson, in his pioneering essay "The
Study of Administration (*Political Science Quarterly*, June 1887) wrote: "It
is the object of administrative study to discover, first, what government
can properly and successfully do, and secondly, how it can do these
proper things with the utmost possible efficiency and at the least possible
cost either of money or of energy." In his *Congressional Government*
(1900), Wilson states that "efficiency is the only just foundation for
confidence in a public officer." President William Howard Taft offered
his panegyric in a 1912 message titled "Economy and Efficiency in Government Service." The Progressive reformers, including Charles Beard
himself, proclaimed efficiency as the goal while they denounced the
spoils system as the enemy. The Municipal Bureau movement, which
had its origins in 1905 and led to the establishment of the New York
Bureau of Municipal Research in 1912, had efficiency emblazoned, fig-
uratively at least, on its banner. The American Academy of Political and
Social Sciences' symposium for 1912 was titled "The Efficiency of City
Government." Even such an unlikely source as Louis Brandeis, the fa-

mous New York lawyer and United States Supreme Court justice, whose "Brandeis Brief" is famous for introducing sociological arguments on behalf of the poor into court proceedings, was a believer. In his article "The Fruits of Efficiency," Brandeis hailed scientific management, whose centerpiece was time and motion studies.

As an extension, or perhaps as precondition, of their belief in efficiency was these writers' acceptance of private enterprise as a basically good institution, and of the corporate form as the model *par excellence* for the public sector to emulate. In his 1927 article, W.F. Willoughby identifies the private corporation as the correct model for a portion, at least, of national government. In his schema Congress is the equivalent of the board of directors of the corporation, the President is the equivalent of the Chief Administrative Officer, and several federal departments would become independently incorporated with Congress acting literally as a holding company.[3]

Writing in the 1930s, Marshall Dimock also stated the case for government-owned corporations, which, Dimock believed, would enjoy "the elasticity and autonomy which are required for efficient and progressive administration."[4] Unlike Willoughby, who saw room for government corporations only for limited functions, including revenue generation, management of public domains, and supplying materiel to government, Dimock saw corporations-in-place-of-departments as serving a wide variety of functions, and cited further advantages: a government corporation can be sued, is free of bureaucratic ponderousness (that is, it is more efficient), displays greater innovativeness, and is less inclined to use coercive power to achieve its ends. Leonard White, writing in 1926, also saw the private corporation as a correct blue print for government organization.

The Progressive reformers, who fought the battle against municipal corruption, likewise saw the private corporation and its efficiency as the ideal organizational framework for local government. Indeed the modern City Manager form of government seems to have been drawn up under the influence of the corporate ideal. Richard Spencer Childs, former President of the National Municipal league and originator of the Council-Manager plan, describes how he was inspired by the possibilities of a corporate organizational form, in which a city manager takes the place of the corporation's chief executive, while reading a newspaper editorial one day.[5] Childs' anticipations of a more efficient local government were correct: within a year twelve cities had adopted the Council Manager plan, and all reported significant improvements in operations including lower taxes and less Commission (Council) meddling in administrative affairs.

The Progressive reformers, well known for their attacks on business corruption of politics and private monopolies, never attacked the business system per se. As Dwight Waldo remarks,

The early reformers and the pioneers in public administration accepted the business example enthusiastically and practically without reservation.[6]

Waldo also writes that "Much as public administration owes to the stimulus of Progressivism and reform, its Founding Fathers seem hardly to have been touched" by muckraking critics of business. Even during the Great Depression, Waldo notes, leading public administrationists offered "hardly a suggestion as to what might replace business spirit, organization, and methods in government."

These early writers laid the groundwork for the giants of the 1930s and 1940s, whose concern for efficiency was, if anything, more explicit than their predecessors'. In their pathbreaking *Measuring Municipal Activities*,[7] written in 1938, authors Clarence E. Ridley and Herbert A. Simon state their thesis plainly: it is the administrator's job to "maximize the attainment of government objectives ... by the efficient employment of the limited resources that are available to him."[7] The authors give a clear definition to efficiency: it is "the accomplishment relative to available resources."[8] In 1937 Luther Gulick wrote: "In the science of administration, whether public or private, the basic 'good' is efficiency." From these beginnings have come the performance management methods and writings of both practitioners and academics in the past decade.

Leonard White is considered, with Luther Gulick and Herbert A. Simon, to be a founder of contemporary public administration; and like the other two men belongs in the school of those with a major concern with efficiency. In his *Introduction to the Study of Public Administration*[9] White defined public administration as simply the study of "the management of men and materials in the accomplishment of the purposes of the state." Throughout his writings White is primarily concerned with the efficient utilization of resources and the elimination of waste and inefficiency.

Although White, Gulick, and Simon brought an explicit concern for efficiency to *public* administration, French industrialist Henri Fayol and onetime American plant engineer Frederick W. Taylor reified efficiency into religion, first in the private sector. Industrial engineering and operations management, which sprang from their work, are described elsewhere in this volume.[10] For Fayol and Taylor, efficiency was not one object among many; it was the whole object. Industrial engineering has penetrated public administration *practice* for years, primarily in public works, maintenance, and engineering; and in progressive jurisdictions in the 1980s, has penetrated every department of local government.

It is true that the for-profit corporation, hired on contract as an "outsider" to deliver public services, is a far cry from the government-owned, no-profit corporations advocated by Willoughby and Simon, or even the manager-as-CEO paradigm seen by Childs and many others. No theorist through the 1940s ever contemplated private sector contracting as a major tool of public administration. Yet the motivation, the bottom line that unites the generations is the word: efficiency. Were Mssrs. Wilson, White, Simon, and the other early writers still with us, they would surely be writing about (and perhaps, although not necessarily, defending) this recent exotica.

Contracting also stands in a special relationship to the Public Choice school of political philosophy.[11] If this broad philosophy can be reduced to a few major principles they would include the following: (1) minimal cost in local government; (2) the right of citizens to choose that locality which offers the most desired "basket" of services; (3) from this, the right to incorporate municipalities with minimal services, or contracting for many services, as is the case with some 50 municipalities in Los Angeles County; and (4) the notion that human action is primarily based on economic self interest. Because it is in the interest of the citizen taxpayer to keep his taxes as low as possible, Public Choice tends to support methods that lead to that result, including multiple local jurisdictions in place of consolidated metropolitan services.

Finally it should be noted that the contracting technique, recast as "privatization," is used by contemporary philosophers and practitioners who wish, for philosophical reasons, to see the government sector reduced.[12] This helps to explain why contracting has been expanded in this decade to such nontraditional areas as fire and police. However, it is of real importance to realize that, although contracting can be put to the service of any philosophy, it nevertheless remains, as a subject and as a method, distinct from all political philosophies, including those of its advocates and detractors. It is, simply, a method, deserving of practical examination. It is that examination that concerns the rest of this chapter, which seeks answers to two practical questions: How good is contracting? How far can it be carried?

WHO CONTRACTS AND WHY?

We start with the question: Who contracts? And with the answer: Everyone. In the most recent national survey of local contracting,[13] no less than 99% of respondent local governments indicated that they had used contracting for the provision of at least one service in the past five years.[14] The total value of contracts in the 1987 survey, for all respondent governments, was $1 billion. Some 21% of respondents contracted less than $100,000 of services; 22% contracted over $1 million, and the rest were scattered in between, with the most (26%) contracting between $100,000 and $300,000.[15]

To find out why local governments contract out (or privatize), the

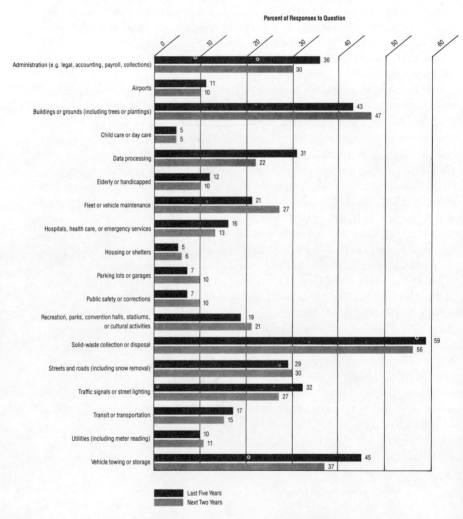

Figure 1.   Services Contracted Out
Which Services Has Your Government Contracted Out
In the Last Five Years? Which Services Does It
Plan to Contract Out In the Next Two Years?

Source: Touche Ross & Co., *Privatization in America: An Opinion Survey of City and County Governments on Their Use of Privatization and the Infrastructure Needs.* Reprinted with permission. (For additional information, contact: Irwin T. David, National Director-Public Sector Services, Touche Ross & Co., Washington Service Center, 1900 M Street NW, Washington, D.C. 20036-425.)

1987 survey asked: "To what extent have the following developments heightened your interest in privatization?" Out of the nine categories of answers received, the three most common were the growth in demand for services (65%), taxpayer resistance to tax increases (59%), and the elimination of federal revenue sharing (51%). It is worth noting that four of the nine answer categories deal with federal action: federal elimination of revenue sharing (51%), federal deficit reduction programs (29%), changes in the tax-exempt status of [industrial development] bonds (28%), and the Tax Reform Act of 1986 (20%). The importance of the discussion in the first three chapters of this volume is thus underscored; and the argument, that cuts in federal aid will lead to increases in local government productivity efforts, seems partially substantiated.

A databank of known contracts, including all of the 1,780 responses to a 1982 International City Management Association survey of local contracting, plus an additional 800 examples of contracts, leases, and privatized facilities found at random, has been maintained by the Local Government Center in Santa Monica. The database has some 28,500 entries. Only those entries that are contracts for services are shown in Table 1.

Table 1. Number of Local Government Jurisdictions Contracting for Services, 1987

Service	Number of Jurisdictions*
Residential solid waste collection	702
Solid-waste disposal/landfills	591
Street repair	466
Street/parking lot cleaning	193
Street light operation	698
Parking lot/garage operation	283
Emergency medical service	605
Vehicle towing and storage	1,130
Day care facility operation	355
Programs for the elderly	605
Operation/management of hospitals	248
Operation of mental health/retardation facilities and programs	296
Recreation services	512
Park landscaping/maintenance	252
Building/grounds maintenance	386
Building security	152
Data processing	370

Note: *Jurisdictions includes municipalities, counties, and special service districts.

Source: Privatization Database, Local Government Center.

The 1987 Touche-Ross/ICMA survey, in contrast, covered not only contracted services, but also "privatized" facilities. The survey defines privatization as the process whereby "a private sector organization builds or acquires a facility, such as a sewage-treatment plant, and then owns and operates the facility for the government." Large private capital expenditures are typical in facility privatization, and the survey shows that such measures have been employed within the past five years by 32% of

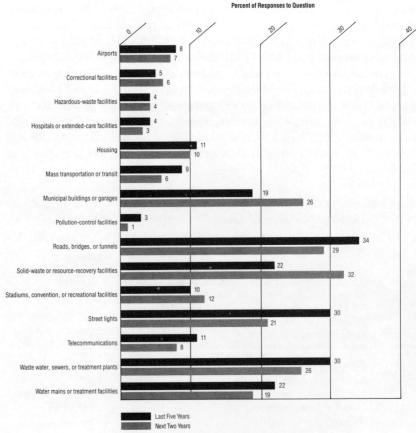

Percent of Responses to Question

Facility	Last Five Years	Next Two Years
Airports	8	7
Correctional facilities	5	6
Hazardous-waste facilities	4	4
Hospitals or extended-care facilities	4	3
Housing	11	10
Mass transportation or transit	9	6
Municipal buildings or garages	19	26
Pollution-control facilities	3	1
Roads, bridges, or tunnels	34	29
Solid-waste or resource-recovery facilities	22	32
Stadiums, convention, or recreational facilities	10	12
Street lights	30	21
Telecommunications	11	8
Waste water, sewers, or treatment plants	30	26
Water mains or treatment facilities	22	19

Figure 2. Facilities Privatized
Which Facilities Has Your Government Privatized
In the Last Five Years? Which Facilities Does It
Plan to Privatize In the Next Two Years?

Source: Touche Ross & Co., *Privatization in America: An Opinion Survey of City and County Governments on Their Use of Privatization and the Infrastructure Needs.* Reprinted with permission. (For additional information, contact: Irwin T. David, National Director-Public Sector Services, Touche Ross & Co., Washington Service Center, 1900 M Street NW, Washington, D.C. 20036-425.)

the respondent governments. Another 24% of respondent governments had sold some government assets within the past five years.

THE HISTORY OF CONTRACTING: AN EXPANDING SCOPE

Since 1945 local contracting has gone through three phases, defined by the scope or range of services that are contracted. In the first phase, lasting into the 1970s, local contracting focused on "hard" services with tangible products for which results were easily monitored. Refuse collection, street repair, utilities, vehicle towing, and some buildings and grounds maintenance were frequently contracted across the country in cities of all sizes. In small towns, contracting for record keeping and legal services were, and continue to be, common.

In the 1970s, as a result of both federal and local influences, and encouraged by the "Alternative Services" writing of the International City Management Association (ICMA) and others, the scope of contracting began to broaden from tangible services to social services, from "hard" to "soft." Cities and counties began to contract for childcare, drug and alcohol treatment programs, and many others. The 1982 survey by the International City Management Association showed how far social services contracting had progressed by the beginning of this decade.

Most of the contractors for these "soft" services, as Table 2 indicates, were nonprofit organizations, less suspect in the eyes of local officials because of the absence of a profit motive. But not all were so. Of the 59 services covered by the 1982 ICMA survey, each was contracted to a private, for-profit business by at least one of the 1,780 respondent local governments. In 23 of the 59 services, private for-profit companies received 10% or more of all contracts; in 14 of these services, private for-profit businesses received a quarter or more of all service contracts.[16]

Of prime significance was the fact of the shift to contracting of services which hitherto had been considered strictly the preserve of government. Police departments began to contract for clerical and laboratory functions; private businesses increasingly came to rely on private guard service. Jails and fire services began, on a small scale, to be contracted. Even city managers themselves have recently been hired on contract in smaller jurisdictions in Pennsylvania and Connecticut, where "circuit rider" managers are used by local jurisdictions needing only parttime administrators. The growth in the scope of contracting has continued into the 1980s, sharply narrowing the definition of "strictly governmental services" and alarming some theorists and practitioners that government

Table 2. Local Contracting for Social Services in 1982

Rank*	Service	Number of Localities Reporting	Percent Contracting with		
			Businesses	Neighborhoods	Nonprofits
1	Drug/alcohol treatment programs	626	6	4	41
2	Operation of mental health programs facilities	512	7	3	40
3	Day-care facility operation	436	35	6	37
4	Programs for elderly	1189	4	4	29
5	Public health programs	721	8	2	27
6	Operation/management of hospitals	361	30	1	27
7	Child welfare programs	558	5	2	24
8	Animal shelter operation	1225	13	1	18
9	Operation/management of public elderly housing	602	13	1	18
10	Insect/rodent control	1037	14	0	5
11	Animal control	1482	6	0	9
12	Sanitary Inspection	439	1	0	6

Note: *Percent columns are nonadditive. Each service is ranked by the highest percentage in any of the three columns; in case of a tie, the service with the larger number of localities reporting is ranked first.

Source: 1982 ICMA Survey; corrected and reprinted in John Tepper Marlin, ed., *Contracting Municipal Services* (New York: Ronald Press, 1984), p. 113, Table A.4. See note 12.

itself, and perhaps the Constitutional rights of citizens, might be contracted away.[17]

In the 1980s a second profound enlargement of the scope of contracting occurred, the rise of "infrastructure privatization." Prodded by growing service demands and cutbacks in federal grants and tax deductions, local governments have increasingly been inviting the private sector to design, finance, build, and own (or operate, on long term lease) such "public" facilities as wastewater plants, water systems, bridges, and roads. In several cases the private sector simply took over antequated facilities and brought them up to federal standards while operating them on a day-to-day basis. A summary of facility privatization is given in Figure 2.

Since 1985, private wastewater plants have been completed for several cities, including Chandler, Arizona and Auburn, Alabama. Both of these have been a clear success. Construction began on the two new wastewater plants, and 27 miles of interceptors, at Auburn in November 1984, a month before the final sale of bonds. The larger plant (5.4 million gallons per day) was completed on December 28, 1985, just over a year later, a period of financing and construction which was one-third to one-fifth the time a public entity would have required in the same circumstances.[18] The brevity of the project planning, finance, and construction cycle is a likely source of savings for any privatized project.

CONTRACTING AT THE STATE AND FEDERAL LEVELS

State governments have contracted for services since at least 1945, although at a slower rate than local governments. Like municipalities, states began contracting for non-client services, including custodial, engineering, highway maintenance, and security services, and have more recently moved to contract human services. Florida now contracts the operation of its South Florida State Hospital, which includes mental health services,[19] and Kentucky now contracts for the management of its Outwood Mental Retardation facility.[20]

States are increasingly becoming interested in contracting correctional facilities. Some states have contracted half-way houses, prerelease centers, and work furlough centers to private nonprofit and for-profit organizations. Many states have contracted out auxiliary services for correctional institutions, such as food provision and medical care. Two states, Kentucky and California, have contracted out the basic operation and management of prisons.[21] Kentucky's state prison contractor even owns the facility in which inmates are housed.

An important aspect of state involvement has been the passage of statewide enabling legislation. This legislation enables *local* governments to contract for certain services. Colorado, New Mexico, and Texas have passed such legislation, allowing local contracting for the operation and maintenance of local jails. New Jersey's legislation allows local contracting for wastewater treatment services, water supply facilities, and resource recovery plants.

The federal government first announced its contracting policy in 1955. In that year the Eisenhower administration announced that henceforth the government would neither begin nor continue to produce any product or service "if such product or service can be procured from private enterprise through ordinary business channels."[22] Lacking any legislative enforcement, this administrative policy has been largely flouted. In 1967, 60% of the commercial goods and services required by the federal government were delivered by private companies; by 1981, that share had fallen to 40%.[23] Both federal public employee unions and department managers have successfully pressured Congress to pass legislation forbidding contracting or at the least making it very difficult. No less than 13 pieces of such legislation were passed in the years 1978 through 1984. A major piece of legislation intended to neutralize these obstacles, the "Competition Savings Act of 1987," failed of passage like all its predecessors. In the same year the General Accounting Office report estimated that the Competition Savings Act could have saved the government from $2 billion to $3 billion annually.

Despite these barriers, contracting in Washington has grown. In the fiscal year 1984 the Defense Department held some 257 "competitions" between in-house and private sector suppliers. The private sector came in with the lowest bid in 108 cases, 42% of the total.[24] Support services, including custodial, buildings and grounds, food service, and security creeps forward yearly. Since the 1970s, the scope of contracting has broadened. The Urban Mass Transit Administration (UMTA) has used its local grants program to promote competitive contracting of local bus service.[25] The Department of Housing and Urban Development (HUD) now has a pilot program to encourage contracting of project management to tenants of public housing, and has recently begun to sell federally-owned housing units to low income tenants. The first such tenant-owner is pictured on page 24 in Chapter 2.

LOCAL CONTRACTING OVERSEAS

In Japan, local level contracting came into existence in the 1940s and is encouraged on a nationwide basis by the Ministry of the Interior.[26] As a result, Japan's 669 cities, called *shi*, have a blistering rate of contracting out: where a city provides a service, and the service can be separated out for contracting, the service is contracted 46.6% of the time. The total of services contracted in Japan is shown in Appendix 1.

On the European Continent there has been less local level contracting than in the United States. Yet there are striking examples. In Sweden, firms indirectly owned by the Swedish government provide limited private guard service to supplement public police at detention facilities.[27] In Denmark, the family-owned Falck company has, for several decades, provided fire protection and basic ambulance service to the majority of Denmark's population.

Central Europe has also shown some interest in contracting. In Switzerland, smaller towns contract for private police services to supplement regular public police.[28] In West Germany, where service contracting is more common, many cities contract for refuse collection, custodial service, window cleaning, street cleaning and maintenance, and park maintenance. Some German cities contract for the operation of hospitals, taxibus service, swimming pools, and the management of senior citizen residences. Contract police patrol the subway in Munich, Germany.[29]

In France, contracting for the supply and distribution of city water began in the nineteenth century. Some of France's present-day water companies are considered among the most advanced in the world. In 1985, Paris contracted its water distribution system out to two firms, one for the Right Bank and the other for the Left Bank of the Seine.[30]

DOES CONTRACTING SAVE MONEY? SOME RESEARCH EVIDENCE

The city that is starting to contract can expect *additional* costs, beyond that of in-house delivery, at two points: (1) the start-up period, and (2) during the life of the contract as the city hires or trains monitors. Prior to start-up are the time-costs of scoping the contract and letting the bids; after that, when the new provider begins his work, the usual experience is to have additional service costs until the contractor is broken in. Likewise, contract monitoring requires the assignment, and usually the training, of special city staff, as well as a time commitment by top management to read the service reports. The failure to anticipate and prepare fully for these additional costs is a major source of unnecessary grief in contracting.

A study in the mid-1970s by E.S. Savas shows a greater cost for *franchising* solid waste collection, and for *wholly private* service delivery. In franchising, the city turns the business over to a private company. But the same study found collection less expensive when contracted out than when delivered by city employees. The annual cost-per-household figures are: franchising, $27.94; municipal, $24.41; contract, $22.42; and fully private, $35.91.[31]

The remainder of the empirical investigations show significant cost savings through contracting. The 1977 study by the Institute of Local Self Government (ILSG) showed that the cost of contract fire services in Scottsdale, Arizona was about half that of comparable municipal fire departments.[32] A study by James C. McDavid, conducted in 1981–1982 and published in 1986, looked at solid waste collection in 126 Canadian communities. It found that costs per household were significantly higher where cities collect their own residential solid waste, that public crews tend to be less productive, and their equipment less efficient as well.[33] A 1984 study by the Department of Defense, which focused on food provision, audio visual services, data processing, and other support services, showed savings through contracting of at least 22% with "no adverse impacts on readiness" and "very few problems with performance."[34]

Table 3.   Empirical Studies of Cost Savings With Contracting, 1976–1986

Service	Author/Date	Percent More/Less When Provided In-House	Percent More/Less When Provided Through Contractor
Solid waste collection	Savas (1976)	68 (more)	
Fire protection	ILSG (1977)		50 (less)
Solid waste collection	McDavid (1983)	51 (more)	
Street cleaning	Stevens (1984)	43 (more)	
Janitorial service	Stevens (1984)	73 (more)	
Refuse collection	Stevens (1984)	28–42 (more)	
Payroll processing	Stevens (1984)	no difference	
Traffic signal maintenance	Stevens (1984)	56 (more)	
Asphalt paving	Stevens (1984)	96 (more)	
Turf maintenance	Stevens (1984)	40 (more)	
Street tree maintenance	Stevens (1984)	37 (more)	
School bus transportation	McQuire and Van Cott (1984)	12 (more)	
Support services (audio-visual, food provision, data processing)	U.S. Defense Department (1984)	minimum 22 (more)	
Bus transportation	Perry and Babitsky (1986)	no difference	

The 1984 study by Barbara Stevens for the U.S. Department of Housing and Urban Development (HUD) looked at eight services provided by 20 cities in the Los Angeles SMSA. Ten cities offered service through public employees, and 10 matched cities offered the same service through contract management. The ten pairs were chosen for similarity of size, tax base, and other indicators, so that the city providing the service through local government and the city providing the service through a contractor would be as nearly equal as possible. All 121 cities in the Los Angeles SMSA were used as the universe from which the ten matched pairs were selected.[35]

The 1984 McGuire and Van Cott study examined 275 respondent school districts in Indiana, of which 144 provided transportation solely with district-owned buses, 49 utilized private contractors exclusively, and 82 used a combination. The private-contract districts showed a saving of 12% over district buses.[36] The 1986 Perry and Babitsky study[37] found no difference in efficiency between public transit systems and contract managed systems. The workforce, in contracted transit systems, remained under civil service rules.

The 1987 ICMA/Touche-Ross survey showed that, within the previous five years, 40% of responding local governments had achieved savings of 20% or more, while only 2% had lost money. These figures correspond broadly with the findings of the empirical studies summarized in Table 2, and are shown in Figure 3.

SUCCESS STORIES

How much have specific cities saved by contracting? The record is a strong one, and the following pages will examine it in half a dozen services.

The medium size city of Covington, Kentucky, reduced the cost of refuse collection by thirteen and one-half percent after switching from in-house to private collectors. The small city of Pekin, Illinois, reported similar savings after contracting the same service.[38] Phoenix, after severe initial problems in the early 1980s, has reduced its total refuse collection budget by 7%, a cost avoidance of $1.3 million, as a result of contracting out collection in some parts of the city.[39]

Wheeling Township, Illinois, was able to cut its road maintenance budget by a stunning 50%, from $326,000 to $171,000, by abolishing its street repair department and hiring a private contractor to take over the function.[40] Santa Fe Springs, California, contracted out street maintenance to a private firm and achieved savings of 33%.[41] Lafayette, California, contracted out its entire public works department to a private firm, and estimates its future savings at 25%.[42]

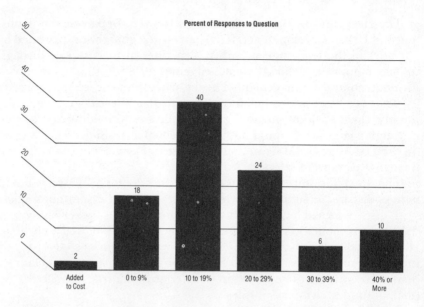

Figure 3. Cost Savings Achieved by Contracting Services Out
If Your Objective in Contracting Services Out Was to Cut Costs,
How Much Did You Save?

Source: Touche Ross & Co., *Privatization in America: An Opinion Survey of City and County Governments on Their Use of Privatization and the Infrastructure Needs.* Reprinted with permission. (For additional information, contact: Irwin T. David, National Director-Public Sector Services, Touche Ross & Co., Washington Service Center, 1900 M Street NW, Washington, D.C. 20036-425.)

A number of cities, counties, and special districts have also contracted out some of their bus and paratransit service to the private sector. One of the most innovative is the Tidewater Transit District located in Norfolk, Virginia. The district instituted a ridesharing program by contracting with private operators, and contracted with local taxicab firms to provide service along lightly traveled bus routes.[43] A number of transit districts and large-city municipal departments, including Los Angeles and Phoenix, contract out for some or all bus service. But the leader is the Dallas Area Rapid Transit (DART) district which has contracted out its entire commuter and regular-route service. DART itself estimates a savings of from 15% to 18% over what it would have cost if the district had provided the service directly.[44]

Public safety services have also been successfully contracted. Santa Barbara County, California, contracts for full ambulance and emergency medical service to 911 Emergency Services Inc. The firm collects about 80 percent of its billings, a much higher rate than most local governments who provide the same service, and provides substantially

FIREFIGHTERS AND PRIVATE BUSINESSMEN. Chief Bret Fillis (left) and CEO Phil Turnbull of the privately owned Valley Fire Service, Grants Pass, Oregon. Funded by Turnbull and friend Don Baker after a user survey by a local college, Valley Fire serves an unincorporated area of over 200 square miles. Service is by subscription. The company has two stations and eight pieces of rolling stock. It maintains 6 men on duty and up to 31 on call.

Source: Photo by Timothy Bullard/*Daily Courier*. Reprinted, with permission, from the Valley Fire Service, Grants Pass, Oregon.

user-paid service with a minor subsidy from the county to finance service to the indigent.[45] Nearly three dozen cities and counties contract for full fire service, or for limited service at airports. These jurisdictions range in size from tiny Paradise Valley, Arizona, to Scottsdale, Arizona and Knox County, Tennessee.[46]

A few pioneering small cities have even successfully contracted for basic police protection for up to five years, usually using fully trained, state-certified officers supplied by the private firm. Oro Valley, Arizona, and Reminderville, Ohio, are two of the most recent examples. One study of contracted police services in Reminderville estimated savings of 50%, with a higher level of service, in comparison to county-supplied police services. Even though the Oro Valley and Reminderville efforts were successful, negative publicity and political pressure forced an end to them.[47]

A great deal of contracting is now occurring in the health and human services area. Sonoma County, California, was one of the first to contract out the management of its county hospital, achieving a savings of approximately 50%.[48] A number of local governments, including San Diego county and Alameda County, California, contract out the provision of mental health services.[49]

Contracting has also been successfully applied in the areas of recreation and parks. Ventura County, California achieved savings on the order of 20% by contracting its park maintenance function.[50] The Hesperia Park District in California has contracted out recreation services to the local YMCA, achieving a budgetary savings of 37%.[51] Several California jurisdictions are achieving significant savings by leasing the operation and maintenance of their municipal golf courses.[52]

Because contracting has been the longest established in the areas of support services, contracting in these areas is probably greater than for any other services, and the savings among the largest. Little Rock, Arkansas contracted out its city hall janitorial services and achieved a savings of nearly 50% over previous in-house costs.[53] Cypress, California contracted out its custodial service in 1984, with a savings of about 20%.[54] Los Angeles County has contracted out some park security to a private firm for an estimated savings of 48%. Shasta County, California, contracted out its entire public defender services to a local law firm for a savings of about 33%.[55]

WHEN CONTRACTING FAILS

To this point we have been looking at the theory, usage, and success stories of service contracting. In this section we look at contracting failures. A thorough reading of the anticontracting literature, published by the American Federation of State, County, and Municipal Employees (AFSCME)[56] will dispel any illusions about the "guaranteed success" of contracting, and will increase the chances of successful outcomes.

There are three main areas in which contracting out may result in failure: (1) processes and procedures leading to the selection of a (poor) contractor; (2) the development of the contract and service standards, or specifications; and (3) contract administration and monitoring.

Contractor Selection

The choice of the wrong contractor is one of the most common failures in contracting. This happened in Cypress, California, when the city first contracted out custodial services. Cypress found that the contractor could not meet the performance requirements of the contract due to undermanning and insufficient supervision of workers. In response, the city instituted a combination competitive bid/negotiated bid process to insure that the lowest cost *and best qualified* bidder was selected. After cancelling the first contract the city solicited other contractors and thoroughly checked their references. The new contractor agreed to perform the work at the same price as the first firm.[57]

Garden Grove, California, contracted out its street sweeping operation to a private firm for a five year period. During the term of the contract, the contractor threatened the city with default due to large increases in labor and gas prices, even though the contract allowed for a 7% increase based on increases in the Consumer Price Index. To deal with this problem, city officials decided to cancel the contract and rebid street-sweeping on a different basis. They divided the city into two districts and awarded two contracts, one of which went to the former contractor.This change resulted in several benefits. The city developed a list of potential future bidders. It created a competitive situation in which one contractor provided a yardstick for measuring the other's performance. And, with two districts, smaller firms were enabled to bid.[58]

To help ensure that a qualified bidder gets the contract, cities can institute a prebid qualification process. This can include a Request for Qualifications (RFQ) form and reply, on which potential bidders are asked to submit a detailed statement on their capacity and history; and a personal, on-site inspection of potential contractors, including inspection of their books by city officials, to guarantee veracity in reporting.

Writing Measurable Specifications

The AFSCME literature offers the example of Cambridge, Maryland, when that city contracted the operation and maintenance of its waste-water treatment plant. AFSCME notes that the contractor refused to change to a less expensive treatment process as requested several times by the city, but notes further that the existing treatment process was mandated in the contract. AFSCME correctly concludes that, once the contract is signed, there is no way to make improvements in the delivery process unless the contractor does so willingly or the contract expires.[59] A well-drawn contract would have avoided the problem.

Another, more typical problem with specifications and service standards is that they are drawn so loosely that they do not bind a contractor to a definite standard of service. Phoenix encountered this problem when, in 1978, it first contracted its custodial service. Its first contractor gave a very low level of service. Because then Phoenix has made a number of changes in its bidding process, "tighten[ing] and chang[ing] contract specifications to limit the ability of the contractor to challenge what is an acceptable level of performance. . . . [Original] contract specifications did not clearly identify minimum levels of service."[60]

Contract Monitoring and Administration

The Phoenix custodial contract again provides an illustration. Four out of six of the custodial supervisors whom the city hired as contract monitors were later rated inadequate by a consultant. Even after developing a monitoring skills improvement program for the four employees, the city had to transfer three of them to other departments. Such a monitoring training program, and careful screening of potential monitors, are necessary in any substantial contracting program. Phoenix found that "inadequate performance [became] less of an issue . . . as the city improved its contract monitoring capability and specifications to guarantee a minimum level of performance."[61]

CONCLUSIONS

As theory, contracting has a legitimate place as a successor to the tradition of economy and efficiency. It is now a widely accepted method for reducing the cost of local public services, and together with the other methods outlined in this volume, is an important potential part of any local government productivity improvement program. As the pool of experienced contractors grows, the question of public v. private will recede, and the practical question, of which provider can do the best job at least cost, will increasingly dominate. Given the steady growth in demand for local services, and the parallel diminution of aid from the federal government, it seems likely that contracting will continue to increase in the near future, both in numbers of contracts and in the kinds of services contracted.

APPENDIX 1:
NUMBER OF JAPANESE CITIES CONTRACTING OUT AND FREQUENCY OF CONTRACTING

		Cities Contracting Out	
Services Supplied by Contractor		Number	Frequency (%)[a]
Cleaning of:	Offices	507	75.8
	Corridors	566	84.6
	Windows	505	75.5
	Bathrooms	560	83.7
	Machine rooms	266	58.1
	Indoor parking	165	47.1
	Courtyard and garden	260	48.5
	Office grounds	277	49.6
	Outdoor parking	238	42.7
Security:	Day and night	104	46.4
	Nighttime only	271	68.1
	Daytime only	147	43.9
Telephone switchboard operator		175	27.0
Information services		73	14.5
Elevator maintenance		98	36.6
Heating and cooling		288	47.7
Shorthand (steno)		230	49.3
Resident registration record		46	6.9
Typing work		142	21.2
Printing work		311	46.5
Microfilms		205	82.7
Computing of:	Tax assessment rates	462	69.1
	Tax to be collected	216	32.3
	Payroll	377	56.4
	National pension	334	49.9
	Child allowance	128	19.1
	Water charges	357	55.3
	Sewer charges	168	57.5
	Other statistics	119	17.8
Human waste collection		232	53.0
Refuse collection:	General waste	302	46.7
	Gross waste	192	36.4
	Non-Combustible	290	50.0
	Dangerous materials	128	44.8
	Industrial waste	15	11.8
Fee collection:	Nightsoil charges	126	36.3
	Sewer charges	159	54.5
	Water charges	390	60.4
School lunches:	Cooking and transportation	49	10.8

(continued)

APPENDIX 1   (*Continued*)

Services Supplied by Contractor	Cities Contracting Out	
	Number	Frequency (%)ᵃ
Cooking only	8	1.3
Transportation only	128	28.1
Citizen awareness surveys	126	36.0
Water meter reading	365	56.5
Design of major public facilities	419	81.8
Surveying and mapping of roads	475	78.3
Publications distribution	373	55.8
Home service for disabled	185	32.2
Overall Average	246	46.6

Note: ᵃCities contracting out/cities with contractable services.

Source: Japanese Ministry of Home Affairs. Reprinted from John Tepper Marlin, *Privatisation of Local Government Activities. Lessons from Japan* (New York: Council on Municipal Performance, 1982).

APPENDIX 2:
RESEARCH ORGANIZATIONS ON CONTRACTING OUT AND PRIVATIZATION[62]

Academy for State and Local Government
444 N. Capitol Street, N.W.
Washington, D.C. 20001
(202–638–1445)

One of the Academy's activities is the publication of Urban Innovation Abroad, which includes a regular section on privatization abroad. Many of the articles have been reprinted in *Public/Private Partnerships and Privatization Initiatives from Abroad,* compiled in 1986 and published in early 1987 by the Academy.

Adam Smith Institute-U.S.A. (ASI)
305 Ninth Street, S.E.
Washington, D.C. 20003
(202–544–8071)

The Adam Smith Institute, both at its headquarters in Great Britain (London) and its U.S. office (Washington, D.C.) provides continuous privatization research. ASI-London publications include how to use the proceeds of asset sales to cut taxes, privatizing libraries, the liberalization of laws regulating liquor sales and consumption, and the replacement of student grants with student loans. ASI-U.S. publications include Peter Young, "Privatization: A Hot Topic in the Tropics," *The Privatization Review* (Fall 1986). Young has also published "Privatization in Great Britain," *Government Union Review* (Spring 1986); and "Privatization in Lesser Developed Countries—A Solution that Works," *Journal of Economic Growth*, 1, 3 (Fall 1986).

American Legislative Exchange Council (ALEC)
214 Massachusetts Avenue, N.E., Suite 400
Washington, D.C. 20002
(202–547–4646)

In January 1986, ALEC sponsored a 5-state privatization tour by Dr. Madsen Pirie, a renowned privatization expert from Great Britain (and a privatization advisor to Prime Minister Margaret Thatcher). Pirie spoke to state legislators in Idaho, Illinois, New Mexico, Ohio, and Washington. A report on Pirie's tour was contained in ALEC's bi-monthly newsletter, *First Reading,* titled "Privatization in the States: Adam Smith Would Have Loved It" (March/April 1986).

In the *1987–88 Sourcebook of American State Legislation,* published in late 1986, ALEC supplies model legislation for two privatization proposals:

1. The Nongovernmental Corrections Facilities, Programs and Services Act.   This legislation seeks to increase the role of the private sector in corrections by expanding opportunities to provide such services as prison management, alternative incarceration programs for nonviolent offenders, and probation and parole administration.
2. The Government Efficiency Act.   This legislation seeks to create opportunities for state governments to accurately assess the cost of providing public services and, if it is determined that the private sector can more efficiently provide the service, facilitate contracting out to the private sector.

One of the major privatization activities of ALEC in 1986 was the publication in the January 1986 issue of *State Factor,* of a lead article, "Privatizing the Public Sector: An Initiative for Service and Savings," including a special section on applying privatization to state level services. ALEC also publishes a special Privatization Info-Pak for state legislators.

Cato Institute
224 Second Street, S.E.
Washington, D.C. 20003
(202–546–0200)

Besides holding several policy forums relating to privatization in 1986, Cato issued eight different privatization studies in 1986 as follows:

- *The Bonneville Power Administration: The Worst Mess By a Dam Site,* by Peter D. Cooper. Cato Policy Analysis. Washington, D.C.: Cato Institute, February 6, 1986.
- *Deductible IRAs Are Best for Workers,* by Peter J. Ferrara. Cato Policy Analysis. Washington, D.C.: Cato Institute, June 3, 1986.
- *Market Solutions to the Education Crisis,* by Myron Lieberman. Cato Policy Analysis. Washington, D.C.: Cato Institute, July 1, 1986.
- *Privatization: The Worker Buy-out Option,* by Peter Young. Cato Policy Analysis. Washington, D.C.: Cato Institute, July 28, 1986.
- "Currency Competition Versus Governmental Money Monopolies," by Roland Vaubel. *Cato Journal,* Winter 1986.
- "Intergenerational Transfer and Super IRAs," by Peter Ferrera. *Cato Journal,* Spring/Summer 1986.
- Institutional Requirements for Stable Free Banking," by Hugh Rockoff. *Cato Journal,* Fall 1986.
- "Public Mass Transportation and the Private Sector," by Ralph Stanley. *Cato Policy Report,* March/April 1986.

Center for the Study of Market Alternatives
Freedom Plaza
1920 East Hazel at Michigan
Caldwell, ID 83605
(208–454–1984)

The Center for the Study of Market Alternatives (CSMA) was involved in several privatization activities in 1986. These included testimony before the Idaho legislature and sponsorship of a presentation before the Idaho legislature by Dr. Madsen Pirie in connection with his privatization tour. CSMA staff also appeared before civic groups and on a variety of radio shows.

One of the major privatization publications issued by CSMA in 1986 was *Privatizing Education in Idaho,* by Alan Dalton.

Citizens for a Sound Economy (CSE)
122 C Street, N.W., Suite 700
Washington, D.C. 20001
(202–638–1401)

CSE pursued an active privatization program in 1986 including papers and congressional testimony relating to the privatization of federal power marketing administrations, the Coast Guard, military commissaries, Amtrak, and Conrail. Following are a list of some of CSEs' 1986 privatization publications:

- *Power Marketing Administrations: The Case for Privatization*, by Timonthy P. Roth. Issue Analysis No. 8, January 1986.
- *An Answer to the Critics: Why the Federal Power Marketing Administrations Should be Sold*, by Michael Becker and Jeffrey C. Smith. Issue Alert No. 6, April 9, 1986.
- *Amtrak and Congress: Still Taking the Taxpayers for a Ride*, by Jerome Ellig. Issue Alert No. 10, September 5, 1986.

Council of State Governments (CSG)
Iron Works Pike
P. O. Box 11910
Lexington, KY 40578
(606–252–2291)

The Council pursued a number of privatization activities in 1986, including primary sponsorship of a "Contracting for Services Conference in Atlanta," April 24–25, 1986. The conference included workshops on contract administration and the contracting out of various state and local services such as waste management, support services, hospital and health care, and prisons.

CSG also participated in nationwide surveys in 1986 seeking information on privatization initiatives in state governments and on the contracting out of state correctional facilities.

CSG also provided consultation services to state governments, and in cooperation with the Urban Institute, initiated alternative service-delivery projects for two eastern states, Maryland and Delaware.

CSG publications pertaining to privatization included several articles in *State Government News,* including "Privatization: A Public Option?" and "Public-Private Alliances Grow." CSG also published a bibliography, *Alternative Service Delivery and Management Improvement in State Government* and a booklet titled *The Contract Cookbook for the Purchase of Services.*

Council on Municipal Performance (COMP)
55 West 44th Street
New York, NY 10036
(212–730–7930)

The Council on Municipal Performance (COMP) merged with the National Municipal League in 1986. It publishes a useful monthly newsletter, *The Privatization Report*. As described on page 16, the Council also co-sponsored a major privatization conference in 1986, in addition to holding several other conferences in other cities.

Heartland Institute
59 East Van Buren, Suite 810
Chicago, IL 60605
(312–855–1440)

One of the Heartland Institute's major activities, beside publishing a number of privatization studies, was the sponsorship in July 1986 of a conference on applying privatization techniques to the budgets of Chicago, Cook County, and the State of Illinois and estimating the resulting cost-savings. The Institute also played an important role in Chicago Mayor's Blue Ribbon Committee report released in November 1986. Some of the major privatization studies issued by the Institute in 1986 and 1985 included:

- *Public vs. Private Economic Activity: A New Look at School Bus Transportation,* by Robert A. McQuire and T. Norman Van Cott.
- *Access to Quality: Private Schools in Chicago's Inner City,* by Joan Ratteray.
- *Comparison of Privately and Publicly Owned Sports Stadiums,* by Dean Baim.
- *Privatization of Public Functions: Promises and Problems,* by Calvin Kent. Heartland Policy Study.

The Heritage Foundation
214 Massachusetts Avenue, N.E.
Washington, D.C. 20002
(202–546–4400)

For some years, the Heritage Foundation has been among the leading national think-tanks on privatization. In 1986, privatization research published by the Heritage Foundation included the following:

- *How to Get Privatization Back on Track,* by Stuart M. Butler. Heritage Background-er No. 550, December 3, 1986.
- *Cutting the Deficit by Selling Federal Power Marketing Administrations,* by Milton C. Copulous. Heritage Background-er No. 485, February 13, 1986.
- *Privatizing Federal Services: A Primer,* by Stuart M. Butler. Heritage Backgrounder No. 488, February 20, 1986.
- *How to Privatize Federal Services by Contracting Out,* by Steven Moore, Heritage Backgrounder No. 494, March 13, 1986.
- *Controlling Catastrophic Health Costs: Otis Bowen's Grand Opportunity,* by Peter Ferrara. Heritage Backgrounder No. 499, April 3, 1986.
- *Cashing in on the Federal Quarter-Trillion Dollar Loan Portfolio,* by John Buttarazzi. Heritage Backgrounder No. 541, October 28, 1986.
- *Rx for Ailing U.S. Mass Transit Policy: A Dose of Competition,* by Steven Moore, Heritage Backgrounder No. 542, October 29, 1986.

In addition, the Heritage Foundation published several articles on privatization in various of its newsletters, including a *Backgrounder Update* titled, "Why Reagan Should Give a Green Light to Private Space Launchers" (No. 20, August 8, 1986); and "Freeing National and Dulles Airports from their Federal Burden," by James Gattuso (No. 127, July 28, 1986).

In its magazine, *Policy Review,* the Heritage Foundation published several articles on privatization in 1986, including "Time to Privatize Money," by Richard Rahn (No. 36, Spring); and "The Privatization Revolution: What Washington Can Learn from State and Local Government," by Philip E. Fixler, Jr. and Robert W. Poole, Jr. (No. 37, Summer).

Hubert H. Humphrey Institute
909 Social Sciences
267 19th Avenue South
Minneapolis, MN 55455
(612-373-2653)

Major activities of the Institute's Public Services Redesign Project in 1986 included the publication of an essay by Senior Fellow Ted Kolderie, *What Do We Mean by Privatization?* in the Contemporary Issues Series (No. 19) of the Washington University Center for Business and reprinted in the summer 1986 issue of *Public Administration Review.* Another activity was participation in a project called Public School Ini-

tiatives, that seeks to foster the contracting out of instructional services
to private teaching practices.

International City Management Association (ICMA)
1120 G Street, N.W.
Washington, D.C. 20005
(202–626–4600)

In 1986, the International City Management Association (ICMA) followed up on its seminal 1984 report, *Rethinking Local Services: Examining
Alternative Service Delivery Approaches,* with the inauguration of a new
program to apply many of the ideas in *Rethinking* to local governments in
the Philadelphia area. The ICMA also devoted almost its entire December issue of *Public Management* to privatization.

Law and Economics Center
University of Miami
P.O. Box 248000
Coral Gables, FL 33124
(305–284–6174)

In 1986, the Law and Economics Center (LEC) was part of a joint venture (with the Local Government Center) that undertook the Florida
Privatization Research Project. LEC staff participated in several privatization conferences and published several papers on the subject.

Manhattan Institute for Policy Research
131 Spring Street
New York, NY 10012
(212–219–0773)

The Manhattan Institute engaged in several privatization activities in
1986, including the publication of a New York Perspective on privatizing
public housing, "New York City vs. Its Housing," as part of its project on
New York's Economic Future. The study advocates the divestiture of
New York City-owned housing acquired by the city through tax delin-
quency sales.

National Center for Privatization
P.O. Box 14151
Shawnee Mission, KS 66125

In 1986, the Center continued the publication of its newsletter *Private
Solutions,* including surveys of newsletter recipients.

National Center for Policy Analysis
7701 N. Stemmons, Suite 800
Dallas, TX 75247
(214–951–0306)

The National Center for Policy Analysis issued several major privatization studies in 1986. The first was *Privatization Around the World: Lessons
for the Reagan Administration,* by Peter Young (NCPA Policy Report No.
120). The second was *Privatizing the Welfare State,* by John Goodman and
Michael D. Stroup (NCPA Report No. 123, June 1986). Finally, in October 1986, NCPA issued a study advocating the privatization of public
lands, *Destroying the Environment: Government Mismanagement of Our Natural Resources,* by John Baden (NCPA Report No. 124).

Political Economy Research Center
502 South 19th Avenue, Suite 211
Bozeman, MT 59715
(406–587–9591)

In 1986, the Political Economy Research Center (PERC), which spe-
cializes in the application of privatization to land and natural resource
issues, was involved in several privatization activities. The most important event was the sponsorship of a major conference on Privatization
and Public Policy in September 1986.

The Privatization Council Inc.
1101 Connecticut Avenue, N.W.
Washington, D.C. 20036
(202–857–1142)

The Council continued the publication of its quarterly journal, *The Privatization Review,* that contains practical information and case studies on
privatization.

The Council sponsored or co-sponsored several privatization conferences in 1986, including a National Conference on Privatization Opportunities in New York, October 1986; as well as participating in several smaller conferences.

Another major activity of the Council in 1986 was the publication in
April 1986 of a *Compendium of Privatization Laws* and a November 1986
update of same.

Reason Foundation
2716 Ocean Park Boulevard, Suite 1062
Santa Monica, CA 90405
(213–392–0443)

The Reason Foundation's privatization program maintained a high level of visibility in 1986 with the publication of a number of reports and articles. *Reason* magazine, the Foundation's flagship publication, published "Buying Out of Socialism," by Madsen Pirie (January), detailing Margaret Thatcher's privatization successes; and Mark Frazier's report on the privatization-minded French government, "The French Revolution of 1986" (November).

Privatization was one of the topics covered in a 6-part TV program, "The New Enlightenment," co-sponsored by the Foundation and aired on Channel 4 in Britain in November–December 1986. The Foundation also issued the first of six Federal Privatization Project papers commissioned in 1986, *Privatizing the Air Traffic Control System*, by Robert W. Poole, Jr. (November 14, 1986).

The Foundation's Local Government Center continued publication of *Fiscal Watchdog* (now called *Privatization Watch*), which reports on the latest privatization developments, and continued the expansion of its computerized Privatization Database and Directory of Private Service Providers. The LGC researched and published three papers in 1986 for the Pacific Basin Development Council: *Contracting Out School Transportation Services, Employee Options Under Privatization, and Federal Barriers to Privatization in the American Pacific Territories*.

The major privatization project was LGC's Florida Privatization Research Project, a joint venture with the Law and Economics Center at the University of Miami. The study developed new hands-on tools for local officials, including a Computerized Privatization Information System and Privatization Candidate and Budget Analysis programs for use on personal computers.

Another result of the Florida study was the development of the LGC's third privatization database, the Privatization Bibliographic Database, listing over 500 books, studies, reports, and articles. (The Privatization Database list 28,500 examples of privatization by U.S. cities, counties, and states. The Directory of Private Service providers lists over 600 companies that privately provide public services, including relevant trade associations and consultants.)

Sequoia Institute
1822 21st Street, Suite 200
Sacramento, CA 95814
(916–454–4505)

The Sequoia Institute worked with the U.S. Agency for International Development (A.I.D.), assisting that agency in holding the 1986 A.I.D. privatization conference (see page 15) and in developing a database to track Third World privatization projects. The Institute also began publishing *Sequoia Education Newsletter,* that includes coverage of privatization developments in education. In 1986, the Sequoia Institute merged with another public-policy think tank, the Institute for Contemporary Studies, headquartered in San Francisco.

Urban Institute
2100 M Street, N.W.
Washington, D.C. 20037
(202–833–7200)

The Urban Institute for several years has been involved in researching alternative service delivery and privatization. Several new Urban Institute publications were published in 1986 and in recent years, including:

- *Privatizing the Delivery of Social Welfare Services,* by Marc Bendick, Jr., May 1985
- *The Two Faces of Contracting,* by Harry P. Hatry, June 1986.
- *Social Welfare Policy and Privatization: Theory and Reality in Policy Making,* by James C. Musselwhite Jr. and Lester M. Solomon, 1986.

APPENDIX 3:
TRADE ASSOCIATIONS

In 1986, trade associations representing companies that privately provide public services were also increasingly active. The following is a list of some of the trade associations active in promoting privatization and, where applicable, a brief summary of their activities in 1986.

American Ambulance Association (AAA)
3814 Auburn Boulevard, Suite 70
Sacramento, CA 95821
(916–483–3827)

Besides publishing occasional articles on privatization in its *Ambulance Industry Journal* (issued five times a year) and its monthly *Industry News,* one of AAA's major privatization activities is the development of model legislation to promote private provision of ambulance and emergency medical service. Another activity which has the effect of promoting privatization is AAA's accreditation program to set industry standards for "safe, efficient and ethical conduct to improve the quality of care and instill public confidence in [the] industry."

American Water Works Association
6666 West Quincy Avenue
Denver, CO 80235
(303–794–7711)

The American Water Works Association (AWWA) is composed of investor-owned utilities and publishes occasional articles on privatization in its
monthly *AWWA Journal* (in February 1986, virtually the entire issue was
devoted to privatization) and a monthly newsletter for its members,
OpFlow. Further, it publishes *AWWA Mainstream* as a monthly news and
feature publication.

Association for Commuter Transportation
1776 Massachusetts Avenue, N.W., Suite 521
Washington, D.C. 20036
(202–659–0602)

Nineteen eighty-six meant both setbacks and advances for car- and van-
pool programs. Setbacks included the end of the energy tax credits for
car- and van-poolers. But a recent positive trend in the last few years has
been the emergence of third-party operators, instead of direct employers. Unfortunately, a 1986 shakeout of the five private firms providing for-profit van-pool services in more than one state, left basically two
major companies in the business, operating about 3,000 vans throughout the nation. Such developments are kept track of in ACT's monthly
newsletter called *ACT Now* and through its information-exchange
service.

Federation of American Health Systems (FAHS)
1405 North Pierce, Suite 308
Little Rock, Arkansas 72207
(501–661–9555)

The Federation changed its name in 1986 from Federation of American
Hospitals to the Federation of American Health Systems, in order to
better reflect changes in private health care. FAHS tracks privatization
developments through its bimonthly magazine called *Review*; a biweekly
newsletter on Washington events, *Hotline*; and a monthly updating of
legislative and regulatory activities at the state level, *State-to-State*. One of
the major trends in 1986 (continuing from 1985) was the privatization or
partial privatization of teaching hospitals.

National School Transportation Association
P.O. Box 2639
Springfield, VA 22152
(703–644–0700)

The National School Transportation Association (NSTA) is composed of numerous private firms and related parties involved in the provision of school bus transportation on a contract basis. Privatization information on this industry is published in a quarterly magazine called *National School Bus Report* and a monthly newsletter called the *NSTA Newsletter*. One of the major privatization articles published by *National School Bus Report* was in the March 1986 issue, "Anatomy of a Contract" by Ed Greene.

National Association of Water Companies
1725 K Street, N.W.
Washington, D.C. 20006
(202–833–8383)

The National Association of Water Companies (NAWC) is a nonprofit trade association consisting of private and investor-owned community water-supply firms. NAWC representatives advise that the 1986 Tax Reform Act will have a major negative effect on water utilities serving populations of 10,000 or less (98% of estimated private providers). This and other privatization developments are analyzed in NAWC's quarterly magazine called *Water*. One of the major subjects covered by *Water* is the effect of regulation on private water supply. Major 1986 articles on the subject included "Perspectives on Utility Rate Regulation," by Fred R. Meyer (Fall 1986) and "Seizing Assets: Slow and Subtle," by Steve Hanke (Spring 1986).

Private Sector Fire Association
P.O. Box 1512
Elk Grove Village, IL 60007
(312–690–6550)

The Private Sector Fire Association (PSFA) is composed of companies that provide fire protection services on a contractual or subscription basis. Besides its annual meeting, PSFA operates mostly as an information clearinghouse for private provision of fire protection. It has published one pamphlet, *Questions and Answers About Private Sector Fire Services*.

United Bus Owners of America (UBOA)
1275 K Street, N.W., Suite 800
Washington, D.C. 20005–4006
(202–424–5623)

UBOA follows privatization developments at the federal, state, and local levels in its semi-monthly newsletter called *The Docket*. Probably the most significant UBOA privatization activity in 1986 was its strong participation in the Coalition for Competition in Public Transportation, which successfully promoted the passage of a mass transit appropriations bill that contained language promoting competitive contracting of bus services.

Other trade associations:

Airport Operators' Council International
2033 M Street,
Washington, D.C. 20036
(202–296–3270)

Airport Ground Transportation Association
1114 Clinch Avenue
Knoxville, TN 37916
(615–525–1108)

American Association of Airport Executives
2301 M Street, N.W., 4th Floor
Washington, D.C. 20037
(202–331–8994)

Association of Data Processing and
   Service Organizations
1300 N. 17th Street, Suite 300
Arlington, VA 22209–3899
(703–522–5055)

Building Service Contractors Association
8315 Lee Highway, Suite 301
Fairfax, VA 22031
(804–698–8810)

Business Alliance on Government Competition
1615 H Street, N.W.
Washington, D.C. 20062
(202–463–5500)

Center for Nonprofit Organizations
203 W. 25 Street, 3rd Floor
New York, NY 10001
(212–989–9026)

Contract Services Association
650 14th Street, N.W.
Washington, D.C. 20005
(202–347–0600)

International Facility Management Association
3970 Varsity Drive
Ann Arbor, MI 48104
(313–944–0660)

Institute for Resource Recovery
1730 Rhode Island Ave., N.W., Suite 1000
Washington, D.C. 20036
(202–659–4613)

National Association for Child Care Management
1800 M Street, N.W.
Washington, D.C. 20036
(202–659–5955)

National Association of Private Residential
  Facilities for the Mentally Retarded
6269 Leesburg Pike, Ste. B–5
Falls Church, VA 22044
(703–536–3311)

National Association of Private Psychiatric
  Hospitals
1319 F Street, N.W., Suite 1000
Washington, D.C. 20036
(202–393–6700)

National Contract Sweepers Association
1730 Rhode Island Ave., N.W. Suite 1000
Washington, D.C. 20036
(202–659–4613)

National Council of Investigative and
  Security Agencies
1133 Fifteenth Street, N.W.
Washington, D.C. 20005
(202–293–5913)

National Restaurant Association
311 First Street, N.W.
Washington, D.C. 20001
(202–638–6100)

National Solid Wastes Management Association
1730 Rhode Island Avenue, N.W., Suite 1000
Washington, D.C. 20036
(202–659–4613)

APPENDIX 4:
SPECIALIZED CONSULTING ORGANIZATIONS

Parsons Municipal Services Inc.
100 West Walnut Street
Pasadena, CA 91124
(818–440–3141)

Municipal Development Corporation
180 Maiden Lane
New York, NY 10038
(212–968–1400)

NOTES AND REFERENCES

1. The discussion of economy and efficiency draws heavily from the following: Dwight
Waldo, *The Administrative State* (New York: Ronald Press, 1948); Albert Lepawsky,
Administration (New York: Alfred A. Knopf, 1949); and Keith M. Henderson, *The Study of
Administration* (Lanham, MD: University Press of America, 1983). For other useful histories
of this subject, see James W. Fesler, ed., *American Public Administration: Patterns of the Past*
(Washington, D.C.: American Society for Public Administration, 1982); and Frederick C.
Mosher, ed., *American Public Administration: Past, Present, Future* (University, AL: University
of Alabama Press, 1975).
2. Woodrow Wilson, "The Study of Administration," *Political Science Quarterly*, 2, 2
(June 1887): 191–222; and "Democracy and Efficiency," *Atlantic Monthly* (March 1901),
pp. 289–299. Frank Goodnow, *Politics and Administration* (New York: Macmillan and Company Ltd., 1900).
3. W.F. Willoughby, "The National Government as Holding Company," *Political Science Quarterly*, 32, 4 (December 1917): 505–521.
4. Marshall Dimock, "Principles Underlying Government-Owned Corporations,"
Journal of Public Administration, 13 (January 1935): 51–66.
5. Richard Spencer Childs, *Civic Victories* (New York: Harper, 1952).
6. Dwight Waldo, *The Administrative State*, p. 75.
7. Clarence E. Ridley and Herbert A. Simon, *Measuring Municipal Activities* (Chicago,
1938).
8. *Ibid.*, p. 125.
9. Leonard D. White, *Introduction To The Study of Public Administration* (New York:
Macmillan Company, 1939).
10. See Chapter 9 ("Methods Improvement and Work Measurement: Industrial Engineering For Local Government").
11. The seminal article on the application of public choice to local government is
Charles Tiebout, "A Pure Theory of Local Expenditures," *Journal of Political Economy*, 64, 4
(October 1956): 416–424. See also Vincent Ostrom and Elinor Ostrom, "Public Choice: A
Different Approach to the Study of Public Administration," *Public Administration Review*, 2,
31 (March/April 1971): 204; and Gary J. Miller, *Cites By Contract. The Politics of Municipal
Incorporation* (Cambridge, MA: MIT Press, 1981).
12. See Madsen Pirie, *Dismantling The State. The Theory and Practice of Privatization*
(Dallas, TX: The National Center for Policy Analysis, 1985); and John C. Goodman, ed.,
Privatization (Dallas, TX: National Center for Policy Analysis, 1985). See also Robert W.

Poole, Jr., *Cutting Back City Hall* (New York: Universe Books, 1980); Philip E. Fixler, Jr. and Robert W. Poole, Jr., "The Privatization Revolution: What Washington Can Learn from State and Local Government," *Policy Review*, 37, 2 (Summer 1986); R. Q. Armington and William D. Ellis, *This Way Up. The Local Official's Handbook for Privatization and Contracting Out* (Chicago: Regnery Gateway, 1984); and E.S. Savas, *Privatizing The Public Sector* (Chatham, NJ: Chatham House Publishers, 1982). A very useful volume on the practical technique of contracting services is John Tepper Marlin, ed., *Contracting Municipal Services. A Guide for Purchase From The Private Sector* (New York: Ronald Press/Wiley, 1984).

13.   This survey was jointly sponsored in 1987 by Touche Ross, the International City Management Association (ICMA), and the Privatization Council of New York (now Washington, D.C.). Mailed to all cities with a population of over 5,000 ($N = 4,360$) and all counties with a population over 25,000 ($N = 1,358$), the survey drew 1,086 returns, a return rate of 19%. Henceforth this survey will be referred to as "the 1987 survey."

14.   Touche Ross, the International City Management Association, and the Privatization Council jointly sponsored a nationwide survey of local government contracting, with a response from 1,086 local cities and counties. Results are available from any of the three sponsoring organizations. This study is referred to throughout this chapter as "the 1987 survey." Source: Touche Ross, *Privatization In America* (New York: Touche Ross, 1987).

15.   *Ibid.*, page 12, Figure 8.

16.   Commercial waste collection (41%); residential waste collection (34%); tree trimming/planting (30%); solid waste disposal (26%); street repair (26%); paratransit system operation (22%); traffic signal installation/maintenance (25%); vehicle towing/storage (78%); ambulance service (23%), and day-care operation (33%). Source: Harry Hatry and Carl Valente, "Alternative Service Delivery Approaches Involving Increased Use of the Private Sector," *The Municipal Yearbook 1983* (Washington, DC: International City Management Association).

17.   Harold J. Sullivan, "Privatization of Public Services: A Growing Threat To Constitutional Rights," *Public Administration Review*, 47, 6 (November–December 1987): 461–468.

18.   Telephone interview with Mr. Douglas Watson, City Manager of Auburn, Alabama, June 1986. Mr. Metcalf stated that he had "nothing but the highest praise" for the consulting engineers who managed the project.

19.   Harry P. Hatry and Eugene Durman, *Issues In Competitive Contracting* (Falls Church, VA: National Institute of Governmental Purchasing Inc., August 1985), p. 10.

20.   Harry P. Hatry, *A Review of Private Approaches for Delivery of Public Services* (Washington, D.C.: Urban Institute Press 1983), p. 20.

21.   Mark A. Stein, "California's First 'Private Prison' Is Open for Business," *Los Angeles Times* (May 29, 1986); and *State Government News* (Frankfort, KY: Commonwealth of Kentucky, December 30, 1985).

22.   William Russell, "OMB Circular A-76: How To Make Contracting Out for Federal Services Harder Than Ever," *Government Executive* (October 1983), pp. 78–81. This policy was promulgated in 1955 in the Bureau of the Budget's BOB *Bulletin 55–4*. In 1966 this circular was renumbered Circular A-76, and has been known ass the A–76 program ever since.

23.   Senator Warren Rudman (Rep. Vermont), "Freedom from Government Competition Act," United States Senate *Congressional Record* (August 3, 1983), pp. 11384–11385.

24.   Bureau of National Affairs newsletter, "Regulatory and Legal Developments," No. 113 (1987), p. A–10.

25.   Urban Mass Transportation Administration, Office of Technical Assistance, *Public/Private Partnerships in Mass Transportation* (Executive Summary) (nd).

26.   John Tepper Marlin, "Privatization of Local Government Activities. Lessons From Japan" (New York: Council on Municipal Performance, 1982), pp. 4–7.

108 PHILIP E. FIXLER, JR. and EDWARD C. HAYES

27. Conversation with Hans Jeppson, Swedish political party official (July 6, 1987).
28. Poole, Cutting Back, pp. 72, 82.
29. Ibid., p. 41.
30. "Paris Contracts Out Water Distribution," Urban Innovations Abroad, 9, 2 (February 1985), p. 3.
31. E.S. Savas, "Policy Analysis for Local Government: Public v. Private Refuse Collection," Policy Analysis, 3, 1 (Winter 1977): 49–74.
32. Roger S. Ahlbrandt, Jr., Alternatives to Traditional Public Safety Delivery Systems: Civilians in Public Safety Services (Berkeley: Institute for Local Self Government, September 1977).
33. James C. McDavid, "The Canadian Experience with Privatizing Residential Solid Waste Collection Services," Public Administration Review, 45, 5 (September/October 1985): 602–608.
34. Robert W. Poole Jr. and Philip E. Fixler Jr., "Privatization of Public-Sector Services in Practice: Experience and Potential," Journal of Policy Analysis and Management, 6, 4 (Summer 1987): 615.
35. Barbara J. Stevens, ed., Delivering Municipal Services Efficiently: A Comparison of Municipal and Private Service Delivery. (Washington, D.C.: U.S. Department of Housing and Urban Development, 1984).
36. Robert A. McGuire and T. Norman Van Cott, "Public versus Private Economic Activity: A New Look at School Bus Transportation," Public Choice 43 (1984): 25–43.
37. James L. Perry and Timlynn T. Babitsky, "Comparative Performance in Urban Bus Transit: Assessing Privatization Strategies," Public Administration Review, 46, 1 (January/February 1986): 57–66.
38. Nancy M. Peterson, "Solid Waste Collection," in This Way Up: The Local Official's Handbook for Privatization and Contracting, R.Q. Armington and William D. Ellis, eds. (Chicago: Regnery Gateway for The American Society of Local Officials, 1984), p. 101.
39. Valente and Manchester, Rethinking Local Services, p. 188.
40. "Lean Streets," Fiscal Watchdog, 69 (July 1982): 1. (Santa Barbara, CA: Local Government Center.)
41. Robert W. Poole, Jr., "Contracts Bring Savings," Fiscal Watchdog, 18 (April 1978): 2.
42. Philip E. Fixler Jr., "Contracting Out Professional Services," Fiscal Watchdog, 108 (October 1985): 1.
43. Philip E. Fixler, Jr., with Michael R. Martin and Robert W. Poole, Jr., Privatization 1986. Annual Report on Privatization of Government Services (Santa Monica, CA: Reason Foundation), pp. 22–23.
44. Robert W. Poole Jr., "Transit Systems," in This Way Up: The Local Official's Handbook for Privatization and Contracting, R.Q. Armington and W.D. Ellis, eds. (Chicago: Regnery Gateway for the American Society of Local Officials, 1984), p. 23.
45. Philip E. Fixler Jr., "Can Privatization Resuscitate Emergency Medical Services?," Fiscal Watchdog, 98 (December 1985): 4.
46. Gary L. Briese, "An Overview of Private Sector Fire Service," The International Fire Chief, 50, 2 (February 1984): 18.
47. Theodore Gage, "Cops, Inc.," Reason, 14, 8 (November 1982): 23–28.
48. "Rx for Sick Hospitals," Fiscal Watchdog, 77 (March 1983): 1.
49. Ralph M. Kramer and Paul Terrell, Social Services Contracting in the Bay Area (Berkeley, CA: Institute of Governmental Studies, 1984), p. 18.
50. Poole, Cutting Back, p. 105.
51. Harry P. Hatry, A Review of Private Approaches for Delivery of Public Services (Washington, D.C.: Urban Institute Press, 1983), pp. 23–24.
52. Poole, Cutting Back, p. 106.

53. James C. Mercer, "Growing Opportunities in Public Service Contracting" *Harvard Business Review,* 61, 2 (March–April 1983): 178.

54. Valente and Manchester, *Rethinking Local Services,* pp. 161–163.

55. "Shasta County Saves $100,000 on Public Defender," *CAL-TAX NEWS,* 1 (September 1985).

56. John D. Hanrahan (uncited author), *Passing the Bucks. The Contracting Out of Public Services* (Washington, D.C.: American Federation of State, County and Municipal Employees, AFL-CIO, 1984).

57. Valente and Manchester, *Rethinking Local Services,* p. 162.

58. *Ibid.,* p. 169.

59. Hanrahan, *Passing The Bucks,* p. 52.

60. Valente and Manchester, *Rethinking Local Services,* p. 190.

61. *Ibid.,* p. 191.

62. The material in Appendices 2 and 3 are drawn from *Privatization 1986* (Santa Monica, CA: The Reason Foundation).

Chapter 6

COMPREHENSIVE
PRODUCTIVITY PROGRAMS:
A LEVERAGED INVESTMENT

Paul D. Epstein and Suzanne Fass

SUMMARY. Productivity improvements can be counted in cash savings, increased revenues, or increased services. Local governments should adopt long-term productivity programs (strategies) with two prongs of attack: short-term operations improvements, with immediate payoffs; and long-term "capacity building" measures, which do not have immediate payoffs but which are crucial to a steady record of productivity improvement. Capacity building measures, looking at those most commonly used today, include staff training, worksite improvements, wellness programs, measurement systems, "organizational development" techniques, and others. Charts and text illustrate how to integrate a productivity strategy into the annual cycle of planning and budgeting, and explain why "outlays" for productivity programs are better called "leveraged investments."

Industrial productivity has been a national concern as foreign competition has increased and Americans' real incomes have fallen. On July 13, 1986, *The New York Times* reported: "When asked the reason for lagging income growth, economists speak with rare unanimity: Slow productivity growth is Public Enemy No. 1." The need for productivity improvement of government services has also become widely recognized as more state and local governments have been squeezed between declining real revenues (due to local economic stress, tax revolts, or reductions in in-

111

tergovernmental funds) and increased needs and demands for public services in an ever more complex society. Fiscal stress often brings on a call to raise government productivity, but in truth the need is constant. Government productivity is important not only when funds are tight. Sustained public service productivity growth through both fat and lean years can help avoid public fiscal crises or make them easier to weather without drastic service cuts.

Industry has traditionally depended on major investments for productivity growth, and stockholders readily accept the idea. But there is no equivalent public idea of *investing in government productivity growth.* Governments, to be sure, have modernized over the years, from the time fire companies and police departments were first motorized to the more recent proliferation of computers to help perform many government functions. But it simply is not in our culture to think of investment as a necessary ingredient for sustained productivity growth of *public* organizations. In a 1982 editorial in *Public Productivity Review,* Editor-in-Chief Marc Holzer complained, "the same businessmen who invest stockholders' millions in the infrastructure of their companies object to investing taxpayers' millions in public organizations. The result only handicaps governments. Government officials are permitted to spend only about one-fifth as much as the private sector on training—on their human capital. In the public sector, purchases of computers, word processors, vehicles, or other equipment are more arduous because of an exaggerated fear of misspending tax dollars."[1]

Traditional investments in new capital equipment and facilities are important to improving public service productivity, but they are only a small part of the answer. Government is a service industry. Services are delivered *by people* (whether government employees, contracted staff, or volunteers) to people. Investments to improve services should be seen as *investments in people*—investments in the "human capital" referred to by Holzer. This does not mean simply adding more service delivery staff to get more services. It means investing in better training, in analytic studies of operations to improve service effectiveness and efficiency (for example, to reduce response times, simplify procedures, and reduce paperwork), in measurement and analysis to determine how to allocate resources to meet community needs more equitably, in organizational studies to provide better management and supervision, and in anything else that *helps people do their jobs better in serving people.*

Studies, training, and other productivity improvement techniques require the time of people with the appropriate technical skills, whether public employees or consultants. A significant part of productivity investment costs are staff costs. Even purchases of computers and equipment to reduce expenses require the time of skilled staff, first to identify automation opportunities and then to analyze operations so the money spent on hardware will produce the intended savings and not be wasted. But as important as investments in skilled staff are for improved government productivity, they are the hardest politically for governments to make and sustain. These jobs are seen as "administrative" positions which lose out in budget battles to service delivery positions, especially in times of fiscal stress. Staff analyst and training jobs (and funds for consultants, which are seen as discretionary) will always be cut before police officers or fire fighters.

It is ironic that in times of fiscal stress, governments are likely to make budget cuts under the banner of productivity which endanger future productivity by reducing training and internal staff expertise. Policymakers must view funds for skilled staff as necessary investments in productivity growth, not as discretionary administrative expenses. Mayors and council members must also believe they can develop public support for these investments so that they will take the political risks of supporting them. They must reverse their usual way of thinking: instead of first seeing the immediate costs and fearing the political consequences of support for the expenditure, they must confidently focus on their investment goals: the returns to be gained. Public support should be forthcoming when it is clear that the community will benefit from improved services or lowered costs as a result of the investment.

THE "RETURN ON INVESTMENT" IN GOVERNMENT PRODUCTIVITY

Any investment analysis requires a way to define and measure *returns on investment*. The "returns" are measurable public benefits which result from government productivity improvements. These benefits can take three forms:

- measurable improvements in service to the public;
- measurable reductions in costs of providing services; and
- measurable increases in revenue to the jurisdiction.

Revenue increases are often ignored in government productivity discussions, but they can be important. Improving productivity of revenue generating activities such as tax audits, fine collections, and fee-generating inspections yields revenues which represent real public benefits because they help fund services or reduce pressure to raise tax or fee-for-service rates.

Of course a government need not improve productivity to increase revenues, reduce costs, or improve services. Generally, any of these benefits can be obtained faster without improving productivity if a government is willing to pay the usual price:

- the usual price of increasing revenue is an increase in taxes or fees;
- the usual price of reducing costs is a reduction in services; any
- the usual price of improving services is a proportional increase in the main operating costs of the services.

A productivity investment produces a return which can be measured in dollars when the above benefits are achieved *without paying the usual price*. When the productivity benefits are cost reductions or revenue increases, the return on investment is simply the dollar amount of the savings or added revenue. When the benefits are improved services, the return on investment is the lowered operating cost—a productivity increase, or "service bonus"[2]—which derives from operating the service more productively. Increasing services by simply pouring more resources into the same old ways of doing business generates greater operating costs in direct proportion to the increase in service. If new methods or equipment produce the same service improvement at a lower increase in operating costs than "doing it the old way," the difference is the amount "less than the usual price"; this is the amount of the cost avoidance, or service bonus. Calculated in terms of dollars, it represents the return on the productivity investment. Because the added services represent a public benefit, the dollar value of this service bonus should be counted as much toward the return on productivity investment as cash savings and added revenue.

An example of a "cost avoidance" return on investment: A city may invest in new, more efficient lawn mowers and use them to mow all the grass in its parks 20% more often that year using the same number of employee hours and the same amount of fuel and maintenance costs as the year before. Assuming that the new level of service performance is maintained annually, the annual return on investment in the new mowers is the dollar value of the 20% added staff time and the added fuel and maintenance costs that *would have been needed* had the extra work been done using the old mowers. Although operating costs remain the same, a net annual increase in service levels, amounting to an annual service bonus, has occurred.

If the city has amortized the costs of the new mowers over their expected useful life, the city can subtract the dollar value of the annual cost avoidance benefits in staff, fuel, and maintenance from the annual cost of the investment, to get an exact measure of its return-on-investment in mowers.

Sometimes real operating costs rise after a productivity investment. *If services measurably increase by a proportionally greater amount than the increase in operating costs, a positive return on investment is still* achieved, and can be calculated as a cost avoidance. In the above example, city policy makers may decide that parks need even more mowing, and to that end to buy new mowers, thereby increasing the annual costs of staff, fuel, and maintenance by 25% while increasing mowing by 50%. In this case the annual return on investment is the difference between the 25% cost increase using the new mowers and the 50% cost increase that would have been incurred using the old mowers. Even though total operating costs rise, real costs are avoided (costs per-service-unit fall) while needed services are increased. In other words, the city still pays *less than the usual price* for the added service. That difference, or cost avoidance, is the return on investment.[3]

FROM INVESTMENT GOALS TO INVESTMENT STRATEGIES

An "investment strategy" is the key to developing public support for government productivity investments. People who work with businesses and financial institutions, or who have personal investment capital, understand the need for financial investment strategies based on specific financial goals. Similarly, governments need productivity investment strategies based on specific productivity improvement goals. As in financial investment strategies, both long- and short-term goals are important. Short-term productivity goals can include improving services and reducing costs over the next one to three budget years. Long-term goals should concern building and sustaining productivity growth for many years to come.

Some improvement techniques lead directly to service operations improvements; by investing in these techniques governments tend to support short-term productivity goals. Other techniques rarely produce early gains but they build the capacity of organizations for future productivity growth; investments in these techniques support long-term productivity goals. Policymakers—particularly elected officials—need not be expert in myriad productivity improvement techniques to participate in developing productivity investment goals. They can demand that their public managers obtain the needed expertise to develop and implement a multi-year productivity investment strategy which produces both early gains and progress toward long-term goals for productivity growth. Policymakers should then be responsible for approving the strategy and developing the public support needed to sustain it.

For an "investment strategy" approach to government productivity improvement to work, several requirements must be met, including:

- systematic measurement of performance and costs of government agencies, including indicators of effectiveness and efficiency of services they provide, regardless of whether service delivery is by government, contract, or volunteer personnel;
- measurable accountability of managers for the performance of their programs, such as reporting against specific cost, revenue, and service performance targets; and
- systematic forecasting, measurement, and tracking of costs and benefits of productivity improvements. Wherever possible, equivalent dollar values should be calculated for service improvement benefits ("cost avoidance") and added to savings and revenue for a total dollar value of "return on investment."

These requirements are a matter of good analysis, creative measurement, and good accounting. There has been plenty of research and practice over the past fifty years or more to prove virtually any public service can be measured in useful, objective ways. Measuring some services is more difficult, more costly, or less precise than measuring others. In practice, governments devise and use affordable measurement techniques for any service when managers believe the measures will help them manage or elected officials believe the measures will help them make policy decisions. Surveys of municipalities done in 1976 and 1982 indicate growing use of management tools which stress performance measurement and accountability, such as program budgeting, management by objectives, and performance monitoring.[4]

TYING PRODUCTIVITY IMPROVEMENT TO THE BUDGET PROCESS

For many years a number of governments have included service performance measures in their budget processes, and that number has been growing. Public documents in the formal budget processes of some jurisdictions, such as Charlotte, North Carolina[5] and Dayton, Ohio[6] highlight key agency performance objectives, report on their achievement and nonachievement, and show past and proposed program costs. These cities give public evidence that they are serious about improving service performance while they control costs.

In developing six consecutive annual expense budgets, including the current one, New York City explicitly targetted hundreds of City agency productivity projects for reduced costs or increased revenues to help balance the budget. These projects have been specially monitored by the City for achievement of savings and revenue goals, and have produced combined savings and revenue which ranged from about $100 million to $240 million in the budget year in which they were designated. Including annually recurring benefits, productivity savings and revenue from these projects in the City's Fiscal Years 1983 through 1986 totaled over $1 billion.[7] Smaller cities can put these numbers in perspective by considering that New York City's annual expense budget is over $20 billion. However, New York does not make a practice of aggregating the cost avoidance totals of numerous projects done by City agencies each year which improve service, as documented through agency service performance indicators. Thus New York's return on productivity investments may actually be much greater than the City's budget figures suggest.

"Short-Term" Investments:
Direct Operations Improvements

Many productivity improvement techniques are well suited to developing recommendations which, when implemented, directly lead to savings, revenue, or service improvements. These include studies which borrow from disciplines such as industrial engineering, systems analysis, operations research, evaluation research, financial analysis, organizational analysis, and performance auditing. These techniques can be in a government's "short-term investment portfolio" because they often start yielding returns within one to two years of the start of a study. If the government agencies or departments studied participate in a cooperative spirit, improvements may start very quickly—in a matter of weeks or months—because the agencies can start changing procedures as soon as problems and solutions are identified, without waiting for a formal study report.

The cost of direct operations improvement investments is the cost of the staff or consultant time required to conduct studies and implement changes. If any new equipment, computer software, or other one-time expenses are required, these are also part of the investment cost. If a change creates new *recurring* expenses (e.g., maintenance costs for new equipment; staff time to monitor performance, or to update work standards or computer programs), these should be subtracted from the net annual return on investment rather than added to the investment cost. In practice, operations improvement projects tend to be good investments because most investment costs are one-time costs and most returns *recur annually* such as recurring savings due to permanent staff reductions. Sometimes there is a large windfall in first year returns, as,

PRODUCTIVITY IN SOLID WASTE: This one-man "side packer" solid waste vehicle, one of a fleet used by San Diego. An Able Co. body rides on a Crane Carrier chassis; driver wheel left and right sides. One man drives and loads waste into side door. Two-man trucks pick up 15.5 tons per route; one man, 10.5 tons, a 50% increase in labor productivity. In use since the late 1970s.
Source: Photo by Kristie Vallance. Permission to reprint granted.

for example, when a tax is audited for the first time in many years. Later annual benefits are smaller. More often benefits are smaller the first year and increase for two or three years before a level annual return on investment is achieved, as happens when staff change procedures and get over a learning curve; or as staff reductions take place gradually through attrition.

Because even the most systematic productivity programs are not managed like investment portfolios, there are no available statistics on "average" returns on investment. But the past fifteen years have seen enough government productivity projects to demonstrate that a real commitment to improvement can bring very large returns. Many operations improvement projects pay for themselves several times over the first year benefits are obtained. But even if it takes several years to pay back the original investment, the annually recurring nature of most benefits makes operations improvement projects excellent investments. If no major capital costs are involved, *annual* returns on investment of *several hundred percent* are fairly common by the second or third year after the start of implementation. Projects requiring capital investments will not always have such high rates of return when the fully amortized capital costs are considered, but if the projects are well selected they will generally produce a return that is significantly greater than the cost of borrowing capital funds.

With such large returns possible, why does every state and local government not have major productivity improvement efforts underway as part of their standard way of doing the public's business? Because unlike managing financial investment portfolios they cannot just research the market and pick out good stocks and bonds, or turn their funds over to a portfolio management expert to invest (as many governments do with their pension funds). Consultants can be used to conduct individual operations improvement studies and help get a productivity program started. On-loan private sector executives may also be a resource in identifying opportunities for improvement. But ultimately a government must implement study recommendations itself, and staff and support an ongoing program. It is hard work that can never be completely farmed out to "experts." To get large productivity returns on a regular basis rather than on occasional projects, a government must make productivity growth a part of its organizational culture. If a government does not build support, acceptance, and skills for improvement throughout its organization it will soon run out of good opportunities to invest in high-return direct operations improvements. That is why other types of investment—"capacity building" investments—are also essential for healthy long-term productivity growth.

"Long-Term" Investments: Capacity Building

For productivity growth to last beyond the immediate returns of the first year's operations improvements, a government's leaders must make it a priority that goes beyond their public pronouncements, beyond their directives to staff, to commitment to explicit long-term investments. These should be investments which support productivity growth even when government leaders cannot give it their personal attention. Managers and employees must see productivity improvement as part of the everyday way of doing business, as something for which they will always have the needed support. That support comes from investments that help build the capacity of government agencies to improve themselves. Capacity building includes investments in such techniques as:

- training;
- assessment of organizations and staff for training and professional development needs;
- work site improvements such as pest extermination, improved heating or lighting, or health and safety hazard removal;
- alternative work schedules such as flextime;
- confidential employee assistance programs to help employees solve substance abuse and other personal problems;
- "wellness" programs to encourage good health and fitness of employees on and off the job;
- employee involvement efforts such as labor-management quality of worklife committees and quality circles;
- organization development and teambuilding efforts;
- incentive and recognition programs such as performance-based raises and bonuses, suggestion awards, and non-monetary recognition and awards;
- performance measurement and information systems that help managers analyze and improve services and resource allocation; and
- technology transfer programs to stimulate adoption of innovations used in other jurisdictions or the private sector.

Capacity building investments, unlike operations improvements, do not improve productivity directly. They should be part of a government's "long-term investment portfolio" because they *improve the organizational environment for productivity improvement.* They make organizations more likely to encourage, accept, and cooperate with productivity initiatives, and more likely to generate new productivity improvements on their own. Some capacity building efforts, either by design or because an opportunity arises, lead to productivity improvements quickly. For example, a "problem-solving team" formed in an organization development project may quickly identify and solve key operating problems. For best results capacity building efforts should be sustained for years because they are most directly *investments in people.* People must feel these programs are not just passing fads but part of a government's serious, long-term commitment to help them improve themselves and the way they do their jobs. Managers and employees who see these programs as commitments respond with better performance and new productivity improvements even when the mayor or city manager is too busy with the latest crisis to exhort the staff to improve productivity.

Many governments use some of the capacity building techniques listed above. Most at least provide some training. But how many governments see capacity building efforts as long-term investments in future productivity growth? Too often they are "nice things to do" when there is ready funding but among the first things to be cut when the budget is tight.[8] A long-term financial investment portfolio may be refined each year as an investor's needs change, but is not intended to be sold off at once for quick returns. Likewise capacity building efforts that are part of a formal productivity investment strategy will not be cut quickly. Instead the government will sustain the investments and refine them regularly to meet changing personnel, organizational, and operations improvement needs. They will be well-targeted to support long-term goals for sustained productivity growth.

Leveraging Investments in Government Productivity

Investments in both capacity building and direct operations improvements *leverage* government resources in that they lead to improved service performance of agencies without proportional increases in agency costs. Capacity building investments, in a sense, are the most highly leveraged. Although they do not directly lead to improved productivity, they help employees and managers perform better and can lead managers to develop their own new operations improvement projects without special new investments or outside expert assistance. This happens, for example, when an agency labor-management committee develops an operations improvement project, and agency staff develop new projects after being trained in productivity improvement techniques. Without investments in capacity building, agency employees and managers will be less able—and probably less willing—to identify new opportunities for investments in operations improvement projects. Without the operating knowledge and cooperation of agency staff, operations improvements are more difficult and expensive, and the well of high-return operations improvement projects will eventually run dry.

Figure 1 shows the three different ways a government can invest in more performance from its departments or agencies, and how they relate to each other. The box on the right represents actual day-to-day performance and costs of agencies in providing services. If a government wants more service performance quickly from an agency, it may choose to "pay the usual price" by simply adding more staff, equipment, or other resources to the agency without taking the time and effort to figure out a better way to increase performance. That is generally the fastest way to clean more streets, inspect more buildings, trim more trees, and increase the level of many services. It is also the most expensive way to increase services, as represented by the triple-thickness arrow leading from "spending as usual," because the extra operating costs must be incurred every year the extra level of service is desired. The middle box represents specific operations improvement projects to improve agency productivity. This improvement approach takes longer because the community must wait for the project to be developed and for implementation to begin before the improvements in service efficiency and effectiveness are realized. However, as indicated by the double-thickness arrow, it is a less costly way to improve services than "paying the usual price" because the investments in staff or consultant time to conduct the projects are leveraged to produce better service performance (in the right-hand box) at proportionally lower cost, and these benefits are likely to recur annually. Finally, the left-hand box represents capacity building efforts. These are often the least costly improvement efforts (hence the single-thickness arrow) and the most highly leveraged (hence the smaller box). Capacity building investments are highly leveraged because they help lower the cost required to implement efficiency and effectiveness improvements, and increase the likely benefits to be achieved. Capacity building makes managers and employees

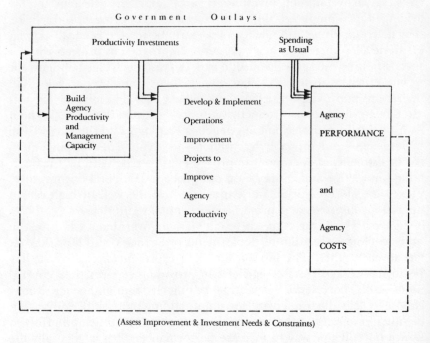

(Assess Improvement & Investment Needs & Constraints)

Figure 1. Relationships Among Capacity Building, Operations Improvement Projects, and Government Agency Performance and Costs

better prepared and more willing to cooperate with special operations improvement projects, and better able to develop operations improvements on their own.

Example: Combining Capacity Building and Operations Improvement

Local governments that sustain significant productivity improvement programs for more than a few years tend to develop a range of improvement approaches. Through a combination of conscious planning and opportunism they develop diverse programs that contain elements of both direct operations improvement and capacity building. Phoenix, Arizona's productivity program once primarily emphasized industrial engineering by a central staff to improve operations, and produced dramatic early savings and cost avoidance. Since the late 1970s Phoenix has added many capacity building approaches including a prize-winning employee suggestion award program, employee attitude surveys, an employee assistance program, incentive pay for managers, and training in productivity improvement techniques for departmental staff. With service departments, rather than the central staff, now initiating most operations improvements, Phoenix reaps the benefits of many more service improvement and cost reduction projects than were generated under its earlier program.[9] Phoenix's suburban neighbor, the City of Scottsdale, also has a balanced approach to improving productivity, emphasizing both capacity building and operations improvement techniques,[10] some of which are described in Chapters 9 and 12 (this volume).

New York City not only emphasizes operations improvements to help balance the budget as described above, but also has an extensive quality of worklife labor-management committee program, employee assistance programs, and wide use of alternative work schedules.[11] New York sometimes directly links capacity building and operations improvement by targeting training in project management and productivity improvement techniques to specific agency staff who are managing improvement projects.[12]

The City of San Diego started two separate improvement programs in the mid-1970s. One used industrial engineering techniques to improve employee efficiency, while the other used organization development and training approaches to improve City organizations. In 1980 the two programs were merged to form the Organization Effectiveness Program, which now provides a wide range of expertise to service departments from one in-house consulting group, including projects which combine direct operations improvements with departmental capacity building.[13]

INCENTIVES TO STAFF
TO IMPROVE PRODUCTIVITY

For any productivity improvement strategy to work, particularly over several years' time, managers and employees must develop a sense that it is better to contribute to productivity improvement efforts than to avoid or obstruct them. Because long-term productivity growth requires active cooperation throughout the organization, the perceived incentives for people to participate must outweigh the perceived disincentives. For example, many governments adopt an "attrition only" rule for eliminating positions as a result of productivity improvements so employees are less likely to feel threatened and more likely to cooperate. Also, since there is little that public managers take more seriously than their agency's budget, measurable performance objectives tied to the budget can increase managers' incentives to improve productivity.

Managers may lead productivity efforts in their organizations but may more easily thwart them. Managers often feel productivity projects take great effort and only result in a tougher management job by raising performance expectations while reducing staff and budget. Many public managers perceive a reduction in staff and budget to be a reduction in stature. Some may feel productivity improvement threatens their future earnings potential since many public compensation plans are based largely on the number of people under a manager's direct and indirect supervision. To overcome this disincentive, top government officials must make managers understand they will be judged on real measurable performance and productivity improvement, not on their ability to "muddle through" with a large staff and budget.

Example: Management Incentive Pay

Phoenix, Arizona[14] and Dayton, Ohio[15] are two cities with considerable experience using performance-based management pay to provide incentives for improving program performance. Probably a great number of jurisdictions could claim to have pay plans that, at least on paper, allow consideration of "merit" in determining salary increases. How well they work to provide incentives to program managers depends on whether measurable service performance objectives are explicitly included in the criteria by which managers are judged. Because Phoenix and Dayton both already had comprehensive performance measurement and improvement programs in place when they started their management incentive pay plans in the 1970s, they were readily able to link performance to pay in ways considered fair and objective. In these cities managers know their future earnings potential is more closely tied to service performance and productivity improvement than to the size of their staffs and budgets.

PRODUCTIVITY INVESTMENT AS PART OF FULLY INTEGRATED SERVICE AND FINANCIAL PERFORMANCE MANAGEMENT

We can now pull together several of the concepts previously discussed into a single management process. Leveraged expenditures, or investments in projects that enhance productivity; and service performance measures and productivity improvement objectives can be combined into a single service and financial performance process, as illustrated in Figure 2.

As shown in Figure 2, a local government's operational, financial, and strategic planning processes are located in the middle of the Figure. They are placed there because budget development and other policy planning should not be done in a vacuum but should be done with the cognizance of agency capacity for improvement and future improvement plans, ideas, and proposals. "Service Management Planning," the middle box, refers to regular targeting of quantified service performance measures by the local government, a process which can be thought of as setting regular service performance objectives. These objectives should be determined in conjunction with development of the operating budget ("Financial Planning") and capital plan ("Capital and Strategic Planning") so the expected resources available to achieve the objectives will be known. Also, proposed capacity building and operations improvement projects of government agencies should be accounted for in all these planning processes. The performance objectives determined in service management planning should reflect projected productivity improvements as a result of those projects which are expected to be implemented. Financial planning should provide for the year-to-year investments needed in capacity building and operations improvement, and should also reflect operating cost reductions and revenue increases which agencies are expected to achieve as a result of their improvement projects. In some cases, high level policy decisions will be needed to decide the extent to which some expected productivity gains will be used to reduce agency costs (as reflected in budget savings) and the extent to which they will be used to improve services (as reflected in higher service performance objectives). Finally, capital and strategic planning should include investments needed for operations improvements, such as large computer systems and new vehicles; and for capacity building efforts, such as capital-intensive worksite improvements, all

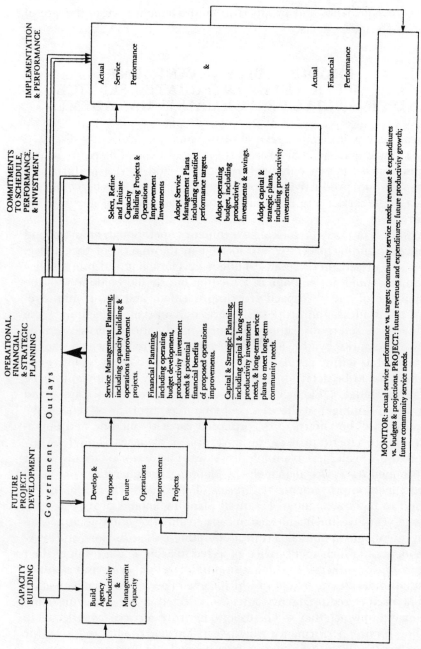

Figure 2. Integrated Service Management and Financial Performance Cycle

of which require capital investments. It also includes other long-term investments such as multi-year training and personnel development programs.

The box to the right of the "Planning" box in Figure 2 features the *commitments* made when the budgets and plans are adopted. Service agencies make commitments to implement selected capacity building and operations improvement projects, to attempt to meet the quantified service performance targets in their service management plans, and to achieve specified savings and revenue increases as a result of selected productivity improvement projects. In return, budget and planning officials and those executives and elected officials who approve budgets and plans make commitments to the service agencies that the investment required for capacity building and operations improvement will be forthcoming. If required funding for a specific project is not made available in the budget, the agency would not have to commit to achieving the productivity gains associated with the project. If the project funds are put in the budget, the agency would be expected to achieve either savings or revenue (specified in the operating budget), or higher service performance targets (specified in service management plans), or some agreed-to combination of these benefits. When the City of New York set out to integrate productivity improvement planning with its budget development process, a key principle made explicit to all agency heads was that mutual commitments would be made among service agencies, the Mayor's Office, and the Office of Management and Budget to provide adequate productivity investment and to achieve agreed-to combinations of savings, revenue, and measurable service improvements.[16]

The box to the left of the "Planning" box in Figure 2 features future development of operations improvement projects, and is shown in sequence to occur *before* the formal planning processes because the ability of a local government agency to develop and propose new projects depends less on a community's formal planning processes than on the agency's capacity to manage and improve itself. The assumption here is that managers and employees of service agencies who deal with service delivery operations and problems each day are in the best position to develop operations improvements and, given the capacity and encouragement to do so, will come up with ideas for improvements throughout the year—not just at times specified in the budget process or other formal planning processes. Some of these ideas will not require special investments outside their existing budgets or other special approvals, so the agencies may decide to implement them on their own without waiting for the formal planning processes to take their course. As a result they might exceed some of their service performance targets or achieve unplanned savings or revenue which (depending on the city's financial accounting rules and procedures) they may be able to reinvest on their own in other service improvements. Those "future projects" which require new investment can be proposed through the formal budget and planning processes, and if approved will result in the commitments for both investment and productivity gains described above.

Agency capacity building is shown on the extreme left in Figure 2 (as in Figure 1) on the assumption that if investments are not made in building agencies' management and productivity capacity, the agencies' managers and employees will be extremely limited in their ability to come up with new ideas for improvement and to develop those ideas into viable operations improvement projects. Capacity building efforts are shown in Figure 2 as the source of a stream of productivity improvements which result in improved services, budget savings, and increased revenue. If the source is not continually replenished with new, highly leveraged, capacity building investment, the stream will eventually run dry.

Finally, Figure 2 shows a feedback loop to each step in the cycle, based on continual monitoring of actual service and financial performance, monitoring and projection of changing community needs and government revenue and expenditure flows, and projection of future productivity growth. This involves periodic reports by government agencies of service performance *versus* their performance targets, regular monitoring of community conditions and analysis of physical and demographic trends, continual accounting of revenues and expenditures *versus* budgets and projections, and periodic projection of future revenues and expenditures. The results of the periodic performance and financial monitoring and projection are generally fed back into the next year's budget and planning processes, but they could be fed back into any step of the performance cycle in Figure 2. For example, if the monitoring identifies a strong need or a good opportunity for improvement, agencies may begin to develop new capacity building or operations improvement projects before the next year's formal planning processes begin.

The integrated service management and financial performance cycle discussed here is not a conceptual ideal incapable of being achieved in practice. Several local governments mentioned in this chapter have achieved the equivalent of this "performance cycle," although they may not have documented it as shown in Figure 2. These are governments which have exhibited exemplary productivity improvement, service planning and performance measurement, and financial management practices. In fact, Figure 2 was derived from a diagram that the New York Mayor's Office developed after reviewing the City's first budget planning cycle which explicitly included agency productivity projects.

The Mayor's Office subsequently used that diagram to help train managers who were responsible for productivity planning in all city service agencies.[17]

INVESTMENT: THE TIME IS NOW

The municipalities cited in this chapter and other jurisdictions around the country—including smaller communities—have each demonstrated parts of a productivity investment strategy. A handful of jurisdictions may actually have all the programmatic pieces in place and need only do the accounting to aggregate the costs of all productivity investments and the dollar value of all returns. But the communities who will gain the most by formally adopting a productivity investment strategy are not those few which have already institutionalized a thorough, balanced productivity program. The many more jurisdictions struggling to start a productivity program, or to keep a modest training program or operations analysis staff going in the face of a budget squeeze, will receive the greatest benefits from their efforts.

It takes political courage by local administrations to propose increasing the costs of capacity building and operations improvement efforts and call it investment in productivity growth. They must have confidence that results will live up to expectations. As time goes on, more public officials will find themselves facing voter reaction to the choice of severe service cuts or stiff tax increases. Those who lead their communities to invest wisely will help avoid such harsh public choices.

ACKNOWLEDGMENT

This chapter is an expanded version of an article by Epstein and Fass, "Build An Investment Portfolio in Government Productivity," *National Civic Review*, 76, 2 (March–April 1987): 96–107.

NOTES AND REFERENCES

1. Marc Holzer, "Constancy and Commitment," *Public Productivity Review*, 3, 6 (1982): 155–156. (New York: National Center for Public Productivity, John Jay College.)

2. The phrase "service bonus" has the same meaning as "cost avoidance"—a phrase we use as well as others writing elsewhere on public sector productivity.

3. Because lower operating costs often mean some capital investment, the difference in operating costs between the "new" and "old" ways of doing business does not represent a free-and-clear return in quite the same way that an outright cash saving, or an increase in revenues *sans* capital outlay, would represent.

An economist would consider operating costs alone an invalid way of looking at "return on investment." Instead he would compare the *marginal* costs between production the old way and production the new way, with "marginal cost" defined as the actual cost of producing a single additional unit (or block of units) of service. Marginal cost includes both operating costs and capital costs, including the cost of money, with equipment depreciated over a certain period (5 years for police cruisers to 25 years for sewage plants).

Increased service levels that do not entail any increase in capital outlays can, after being given a dollar value, be counted as free and clear returns on investment costs, and added together with outright cash savings and/or increased revenues as a "pure return." This is the case in methods improvement studies, in which the investment cost is simply that of hiring a consultant (or accepting an employee suggestion). But if equipment is bought or bonds floated as part of the "new way of doing business," then obviously the cost of equipment and money—and interest rates over 30 years can far exceed the new market value of any structure—must be factored into the rate of return, together with operating costs. Focusing on operating costs, and ignoring fixed (capital) costs, differentiates cities from private corporations.

In many, perhaps most, cases, new equipment *will* lead to lower marginal costs, a lower cost-per-last-unit-of-output. But the issue is not whether true costs (and returns) are higher or lower given the new methods; the issue is whether one is obliged to include capital costs, and not operating costs alone, on *each and every* calculation of "return on (productivity) investment." Only the marginal cost method does this.

4. Theodore H. Poister and Robert P. McGowan, "The Use of Management Tools in Municipal Government: A National Survey," *Public Administration Review*, 44, 3 (May–June 1984): 215–223. (Washington, D.C.: American Society for Public Administration.)

5. *FY87 Objectives* and numerous previous years' *Objectives* documents in the City of Charlotte's budget process (City of Charlotte, North Carolina, 1986 and prior years).

6. *Dayton 1987 Program Strategies: Policy, Financial Plan, Program Budget* and numerous previous years' *Program Strategies* documents (Office of Management and Budget, City of Dayton, Ohio, 1987 and prior years).

7. *The Mayor's Management Report* (September 17, 1986), p. NYCP-3. (Mayor's Office of Operations, City of New York.)

8. In terms of decremental budgeting, both operational improvements and capacity-building programs rate at least a B value rating. See Chapter 4, p. 7, Table 1.

9. *The Phoenix Productivity Program* (Value Management Resource Office Staff, City of Phoenix, November 1985).

10. Richard H. Martin and Alan C. Kapanicas, "Creating a Culture for Productivity in the Public Sector," in *Proceedings of the Fall 1986 Industrial Engineering Conference* December 7–10, 1986 (Norcross, GA: Industrial Engineering and Management Press), pp. 165–171.

11. *The Mayor's Management Report* (January 30, 1987), pp. NYCP-3–NYCP-31. (Mayor's Office of Operations, City of New York.)

12. Nathan Leventhal, "The Koch Administration's Approach to Productivity," *City Almanac*, 16, 3 (October 1981): 6. (New York: Center for New York City Affairs, New School for Social Research.)

13. Trudy J. Sopp, "San Diego Postscript: Anatomy of the Merger Between the City's Productivity Improvement Program and Organization Development and Training Program," in Paul D. Epstein, *Using Performance Measurement in Local Government* (New York: Van Nostrand Reinhold, 1984), pp. 117–120.

14. "Performance Achievement System," *The Phoenix Productivity Program* (City of Phoenix, 1985), pp. 5–6.

15. *Salary Administration Program for Mid-Management, Management, and Executive Employees* (City of Dayton, Ohio).

16. Nathan Leventhal, "Integration of the Productivity Program into the Ongoing Management and Budget Planning Cycles." June 1981 memorandum from Deputy Mayor for Operations Nathan Leventhal to all agency heads, Mayor's Office of Operations, City of New York.

17. Training Materials for Productivity Planning Meetings of May 24 and 25, 1982, Mayor's Office of Operations, City of New York.

Chapter 7

VALUE ANALYSIS
AND THE CITIES

Russell C. Brannen and Edward C. Hayes

SUMMARY. Value Analysis offers local government the opportunity to realize cash savings in the first year. Using a team led by a Certified Value Specialist (CVS) together with city officials, a typical Value Engineered project saves over five times the cost of the analysis itself. The method has been proved beyond question, and while it is employed in many of Fortune 500 corporations it is still not widely employed by local jurisdictions. It is now used regularly for wastewater programs by forty states, by the Defense Department, and by cities as large as New York and as small as Mansfield, Ohio.

WHAT IS IT?

Value Analysis (VA), or Value Engineering (VE),[1] is a method for analyzing any construction project, management process, or purchase item, to systematically reduce costs and/or improve performance. It is based on the insight that projects, processes, and items all perform certain *functions*; that, usually, one of these functions is clearly the *basic function*; that others are secondary, or even undesirable; and that the basic function itself might be accomplished by using different processes, items, or materials. This "function analysis," which began as a way of analyzing methods of purchase and production in the private sector, has now been expanded to the public sector and employed on problems ranging from sewer facility construction to reorganization of a corporate head-quarters.

The classic illustration of VA method is the tieclip which holds a necktie to a shirt. Using the two word description of function preferred by Value Analysts, the function of the tieclip is to "fasten tie." Now if this function is the only one that the analyst wishes to accomplish, and if he or she will take a moment to reflect (or "brainstorm"—the creative phase of Value Analysis), he will realize that the same function can be obtained by using an ordinary paper clip.

Function: FASTEN TIE

	Option 1	Option 2
Item	tieclip	paper clip
Cost	$10.00	1¢

Of course the full list of "functions" of the tieclip—or of public buildings—includes visual attractiveness and security. The paper clip scores zero on these added functions. Yet the examination of projects, programs, and purchases from the standpoint of functions allows the city official to decide which function he really wants—which is basic, and which he can do without. He has a powerful tool for making hard choices.[2]

VALUE ANALYSIS:
ITS GROWTH AND ACHIEVEMENTS

Value Analysis was invented and codified by Lawrence D. Miles, an engineer assigned to the purchasing office at General Electric shortly after World War II. GE asked Miles to discover why post-war manufacturing costs had suddenly shot up. Looking at materials, manufacturing processes, and purchasing practices, Miles found that the "temporary" methods adopted for economy and efficiency during the war had been scrapped when the war was over. The reversion to normal methods had caused production costs to skyrocket.[3]

Putting his discoveries together into coherent form, Miles began a system of function analysis which he began teaching, first to GE's manufacturing and marketing departments, and then to GE's subcontractors, so they could produce at less cost and pass along some of the savings.

In 1957 the U.S. Department of the Navy adopted the first federal VA program. In the 1960s VA spread throughout the Pentagon. In the

LAWRENCE D. MILES, the founder of Value Analysis. VA/VE has shaped our industrial world. Mr. Miles' book, *Techniques of Value Analysis and Value Engineering,* has been translated into 14 languages. He received medals and awards from a dozen countries, and from the United States Navy. State and local governments requesting major Environmental Protection Agency (EPA) grants must first submit their plans for VA analysis.

Source: Reprinted, with permission, from Lawrence D. Miles Value Foundation, Washington, D.C.

1970s the General Accounting Office (GAO), the Environmental Protection Agency (EPA), and the Department of Transportation all began using Value Analysis/Value Engineering. Today some 23 states have VE programs in their transportation programs, 40 states use VE for EPA-financed wastewater treatment plants, and 6 states use it in other departments.

In the United States, the American Society of Value Engineers (SAVE), headquartered in Northbrook (Chicago), has over 1,200 members and chapters in most states. There are Value Engineers in Germany, France, England, Sweden, and Canada, and perhaps 2,500 value engineers in Japan, a country that has taken this born-in-America technique and used it more extensively than American manufacturers.

Value Engineering has been responsible for major cost savings at all levels of government, as the following illustrate:

- Between 1978 and 1984, the U.S. Environmental Protection Agency (EPA) VA program has required a Value Engineer to review all local-government projects in excess of $10 million. In that time VE studies have shaved $235 million from original project plans, at a study cost of $15 million, a return-on-investment of over 15 to 1.[4]

- The U.S. Department of Defense has saved a total of $9.1 *billion* through VE as of 1985. In 1985, DoD's overall return-on-investment for VE programs was 25 to 1. For Army VE projects in that year the return-on-investment was *55 to 1*.[5]

- In VE workshops between 1982 and 1986, the U.S. Department of Transportation gave VE training to 1,465 attendees, primarily state transportation officials; analyzed 247 project studies on projects valued at $1.48 billion; and suggested 383 changes that, if implemented, would have resulted in a saving of $259 million, or 17.5% of total project costs.[6]

- The City of New York, whose VE program began in 1983 under William McElligott, C.V.S., has undertaken seventeen VE studies on capital projects ranging from $5 million to $250 million. For these 17 projects, initial cost savings (through redesign) totalled $125 million on projects originally costing $900 million, a 14% saving. These VE changes have enabled the city to save an additional $11 million in annual debt service, and an additional $11 million in operating costs, for a total annual savings of $22 million, or $345 million over ten years.[7]

- The city of Mansfield, Ohio has had a VA program since the early 1980's. In 1984 two VE reports reduced the projected costs of two construction projects by $300,000. In 1985, using VE methods, the city engineer cut the cost of a new bridge by over $60,000 and won a trip to Paradise Island in the Bahamas.[8]

- The city of Vista, California shaved $7 million from the cost of its jail addition in 1985, after a 40-hour Value Engineering workshop led by the construction firm on the project.[9]

VE has only begun to impact local government in this decade. Yet given its unquestioned success in both private industry and at the state and federal levels, VE will contribute as much to local government cost control in future as the better-known methods of contracting out and industrial engineering.

THE VA METHOD

The method of Value Analysis is based on asking, and getting complete answers to, the following five questions:[10]

1. What is it (the process or item)?
2. What does it cost?
3. What functions does it perform?

4.   What other (item or process) will do the job?
5.   What would that alternate cost?

To analyze a program, process, or item, Value Analysis moves through five formal phases of analysis, with up to as many as twenty separate analytical steps.[11] Figure 1 shows the five phases. In this chapter we shall discuss at length only the first two.

PHASE ONE

The first phase of what Larry Miles called the Job Plan is to gather the data and determine the functions.Functions are divided into two kinds, *basic functions* and *secondary functions*. These are determined using the following guide:

1.   All functions should be expressed as two words—a verb and a noun.

     To state what something does in two words requires considerable thought and refinement, a process that creates a better understanding of the function. A payroll system is designed to "distribute payroll." A fire department has the functions of "suppress fire" and "prevent fire." A sheriff's department has the function of "protect property" and "protect life"; a health department, "protect health." When choosing words that define function, make them as broad and generic as possible. Do not choose words that predetermine the way the function should be performed.

2.   There are only two kinds of functions in any VA study: basic and secondary.

     The basic function is the *most important* function which a product or service is designed to do. A system may have more than one basic function, but care must be exercised that two different elements of work are being done. Taken at a high enough level of abstraction, all departments and programs have one overarching function.

     Secondary functions are all other functions that the program, process, or item performs, subordinate in import to the basic function. Secondary functions may be Required, Aesthetic, or Unwanted (unnecessary).[12]

Following is a list of verbs and nouns that can be used in defining functions for programs and work processes:

Team No. _____

Project No. _____

Phase	Information		Ideation	Evaluation		Definition		Implementation		
Hours	8	4	4	4	4	4	4	4	4	3
Date										

Information

What is it?

What Does it Cost?

What Does it Do?

What is it Worth?

• Determine and analyze costs

Ideation

What else will do the job?

• Apply imagination

Try

• everything

Evaluation

What Does that Cost?

• Organize your ideas

• Define and apply program constraints

• List good and bad features

• Put a dollar sign on

Definition

• Work on specifics avoid generalities

• Verify technical and economic feasibility

• Determine implementation requirements and costs

• Identify and

Implementation

• Prepare a written report

• Consider the use of models

• Discuss report with affected departments

• Include latest forecasts and pertinent data

• Include "breakeven" analysis

138

• Get all the facts from the best source	• anything	all decisions	overcome roadblocks	• Develop flip charts with highlights
• Develop the team approach	Be • creative • spontaneous • fluent • flexible • original	• Exercise judgment	• Challenge requirements	• Make an oral presentation to management
• Define and evaluate function		• Use speciality vendors and own specialists	• Spend department money as you would your own	• Exercise salesmanship, and be diplomatic
	Then - • simplify • magnify • eliminate	• Utilize standard parts and practices	• Develop an implementation plan, with schedules	• Be prepared to spearhead follow-up

Figure 1. Value Analysis Job Plan

Source: Mr. George Bartolomei, C.V.S.

VERBS		NOUNS	
Accept	Instruct	Adjustments	Material
Acknowledge	Maintain	Claims	Order
Advise	Monitor	Computer	Performance
Balance	Notify	Contract	Priority
Certify	Order	Data Delivery	Production
Compile	Post	Failure	Receipts
Edit	Provide	Information	Reports
Estimate	Program	Inventory	Schedule
Identify	Record		Services
	Transmit		Terms

As an optional step in Phase 1, the analyst can lay out a FAST (Function Analysis System Technique) Diagram, showing all aspects of the projected VE process (see Figure 2).

PHASE TWO: CREATIVITY

The second phase, "Ideation," may come as a surprise to the layman, who may view engineers as soulless cement-pourers bent on paving the Everglades or eliminating all windows from public buildings in the name of efficiency. In contrast to this stereotype, the heart of Phase Two is *the exercise of the imagination,* so as to develop superior, creative solutions. Idea stimulation processes such as Association, Brainstorming, and Slipwriting are used to aid in the creation of ideas.

WHAT DO YOU SEE?

Is it a lamp, a table, a wine goblet, or two ladies' profiles? In the "ideation" phase, the ability of city staff, led by VA specialists, to see new patterns to old problems is developed.

The creative process has three broad elements.

- *Imagination.* All people possess this faculty, and it can be devel-

Schematic

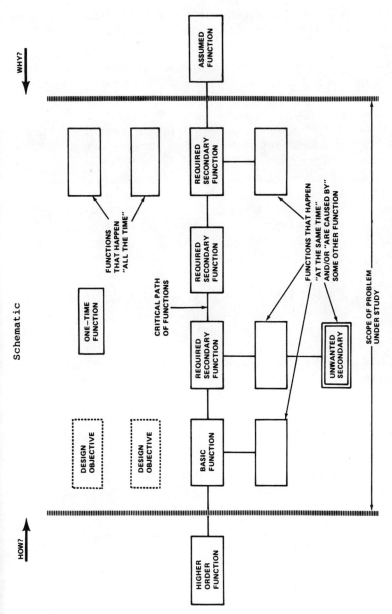

Figure 2. Function Analysis System Technique Diagram

Source: Value Analysis Inc.

141

oped by practice. "Imagination grows by exercise," said W. Somerset Maugham.

- *Inspiration.* During a creative session an idea presented by one person will often stimulate an idea in the subconscious mind of a teammate.

- *Illumination.* This just happens. Like a bubble rising from the bottom of a lake, it comes up, bursts, and there it is.[14]

The creative aspect of VA is not cosmetic. It is essential, and when a good discussion leader is present, the receptiveness of the VA team to new and different ideas is apparent. "Crazy" ideas are welcomed. When a team is loose enough to begin joking ("I know this sounds ridiculous, but . . ."), then the discussion leader is over the hump.

The entire VA effort, including the ideation phase, is a team effort, building on the existing knowledge of program managers and engineers. It is ideas and creativity of city staff that the VE expert is trying to develop, and when the exercise is over, the existing staff has had an enriching experience.

VA AND THE CITIES: SOME EXAMPLES

Mansfield, Ohio

The small town of Mansfield, Ohio (population 53,000) has had an active program in VE, due to the efforts of one interested Councilman.

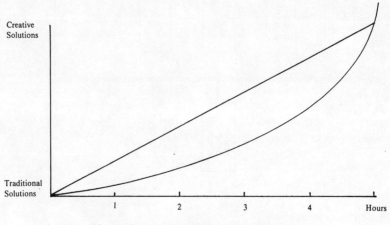

Figure 3. A Parabola of Creativity

The Councilman, Mr. Doug Versau, is associated with the VE program at his place of employment in Mansfield, Therm-A-Disc, a subsidiary of Emerson Electric. The Chamber, other local corporations, and the Mayor and Council have all been drawn to VA through the Councilman's encouragement. Mansfield has had a conference on Value Engineering, funded substantially by the Councilman himself; and a VE Awareness program, through which over 300 of the city's 500 employees have completed a four-hour course in basic VE problem solving methodology. Every employee is seen as able to comprehend and apply the method.

Mansfield has also had an active VE program in its Treatment and Wastewater Collection departments. Sued by EPA in the early 1980s for failure to bring its treatment levels up to standard, the city undertook an expansion of its wastewater treatment plant, and reconstruction of its sanitary sewer to increase its capacity. Two VE reports were made during 1984, at a total cost of $50,000, which resulted in reduction in planned construction costs of $300,000. The studies cost $50,000, a return-on-investment of six to one.

VE is also a major part of the city's permanent Productivity Improvement Program. Erich Eisenloffel, a city civil engineer, was the recent recipient of the Program's first major award. Using VE methods, Mr. Eisenloffel studied alternative methods for replacing a bridge which would fulfill the bridge's basic function of "support traffic." His winning idea called for assembling pre-made concrete pieces at the site, rather than pouring wet concrete, an idea which shaved costs by $23,000. Perhaps more important, this "pre-fab" method of construction reduced total bridge replacement time from 90 days to 30 days, resulting in time savings to companies using the bridge of an additional $40,000. For his efforts the engineer was awarded an all-expense paid trip for two to the Paradise Islands in the Bahamas. A local bank contributed the award.

New York City

The nation's largest city (population 7 million) has a VE unit housed in the Mayor's Office of Management and Budget. The unit has less than fifteen staff, and does not itself do VE studies. Instead it hires outside firms to do the studies, and confines itself to commissioning the studies, insuring their recommendations are implemented, and evaluation. The city has hired at least six firms for such studies and has several on contract at any one time.

What Kinds of Projects?

The program began in 1984 with a study of a proposed new jail facility. The VE study reduced the required amount of floor space by

THE DETENTION FACILITY IN LOWER MANHATTAN. This first project of
New York City's Value Engineering program was given to contracted Value Engineers
in 1984 at the early design stage; they reduced floor space by 66,000 feet with no loss
of capacity. In 17 VE studies on capital projects, New York has saved $125 million,
or 14% of the original projects' costs.
Source: Urbahn Associates Inc., 1250 Broadway, New York. Reprinted with permission.

66,000 feet and eliminated the need for *sixty* full time operating positions. Through early 1987 the city had commissioned VE studies on
seventeen construction projects. Each project had one to two studies,
with total costs per project of roughly $90,000.

Of the seventeen projects, over half have been reconstruction of existing facilities, and the rest, construction of new facilities. These have
included studies of two new jail projects, two police precincts, a new
firehouse, an aquarium addition, and a plaza reconstruction project.[15]

What Have Been The Savings?

Accepted VE changes have resulted in savings of $11 million per year in capital costs, or a total savings in capital costs of $125 for the seventeen projects, whose costs were originally planned at $900 million.

In addition the city will save another $11 million per year in operating costs, for a total of roughly $22 million in savings per year for ten years. The total cost of all VE studies has been approximately $1 million. This figure, plus the annual costs of the VE program, give a final return-on-investment of well over 10 to 1 in 1987.[16]

Why Has VE Saved New York Money?

The city's program has dealt successfully with three main causes of construction over-costs:

1. Loosely defined user requirements. When a hospital is designed, it is the architects and engineers who decide how big the waiting rooms, emergency rooms, and all other areas shall be. Unsure of real requirements, they err on the side of size. The VE process in New York, in contrast, begins its review at the pre-design stage, and brings together the users of the facility, including doctors and administrators, and all whose input is informed. Program requirements are set in 3 to 5 days by actual users.

2. Faulty original estimates of cost. In most government projects, cost estimates usually turn out to be too low. When they are later raised, all hope of instilling cost-control discipline is lost. By spending a full day in refining initial cost estimates the VE workshop deals with this difficulty.

3. Inadequate controls during the design phase. This occurs simply because most government staffs are too small to deal with cost-control during the design phase. Yet this is where the "fat" is designed in or out. The city's VA program oversees the costs incurred during this phase.

By bringing users into the design phase, New York has not only reduced costs, but added space where needed and increased safety features.

The Police Department of Anderson, Indiana

Like police departments everywhere, the department in Anderson, Indiana (population 64,000) is burdened with paperwork. The old saw

"The crook is back on the street before the cop can file his reports" has some truth to it. In particular, a single arrest of a drunk driver under the city's present system requires three hours and thirty-five minutes, 10 forms, and 4 officers. On an annual basis the city's police currently spend 1,287 staffhours on drunk driver arrests.[18]

The VE Seminar

When the city assigned a new person to its Records Division, this new manager made inquiries to the nearby General Motors Fisher Guide Engineering Division, to see if the city could send a police team to the company's October 1985 workshop. The reply was affirmative, and a team consisting of Police Chief Frank Burrows and five other officers and staff of the Police Department attended the weeklong workshop inside the Fisher Guide facility. The workshop was not tailored specially to the police department. It is not uncommon for hospitals and city staffs to "sit in" on VE workshops designed primarily for private companies, just as the Anderson police staff did in this case.

In the Creative Phase, the police contingent formed its own group, with a leader chosen from its own ranks. This group was given overall guidance by the workshop instructor. Using an easel, the team developed numerous ideas to cut paperwork time, all in one afternoon. The entire workshop was tiring; forty hours is a long time. As Assistant Chief Walter L. Smith related, "It requires a spark plug to keep the process moving. The workshop depended for its success on the dynamism of its overall leader."[19] But by the end of the week the police team had refined its ideas and prepared an effective proposal.

The Results

The proposal, which is not yet adopted, is wideranging. It proposes a new drunk driver arrest method that eliminates four (of ten) forms, the need for two officers and the need to transfer prisoners, and 1 hour and forty-five minutes from existing drunk arrest procedures, a proposed total saving of 577.7 hours, or 48.8%. It is conceivable that the introduction of such time-saving methods will encourage officers to perform their primary function: arrest drunk drivers. They would then know their time will not be consumed in nonproductive paperwork.

In the Anderson case, these changes remain largely in the planning stage. According to Assistant Chief Walter Smith, the new system must first be approved by the County Prosecutor, and will require some changes in state law. He is hopeful that these changes will take place and that the full system will be implemented.

VALUE ENGINEERING IN THE PACIFIC NORTHWEST

In the past five years VA has saved the City of Salem, Oregon $335,000 in new construction. Lebanon, Washington incorporated a VA suggested change into its new wastewater treatment plant that saved the town $275,000, or $8 per resident. METRO, the federation of governments in the Seattle/Kings County area, has used value analysis on four wastewater and sewerage projects, and on its Downtown Seattle Transit Program. VE suggestions for the latter program included station design suggestions, revisions to portals, and cut-and-cover ideas. The City of Seattle believes the total savings attributed to VE on its Transit Program amounts to $49 *million*. The VE studies themselves cost under $500,000.

Mandated VE In Washington State Schools

In 1977 the Washington State Legislature established the framework of a local schools cost stabilization program, and the following year Life Cycle Costing (LCC) and Value Engineering were selected as the program's major methods. After a successful pilot VE program in several local districts which had asked for it, VE was mandated for all state school construction for buildings over 50,000 square feet. The local school district chooses the outside VE consultant from a pool of twelve firms that have contracted with the State Superintendant of Public Instruction.[20]

Studies usually cost from $10,000 to $30,000. A typical school renovation VE study, for example, might be conducted by a VE team consisting of a Certified Value Specialist as leader, an architect with renovation experience, structural, mechanical, and electrical engineers, and significantly, an academic administrator responsible for curriculum or for financing. At least five people serve on a typical team.

Of major importance is the fact that the VE study is divided into two parts. The first part lasts two-and-a-half days, during which time the team evaluates both the educational program and the construction site. This gives the team the opportunity to develop programatic changes before the proposed design is examined. The next three and a half days focus on cost estimates and technical issues.

An overall evaluation of the 78 VE school projects through 1986 has been conducted by Harvey C. Childs. This study found that, of the 78 school projects with a total of $248,590,000 in actual bid costs, VE studies had suggested changes valued at just over $38 million. Of these, just over $15 million have been accepted by school authorities, for an overall return-on-investment of 12.87 to 1.[21]

Most school authorities indicated an appreciation of the value of VE on Child's survey. Yet for reasons which the survey did not probe, just over 50% indicated that they would not want to use the VE process again.[22]

VALUE ENGINEERING AND STATE GOVERNMENTS

Value Engineering came to the states in the 1970s. Pennsylvania and Massachusetts were among the first to adopt programs and instruct their own officials in the method. Three states have used VE programs outside their EPA-financed wastewater programs and transportation departments,[23] and no less than 23 states have a Value Engineering function for highways and transit, including California, the District of Columbia, and Nebraska.[24] In California, Caltrans has employed VE to some extent since 1969. Between that year and 1984 the department claims to have realized $80 million in cost reductions.[25]

The state of North Carolina has had success with its program. Established in 1981, the state's Value Determination Program, housed in the Division of Environmental Management (DEM), has, together with other wastewater program initiatives, saved $12 million in construction grants, allowing North Carolina to fund projects while cutting state wastewater staff from 55 positions to 38.[26]

CONCLUSION: SPENDING A DIME
TO SAVE A DOLLAR

Value Analysis will become increasingly popular with local governments for three reasons. First, it works. Its track record is too long and obvious to deny; returns on investment of 10 to 1 are not uncommon. Second, when applied to new buildings, it results in a building that existing officials—the building users—have helped design. It enhances their living quarters' usability, and this guarantees their interest and support. And finally, when VA saves money and cuts positions, it is often saving money not yet spent, and positions that are still in the planning stage. The files of the nation's local civil service commissions contain not one complaint from employees who were never considered for a job.

For those cities still in a cutback mode—and it is important to remember that, despite the relative prosperity of the late 1980s, many cities are unable to keep ahead of inflation- and wage-driven cost increases—VA offers a way to cut existing costs. And it does it by asking a question: "What is the function?" Lawrence Miles may seem an unlikely source of help for our cities, but unlikely sources are welcome when the likely sources have proved insufficient.

APPENDIX:
INFORMATION SOURCES FOR
VALUE ENGINEERING

Professional VA Organizations, Publications, and Curricula

1. The Lawrence D. Miles Value Foundation
    Harold G. "Hal" Tufty, Executive Secretary
    1199 National Press Building
    Washington, D.C. 20045
    (202–347–7007)

    Mr. Tufty independently publishes:
    Value Engineering Digest
    1199 National Press Building
    Washington, D.C. 20045

2. Society of American Value Engineers (SAVE)
    60 Revere Drive, Suite 500
    Northbrook, IL 60062
    (312–480–9282)
    Publications: *Transactions* (of Annual Conference)
                    Value World (quarterly)
                    Interactions (bi-monthly)

Courses in Value Analysis

Correspondence Courses Offered by The Society of American Value Engineers (SAVE-Chicago). To register, contact SAVE.

1. An Introduction To Value Analysis and Value Engineering (14 credits).   Administered by the University of Wisconsin, School of Engineering (1–800–262–6243).

    The basics of VA/VE applied to products and services; for study at home or office.   Text: Lawrence D. Miles, *Techniques of Value Analysis and Engineering*, 2nd ed. (New York: McGraw-Hill, 1966).

2. Basic Value Analysis. Administered by an experienced SAVE member in any state. Available in 6 packets or more; minimum course, six lesson packets, each packet $20. Text: Carlos Fallon, *Value Analysis,* 2nd rev. ed. (New York: Wiley Interscience, 1980).

   An easy introduction, for study at home or in office, using basic items found in any local store as the subject for homework and tests. For those involved in overall administration, purchasing, marketing, and finance.

3. Function Analysis for Architects, Engineers, and Builders (10 CEUs). Administered by the University of Wisconsin, School of Engineering

   Eleven lessons, done at home or office, self-paced. An introduction to Function Analysis (VA) for architects and others. Text: Macedo, *Value Management for Construction* (1978)

The University of Wisconsin-Madison began offering courses in Value Analysis/Value Engineering in 1964. The course described below can be given at the Madison campus or by correspondence. It is open equally to people from industry, service, and government organizations.

1. Value Engineering Specialist Diploma Program (45 credits). A combination of seminars, workshops, and independent study, covering all principles, technical writing, identifying new products for good value, applications to management, design and construction, and principles for architects, engineers, and builders.
   Information: University of Wisconsin-Extension
   Department of Engineering
   Value Engineering Program
   Thomas J. Snodgrass, CVS, Director
   432 North Lake Street
   Madison, WI 53706
   (1–800–262–6243; in Wisconsin: 1–800–362–3020)

Training Films In Value Analysis

The following are offered as films or videos through the Society of American Value Engineers (SAVE), Chicago Office. Rental: $55 per film.

1. *The Evaluation of Function*

   A 27-minute, 16mm color-sound film about Function Analysis, the fundamental technique of Value Analysis. Describes, with an example from an aerospace industry, how to perform the basic steps: determining the function of a part, component, or product; defining its function; distinguishing between basic and secondary functions; and more.

2. *Value Oriented Creative Thinking*

   A 28-minute 16mm color-sound film that explains how to increase the effectiveness of both individual and group thinking.

3. *Value-Oriented Paperwork Management*

   A 26-minute, 16mm color-sound film that shows how to effectively use value engineering and industrial engineering techniques for paperwork simplification.

4. *Applied Value Engineering*

   A 30-minute film of actual value engineering projects conducted by U.S. Army Corps of Engineers, with dollar savings, including swimming pool, hanger doors, gates, bathroom facilities, and more.

Local Information Sources

- *Corporations.* Local private corporations, particularly national corporations, may have Value Analysis units, program, or outside-led workshops. A call to any of them or to the local Chamber of Commerce would be instructive.

- *County, Municipal Departments For Wastewater and Environment.* Because the federal Environmental Protection Agency requires a Value Analysis on all wastewater treatment project applications valued at over $10 million, the local government unit with this responsibility will know available VA resources.

- *State Government Departments of Transportation and Environmental Protection.* Forty states have a VA/VE function in their EPA section, and 23 states have used VE in their Transportation Departments. They should have a list of consultants.

Books on Value Analysis

Lawrence D. Miles, *Techniques of Value Analysis and Engineering,* 1st ed. (New York: McGraw-Hill, 1961; 2nd ed., 1966).

Robert H. Clauson, *Value Engineering for Management* (New York: Auerbach, 1970).

Carlos Fallon, *Value Analysis,* 2nd rev. ed. (New York: Wiley Interscience, 1980; reprinted 1984, 1986).

Reference Sources on Value Analysis

H.B. Maynard, *Industrial Engineering Handbook,* 4th ed. (New York: McGraw-Hill, 1988).

Gavriel Salvendy, ed., *Handbook of Industrial Engineering* (New York: Wiley, 1982).

InfoTrak. This on-line database, available in academic and other libraries, carries entries on local governments that use Value Analysis. Keywords: "Value Analysis" and "Value Engineering."

Consultants in Value Engineering

The following list is partial, and tries to cover recognized VA firms in all parts of the country. The complete list of firms recognized by SAVE is contained in:

Directory of Value Analysis/Value Engineering Consultants
(effective July 1985)

From: Society of American Value Engineers (SAVE)
        600 S. Federal Street, Suite 400
        Chicago, IL 60605
        (312–346–3265)

R.C. Brannen Plus Associates
28717 Osborn Road
Bay Village, OH 44140
(216–871–4684)

CH2M Hill
P.O. Box 22508
Denver, CO 80222
(Locations in 35 cities)
(303–771–0900; 800–525–7964)

Thomas Cook Associates Inc.
16776 Bernardo Center Drive
Suite 203
San Diego, CA 92128
(619–451–6826)

Evolving Technologies Inc.
3725 Talbot Street, Suite F
San Diego, CA 92106
(619–224–3788)

Golden Associates
470 Park Avenue South
New York, NY 10016
(212–481–3400)

Hanscomb Associates Inc.
8 Piedmont Center, Suite 500
Atlanta, GA 30305
(Locations in 10 cities)
(404–262–3638)

Kempter-Rossman International
1199 National Press Building
Washington, D.C. 20045
(202–833–8382)

R.J. Park and Associates
861 Vinewood Ave.
Birmingham, MI 48009
(313–646–4118)

Professional Value Services (PVS)
2222 Park Avenue
Minneapolis, MN 55404
(612–870–8509)

Value Analysis Inc.
4029 Westerly Place, Suite 116
Newport Beach, CA 92660
(714–548–8018)

VEI, Incorporated
10712 North Stemmons Freeway
Dallas, TX 75220
(214–357–0870)

ACKNOWLEDGMENT

Russell C. Brannen, CVS, prepared the first draft of this chapter which is the source of many of the illustrations of VE in action. Edward C. Hayes is solely responsible for the chapter's description of VE methodology.

NOTES AND REFERENCES

1. The terms "Value Analysis (VA), Value Engineering (VE), and Value Management (VM) will be used interchangeably. The abbreviation "VA/VE" is common in the literature.

The essence of VA is *function analysis*. Founder Lawrence D. Miles might have called the method "Function Analysis" except for his desire to show that value—the most product for the least cost—is the purpose of it all. James O. Vogel, "A Brief History of Lawrence D. Miles," *Value World* (January 1986): 4–7.

2.   Value Analysis is emphatically *not* a method for cutting out aesthetic requirements. Founder Lawrence Miles was emphatic on this point: "Inherent in the philosophy of value analysis is full retention for the customer of the usefulness and aesthetic features of the product. Identifying and removing unnecessary cost, and thus improving value, must be done without reducing in the slightest degree quality, safety, life, reliability, dependability, and the features of attractiveness that the customer wants." See Lawrence D. Miles, *Techniques of Value Analysis* (New York: McGraw-Hill, 1966), p. 17.

3.   Specifically Miles found that temporary routings, different methods of manufacture, and new materials developed during the war had resulted in no loss of product useability. He also found that during the war the company dropped the practice of inserting on its blueprints the actual name of parts and of parts suppliers; instead, the wartime prints simply listed "capacity," or function (such as "X number of milliwatts per second"), a practice that had opened up the bidding process to many suppliers. This discovery started Miles on the path of function analysis.

4.   H. Donald Ulrich, "Value Engineering Trims New Construction Costs," *American City and County* (September 1984): 144.

5.   James P. Wade Jr., Assistant Secretary of Defense for Acquisitions and Logistics, "Transmittal of Fiscal Year 1985 Value Engineering (VE) Results," memo (Washington, D.C. Department of Defense, March 17, 1986).

6.   Kempter-Rossman International, "Value Engineering Workshops 1982–86. Final Report" (Washington, D.C.: U.S. Department of Transportation and Federal Highway Administration, July 1986), p. 3.

7.   City of New York, Office of the Mayor, Office of Management and Budget, Value Engineering Program, "A Brief Outline of the Use of Value Engineering In the City's Construction Program," mimeo (September 26, 1986).

8.   James Lichtwalter, Mansfield City Engineer, Interview (April 1987).

9.   John Sauvajot, Assistant Budget Director, San Diego County, Interview (May 1987).

10.   See Lawrence D. Miles, *Techniques of Value Analysis and Value Engineering* (New York: McGraw-Hill, 1966), Introduction and Chapter 1.

11.   William Copperman, C.V.S., of the Hughes Aircraft Company in Los Angeles, lists 16 steps; See W. Cooperman, *The Contractual Aspects of Value Engineering* (4 videocassetts, plus 115 page workbook) (Raleigh: North Carolina State University Engineering Extension Education, 1986).

12.   The information in the two previous paragraphs is distilled from Value Analysis Inc., *Value Analysis/Value Engineering Workshop Handbook*, rev. ed. (Newport, CA: Value Analysis Inc., 1985), pp. 63–73.

13.   *Ibid.*, p. 67.

14.   *Ibid.*, pp. 82–83.

15.   The total list of projects includes the reconstruction of a pool complex, several public school buildings, a subway station, streets, and a hospital; and new construction of high school and community college buildings. See William C. McElligott, C.V.S., P.E., Deputy Assistant Director Office of Management and Budget, and Director of Value Engineering, "Value Engineering As A Budgeting Tool," mimeo (n.d.), pp. 9–10.

16.   New York City Value Engineering Program, "A Brief Outline of the Use of Value Engineering In the City's Construction Program," mimeo (n.d.).

17.   Condensed from William C. McElligott, "Value Engineering As A Budgeting Tool," pp. 11–16.

18. Much of the information on the Anderson police department is from Frank Burrows, Chief, Anderson City Police Department, "VE: Law Enforcement's New Weapon," *Value World* (April–June 1986).

19. Assistant Police Chief Walter L. Smith, Interview (April 1987).

20. Harvey C. Childs, MPA dissertation in progress (The Evergreen State University, Olympia, WA), chapter 4. Mr. Childs did this evaluation while an employee of the State Superintendant of Education.

21. *Ibid.*, p. 48.

22. Jack W. Hill Jr. and Harvey C. Childs, "How To Cut Costs Through Value Engineering," *The School Administrator* (June 1986).

23. Indiana (Public Utilities), Colorado (Administration), and Missouri (Public Building Restoration). In addition the State of Washington mandates VE studies for all local school buildings over 50,000 square feet; and Michigan has used VE studies in its prison construction program.

24. The complete list of states: Washington, Oregon, California, New Mexico, Maryland, District of Columbia, Virginia, New Jersey, Nevada, South Dakota, North Dakota, Montana, Wisconsin, Pennsylvania, Nebraska, Texas, Rhode Island, New York, Minnesota, Illinois, Florida, North Carolina, and Arizona. The programs of these states can be found in U.S. Department of Transportation, Federal Highway Administration, "Summary Report. 1985 Value Engineering Conference, San Diego California" (Washington, D.C.: U.S. Department of Transportation).

25. See Daniel L. Parker, Information Officer, CalTrans, "Value Engineering: A Meeting of Minds Is Saving Money" (1985).

26. "North Carolina [Saves] $12 Million," *Public Works* (January 1985), p. 28.

Chapter 8

TARGET BASE BUDGETING:
THE BUDGETARY PROCESS AS
EXPENDITURE CONTROL

Thomas W. Wenz

The City of Cincinnati is one of many older industrial cities developing tools to manage an increasingly costly service delivery system with declining resources. Looking at the city's expenditure pattern without adjustments for inflation (see Table 1) it would appear that the city has had a steady growth in revenues. But when the figures are adjusted for the Consumer Price Index (see Table One, last column) a different picture emerges. Much of the real decline is due to grants reductions from the federal government, a problem that will intensify in the near future as the federal government phases out General Revenue Sharing (GRS). The Target Base Budget (TBB) process, the structure of the budget, and budget strategies for the future are the tools on which the City Council is depending to minimize the impact of severe expenditure constraints and to maximize service levels.

THE CONTEXT OF TARGET-BASE BUDGETING (TBB)

Cincinnati's general annual operating budget of approximately $166 million can be described as a line-item, performance, program budget, developed by a modified zero-base budgeting method called Target

Base Budgeting (TBB).[1] The City of Cincinnati is, as of 1987, in its
seventh year of using the target base method, and is expanding it from
the operating budget into the capital and community development block
grant project budgets.

Cincinnati has a council-manager form of municipal government. The
financial management responsibilities are shared between the Finance
Department and the Office of Research, Evaluation, and Budget. The
finance staff performs the daily financial operations including accounting, auditing, cash receipts, bond sales, and estimation of revenue and
fund balance positions. Budget staff reports directly to the city manager
in the areas of budget policy development, budget preparation, implementation and monitoring. The programs and service delivery are performed by city departments whose directors are appointed by the City
Manager, or in some cases by special boards or commissions.

The city adapted the TBB method from Tampa, Florida, and has
received many requests for information on it. Requesting cities are as
large as San Diego, California, population one million, and as small as
Forest Park, Ohio (population 23,000), as well as Houston, Texas,

Table 1.   City of Cincinnati General Revenues and Expenditures

Year	Unadjusted for CPI		Consumer Price Index (CPI)[a]	Adjusted for CPI	
	Revenue	Expend		Revenue	Expend
1971	66,340,000	63,328,000	121.3	54,690,849	52,207,749
1972	69,092,000	69,254,000	125.3	55,141,261	55,270,551
1973	84,963,000	78,823,000	133.1	63,833,959	59,220,887
1974	89,562,000	91,142,000	147.7	60,637,779	61,707,515
1975	100,128,000	107,062,000	161.2	62,114,144	66,415,633
1976	103,714,000	111,259,000	170.5	60,829,326	65,313,196
1977	114,130,000	107,923,000	181.5	62,881,543	59,461,708
1978	112,887,000	104,893,000	195.4	57,772,262	53,337,167
1979	120,790,000	115,955,000	217.4	55,561,178	53,337,167
1980	135,836,000	132,582,000	246.8	55,049,838	53,720,421
1981	140,528,000	132,582,000	272.4	51,588,840	53,425,844
1982	144,757,000	155,485,000	289.1	50,071,602	53,782,428
1983	151,702,000	154,645,000	298.4	50,838,472	51,824,732
1984	144,313,000	149,215,000	310.9	46,417,819	47,994,532
1985	159,197,000	155,041,000	321.9	49,455,421	48,164,337
1986[b]	160,745,000	169,420,000	332.6	48,329,826	50,938,064

Notes: [a]Source: Wharton Econometric Forecasting Associates, "Long Term Scenarios February 1985."
              [b]As projected in Appropriation Ordinance Budgets.
Source: City of Cincinnati Department of Finance, *Comprehensive Annual Financial Reports 1980–84*;
              and *Monthly Comparative Statements* (all reporting on non-GAAP basis)

Hampton, Virginia and Thunder Bay, Ontario.[2] The last two cities sent delegations to Cincinnati to study the system. TBB can be used equally well in large or small jurisdictions, and is particularly suited to those governmental units seeking to control or reduce expenditures in the most rational, and least painful, way.

The Target Base Budget Process:
Overview

Cincinnati is on a calendar fiscal year. Annual financial planning begins with the preparation of the Tentative Annual Operating Budget in the month of June prior to the start of the next fiscal year. The tentative budget is a reporting requirement of the State of Ohio, and the tentative revenue and expenditure figures are used by the county for distribution of state tax revenues shared with the local government entities. The revenue forecast is divided into dollar targets which are assigned to city departments. Each department director builds a base budget to match the target by identifying line item expenditures for every budget program, linking their budget requests to performance objectives and evaluation criteria for the fiscal year. The targets have historically (1982–1986) been 4% to 7% less than the departments' previous year's allocations, so the base budgets represent varying degrees of real program and service reductions. The target-base budgeting method calls for setting aside an amount of money termed "discretionary" which serves several purposes: it is a resource to fund department requests for supplements to their base budgets; it is the area of the budget which expands or contracts with resource updates; and it provides a focus area for Council decision making.

As department managers build their budgets, they develop several figures, with brief descriptions of the service level allowed by each, for the "base" budget; a base, plus several figures for additional items, constitutes a discretionary level. In this way the City Council knows exactly what it is buying, in terms of service amounts, when it funds any department at any specific figure.

CONTROL THROUGH THE BUDGET DEVELOPMENT PROCESS

To understand the budget as a control instrument it is helpful first to develop a theoretical framework for understanding budgeting in general.

DEPARTMENT DISCRETIONARY SUMMARY

DEPARTMENT   Recreation (Page 1 of 3)

DESCRIPTION	DIVISION/PROGRAM	PERSONAL SERVICES	NON PERSONAL SERVICES	FRINGE	TOTAL	POSITION IMPACT		CITY MANAGER DISCRETIONARY RECOMMENDATION	
						POS.	FILL	POS.	DOLLARS
1. Close North Avondale Community Center except for self-sustaining activities.	Comm. Act./District 2	68,805	3,100	20,160	92,065	2	2	2	$ 54,740
2. Close North Fairmount Community Center	Comm. Act./District 1	21,644	10,656	7,270	39,570	1	1	1	$ 39,570
3. Close Corryville Community Center	Comm. Act./District 3	26,426	16,310	7,500	50,326	1	0	0	$ 16,310
4. Reduce program activity at recreation centers and swimming pools city-wide.	Comm. Act./District 1,3	114,300	0	25,830	140,130	1	0	0.5	$ 70,070
5. Close swimming pools	Comm. Act./Districts 1,2,3 and Maintenance	60,840	28,324	12,160	101,324	0	0	0	$ 77,750
	Subtotal	$293,015	58,390	72,920	423,325	5	4	3.5	$258,440

1. The closing of this facility would eliminate programs currently serving 382 registered participants with an average annual attendance of 45,000. Among the activities eliminated would be numerous young adult athletic programs, a variety of art programs for all ages and general non-fee programs for youth. Also eliminated would be the after-school program which serves approximately 85 to 100 children between the ages of 5 and 12 years each day. Most of these young people have working parents who depend upon this public service.

2. The closing of this facility would eliminate athletic and art programs currently serving 66 registered participants with an average annual attendance of 10,000.
Unless an alternative site could be located, the loss of this facility eliminates the opportunity to serve 100 children a day in the Federally funded Summer Food Program.
The deep water swimming pool serving North Fairmount is also included as a potential budget cut (Ref. Discretionary Item #5).

3. The closing of this facility would eliminate programs currently serving 192 registered participants with an average annual attendance of 14,000. The potential for vandalism to this recently renovated building would be significant if closed and unsupervised. The 1984 cuts resulted in the closing of the swimming pool which is immediately adjacent to this building.

4. The loss of 17,944 hours of direct programming in areas of art, athletics, day camps, physical fitness, swim lessons and general activities for youth and adults would affect the following communities: Mt. Washington, Oakley, South Fairmount, Lower Price Hill, West Price Hill, Price Hill, Fairmount, Westwood, East Price Hill, Northside, College Hill, Sayler Park and Sedamsville. This budget reducton would impact the hours of operation at 6 community centers and 13 swimming pools.

5. Close 3 deep water (N. Fairmount, Washington Park & Kennedy), 5 shallow water (Grant, Inwood, Dyer, Laurel & Bramble), and 1 indoor (Over-the-Rhine) pools for 42 weeks in the following communities: North Fairmount, West End, Madisonville, Kennedy Heights, Over-the-Rhine and Mt. Auburn. This would affect a total of 2,134 registered participants and approximately 22,000 in attendance at these locations.

160

Budgetary Theory:
The Functions Budgets Perform

Insight on budget theory is adequately provided by Professor Allan Schick, who shows that budgets conserve resources in times of budget reduction, and strengthen claimants demands during times of expansion.[3] Schick also helps us with his useful tri-partite division of the functions of budgeting, as these functions have developed toward full Program Budgeting:

- *Control Orientation.* This was the first concern of municipal reformers at the turn of the century, who promoted the now-familiar line-item budget to create accountability and stop corruption. This orientation asks several questions: how can agencies be held to established expenditure ceilings? What reporting system will insure that fiscal rules are followed?
- *Management Orientation.* In federal budget history, the 1949 Hoover Commission approved the use of goals in budgets, and breaking budgets down by program. It also raised major questions: How should the organization chart be drawn, and staff assigned, to maximize performance?
- *Planning Orientation.* The most recent orientation, this calls for the use of specific written objectives for every program in every department, and asks central questions: What are the long-range goals and policies of the government? What programs should be initiated or terminated, and why?[4]

In this paper we focus on the *control orientation,* although we shall also see that Cincinnati's budget process allows ample scope for the other two orientations defined by Professor Schick.

There are several ways the budget development process in Cincinnati is used to control expenditures and promote conserver values. These include controlling the level of requests, the pricing of line item expenditures, reducing the specific activities associated with line items, controlling employee costs, providing sunset review, and using budgeted reserves. The Budget Office plays a major role in the controls throughout the budget process. It is critical to communicate to departments the reasons and expected outcomes of such control, and whenever possible to decentralize the decisions affecting service delivery levels. The more input line managers have in selecting budget cuts, the more willing they are to accept accountability for resulting negative program service levels. The more informed managers are about the need for controls, the better the controls will work.

Control of Budget Requests

Target budgeting was initially implemented in Cincinnati during 1981 for the 1982 fiscal year. The new process was viewed as a positive way to implement cutbacks forced by resource reductions. Many benefits were anticipated from the capacity of TBB to hold budget requests down. Budget targets were assigned to departments based on projected resources for the coming year, instead of setting arbitrary levels of across-the-board cuts, or allowing departments to request full continuation budgets. This latter practice had put the Budget Office in the unhappy position of having to make cuts.

The targets added up to a total base budget that city officials knew the city could afford. The decisions as to what services would be included in the base budgets were up to the specialists, department staff with experience in the relation between service levels and citizen satisfaction. The process builds in incentives for departments to budget "honestly," without padding their requests, and to seek productivity improvements in order to spread the target dollar amount to maintain as many services as possible.

Generally the department targets represent an across-the-board cut, but important to the success of the process is the practice of allowing departments to make a second request for supplements from "discretionary" funds. These requests compete for funding from a special portion of money set aside for City Council to allocate at its discretion.[5] The departments were provided criteria for selecting programs and services to be placed into competition for discretionary funding. All the actors knew the total of the discretionary funds set aside, and as a result even these secondary budget requests tended to be limited by the process.

The Positive Nature of TBB Controls

The positive nature of the target-base process is evident at three points in the budget process. First, it requires input from department staff to identify candidates for program cuts, thus institutionalizing a participative decision-making approach. Second, the process requires the City Council to distribute the discretionary funds to supplement the basic budgets of high priority programs. This places the Council in the unique, and politically preferable, position of adding money to programs amidst an overall scenario of cuts. Also, this brings Council further into the decision making process by forcing them to set, and adhere to, policy.

Third, the discretionary mechanism provides ultimate flexibility in accommodating variations in the revenue estimates as the budget development process comes to a close. Specifically, the revenue picture may change during Council deliberations or during budget construction. Such changes can cause last-minute additions or cuts, sometimes selected without benefit of clear cost and program impact information. However, with discretionary increments already identified and priced, the Council has good information for any necessary last-minute adjustments. The administration and Council both avoid negative public perceptions of not being prepared to deal with unanticipated dollars that are suddenly "found" in the newest revenue projection. Any revenue estimate is just a snapshot in time, but this is a hard concept for the public to understand. Thus the city appears to be, and in fact is, in control right up to the end of the process, a strongly positive feature of TBB.

The fourth positive aspect of TBB is that it brings focus to the administration's analysis of departmental budgetary needs. Like full-blown zero-base budgeting, several alternative levels of service are represented in the combinations of base and discretionary requests.[6] But unlike zero-base budgeting, the alternative levels are determined by the nature and cost of the additional services that departments want to provide, not by preset percentages or other artificial calculations. This makes the discretionary packages realistic presentations of real service needs and not arbitrary calculator drills. Departments cannot be guaranteed their base budgets exactly as requested because the Budget Office reserves the right to review every base program. But the more rigorous analysis is saved for the discretionary requests, the exact point of focus recommended by budgetary theory.

Moreover, the administration sets up criteria for marginal utility analysis to compare the relative worth of the discretionary requests to each other, and to programs provided in the base, a function that corresponds to Professor Schick's "Planning Orientation" of budgets. These criteria include contribution to economic development, infrastructure maintenance, and protection of public health and safety. Even if a program component was low enough in priority in one department to fall into the discretionary request category, compared to all other discretionary items it may have a greater utility to the city. For example, one more police officer may be the lowest priority item in the Safety Department's budget request, but may have greater utility in Council's eyes than one more inspector in the buildings department.

These positive features of TBB result in a decision process that is quite manageable by the Council and fully understandable by the public. Council members receive a comprehensive budget on the combination of base and discretionary requests for over 200 budget programs, along with the city manager's recommendations for funding. Of course, Council members are not precluded from adjusting any of the budget, but are encouraged by the nature of the presentation to focus adjustment decisions on the discretionary lists.

Line Item Control in Budget Development

Program budget requests are supported by personal and nonpersonal line item detail. The line item, the oldest mechanism for control of expenditures, is used as one representation of all dollar expenditures. Breaking program budgets down into line-items facilitates two kinds of budget cuts: reducing the cost of any one line item, or reducing the overall activities represented by line items. In the area of reducing prices of line items, the city controls in this area when one agency purchases in bulk and then "resells" the supply to departments. The city operates a municipal garage which services all city cars and motorized equipment, either by direct services or by coordinating contracts for repair. The garage purchases all fuel used by the city, negotiating a contract with the supplier, a system which allows purchase at below-retail gas prices. The contractual agreement includes a flexible clause to protect both the supplier and the city from drastic increases or decreases in world prices of petroleum. In 1985 and 1986, when fuel prices have been steadily dropping, Council wanted the administration to "recapture" the excess funds in the base budgets and use the money to fund additional discretionary requests. Council wanted to prevent departments from reaping windfalls through unexpected gas price reductions, when the savings could have greater impact if accumulated city-wide and redistributed on a program priority basis. Because fuel costs are budgeted as a single line item for each department, the Budget Office was indeed able to identify and reduce all the fuel budgets, and transfer this amount of money to the discretionary fund for reallocation.

The other type of line item cut requested by Council was to reduce the city's travel budget by over 20%. Unlike the gasoline example, cutting travel budgets entailed changing planned activities instead of simply taking advantage of a price reduction. In this case the city administration complied by cutting a total dollar amount equal to 20% of the city's travel budget, but cuts were not made across the board. Each department's travel budget (both base and discretionary) was compared to the prior year's actual expenditures, and selective cuts were made in varying amounts, with prior year expenditures providing a benchmark.

This method of making cuts in established base programs was not entirely successful. It reduced the credibility of assigning a target figure to departments, by "arbitrarily" cutting into line items in the base which directors had painstakingly developed to match the target. Targets would lose credibility if Council consistently cut items covered in departments' base budgets instead of focusing on the cuts identified in the discretionary packages. Consequently this "cut line items in the base" approach is not generally recommended by the administration because it runs counter to program budgeting and department control over the important question of which activities will go in the base and which into the discretionary category.

Employee Cost Control

The major dollar cost in any budget comes from wages, salaries, and fringe benefits. In the process of drawing up line items within programs, individual positions and groups of positions in the same classification are identified for each program. Depending on the severity of the budget cut represented by the department's target, directors must reduce the number of positions. Many directors prefer to cut vacant positions from their programs to minimize employee layoff costs and morale problems. Unfortunately random attrition may have little relationship to program priorities. Directors are now being requested to develop long-term staffing plans to try to take advantage of attrition in such a way as to transfer employees filling positions in low-priority programs into vacant positions in higher-priority programs. It should be noted that considerable resistance to preparing such plans is expected, because staff reductions run directly counter to natural organization goals of self-perpetuation and empire-building.

The city administration works very hard with Council members and the press to make clear the difference between positions, which are simply boxes on an organization chart; and employees, who are living people. Otherwise statements about numbers of positions cut from the budget are incorrectly interpreted as the number of layoffs anticipated. Many of the positions cut from the programs were already vacant due to normal or planned attrition. Other vacant budgeted positions existed in the high priority programs into which employees were transferred, further avoiding layoffs while reducing the budget.

Timing is very important when implementing position and employee cuts because it has a critical impact on the net savings to be realized. Cutting vacant positions is simple and the net savings is straightforward. Cutting filled positions calls for assumptions about the number of employees the organization can absorb and how long into the fiscal year other employees scheduled for layoff will be carried on the payroll while City Council negotiates final passage of the budget. Cincinnati is on a calendar year fiscal cycle, but state law allows operations to continue on a temporary basis from January until a deadline of March 31, when a final budget for the year must be passed. For example, if an employee is scheduled to be laid off because the entire program is recommended for phase-out, the city must still pay the employee's wages for the pay periods during which the program continues to operate on a temporary basis. If the program is eliminated, the city must also budget to pay the lump sums for earned vacation balances, and to pay unemployment for 26 weeks since the city is self-insured for unemployment compensation. In 1986 budget development the average cost to lay off a laborer was priced as $10,110, based on an average combined salary and benefits cost of $24,930. The net savings for a layoff effective March 8 would be only $14,820. In fact, unanticipated by the administration, Council held the budget on the calendar longer than expected in 1986, adding another pay period to the cost and further reducing the net savings. The repercussion of delay is to force more layoffs in order to accumulate a total in net savings equal to the amount that must be cut from the annual budget. Therein lies the need for organizational discipline to set a schedule for budget passage, and then sticking with it. Assumptions like layoff costs can be built into budget development, but delayed budgets require last minute adjustments that are more costly in the long run.

The city pays from 30 to 40% of salary figures in employee fringe benefits. The benefits are administered centrally and therefore are budgeted in the nondepartmental accounts separate from the department budgets. These central accounts provide an incentive and opportunity for large savings through expenditure control. In the target budgeting process these accounts are also cut by formula and given targets for the coming year. The targets can generally hold true if minimal fringe rate changes occur, because departments which have received targets based upon the same formula tend to cut enough positions to bring the dependent fringe account costs down to target level. Even better, if during the budget process work on the benefits package pays off and some fringe account rates like health insurance can be adjusted downward, that "savings" can automatically be identified by the budget office for redistribution as additional discretionary funds. Or if rates are still not firm at the time that the final budget is passed, thanks to the conservative approach of budgeting on the high side of uncertain estimates, a savings may be realized during the year once actual (generally lower) rates are known. Again, because the fringes are budgeted in central accounts the costs can easily be tracked and use of any savings can be controlled.

CONTROL THROUGH "SUNSET" AND REPROGRAMMING PROCESSES

The municipal budget cycle has "sunset" provisions built into it, whereby budgets are closed out at the point in time when certain criteria are met. The point in time for annual operating budgets is December 31, with no other criteria needed. Unencumbered funds at that time no longer "belong" to the department because the authorization in the annual appropriation ordinance ends. The unspent, unencumbered money becomes part of the next year's beginning fund balance. The old problem of use it or lose it, which used to cause excessive year-end spending, has in part been addressed in the target calculations.

The base for a department's target calculation is the prior year's Council-approved budget, not the department's actual prior year spending. Therefore, a department is not "penalized" in the target figure for spending under budget in the previous year. In fact, it can be argued that there exists a built-in incentive for productivity improvements because the savings in a base year is not deducted when the target for the next year is calculated. As discussed in the earlier section about travel budget cuts and base budget analysis, prior year spending is used as an indicator by the budget office showing the legitimacy of estimated costs used for items in both the base and discretionary categories of a department's budget request.

In addition to departmental and nondepartmental account savings, unanticipated revenue windfalls not budgeted for use in that year are also gathered into the carry-forward balance for reallocation in the next fiscal year. Cincinnati uses the carry-forward balance, made in part by forced savings brought on by year end closing of the operating budget, as sources for the discretionary fund each year.

In the city's Capital Improvement Program (CIP), five year budgets are developed but authorized in annual increments of around $20 million. Unlike the operating budget, annual capital project authorizations are carried past the end of the year, and can accumulate over a period of several years depending upon the pattern of project expenditures. In conjunction with departments, the budget office performs quarterly "sunset" and "reprogramming" reviews of the several hundred projects on the books. Review criteria include percent of budget spent and project progress as compared to the original completion dates in the project request. Reprogramming reviews are performed on a quarterly basis and are used to redirect funding among authorized projects within a given budget year. Generally, sunset activities close out projects and identify additional resources for the next year.

In both cases the procedure requires ordinances acted upon by City Council because the original project budget authorizations were made by Council. In the reprogramming process, money is transferred from a slowly moving project to one with immediate activity. The assumption is that the slower project may recover its funding in subsequent reprogramming actions, unless the slow pace was an indicator of special problems in the project. All projects are reviewed for reprogramming at the end of each quarter, and the fourth quarter review is a combination sunset-reprogramming consideration.

The city uses the sunset and reprogramming procedures in the Community Development Block Grant (CDBG) program. Ninety percent of CDBG money is in project budgets. Historically the city received approximately $15 million a year in CDBG funds to address low income needs and problems of urban blight.

In 1983 the city received an additional $6,061,000 in special CDBG funds, authorized by Congress in the Jobs Bill legislation (Public Bill 98–8). The Jobs Bill was intended as a one-time shot in the arm to stimulate the economy and provide jobs immediately to address high national unemployment figures. In addition to the regular CDBG requirements only one more string was attached by the federal government—to spend the entire $6 million by September 30, 1985 or return the unspent portion to HUD. This "no-exception" sunset provision caused the city to approve money in projects with the potential to move quickly, and to monitor that group of projects closely and constantly. At the time Cincinnati's Jobs Bill projects closed, none of the money had to be returned to the federal government, indicative of the influence of enforced sunset control.

Budgeted Reserves

City Council made new commitments in 1984 and again in 1985 to build reserve funds by passing resolutions and ordinances with specific savings goals identified. Previously the city's reserve was carried in the Permanent Improvement Fund, a separate fund which generally received little if any scrutiny from Council. It tended to grow with interest rate increases and recede when Council needed to balance the gap between annual revenues and annual expenditures. The size of the Permanent Improvement Fund grew from $1.5 million in 1977 to $8.5 million in 1981, but was spent down to less than $2 million again by 1984. As one city official stated, the city does not collect taxes to create a savings account but to provide services. Yet the prospect became grim for future budgets because the one-time resources in the reserve had been used to balance the budget.

Future expenditures were projected to outpace revenues to such an extent that the City Council placed an increase to the city income tax on the ballot in the spring of 1984. The increase was soundly defeated by the voters. As a follow-up in response to apparent citizen perceptions about lack of efficiency in municipal government, the mayor convened a special review committee of Cincinnati business people, whose time was donated by their employers. One of the committee's subsequent recommendations was that in order to operate in a business-like manner the city should have a reserve fund set aside for emergency purposes, commensurate in size to the city's $166 million operating budget. Coincidentally, the city's historically superior bond rating dropped in 1984. The city's finance director indicated to Council that although many factors are considered in the bond rating review, it was possible that successive years of annual spending above annual receipts and using the reserves to bridge the gap may have influenced the rating drop. In the light of this City Council passed a resolution establishing interim and permanent levels for the reserve fund known as the Permanent Improvement Fund. The goal was to reach a level equal to at least 5% of the annual operating budget by 1986.

The reserve serves several purposes. It limits the use of one-time resources to balance the operating budget by forcing a contribution to savings instead of covering on-going operations. It also increases annual investment earnings by increasing the cash balance; reduces the long term cost of capital project funding if the bond ratings improve; and serves as an emergency source of funds for crisis situations. To date the Permanent Improvement Fund balance is $5 million and projected to reach the 5% goal by December 1986. The city's bond ratings remained unchanged in 1985 but may be adjusted upward when the 1986 ratings are announced. The heated political debates comparing the virtues of carrying a surplus versus spending every available dollar each year have been resolved in Cincinnati for now, with a compromise position of a controlled reserve set at a level that floats with the level of annual revenues. By setting a threshold above which additional expenditures must give way to building the reserve, the Council has determined the balance point between pressures to spend and the need to budget conservatively.

In 1986 Council passed another measure to use reserves to control the budget. The city administration characterized 1986 as the transition year to prepare for the impact on Cincinnati of the elimination of federal General Revenue Sharing (GRS) money in 1987. Council decided to set up a new budget reserve as another tool to meet the challenge of drastic reductions anticipated in 1987. During the final stages of preparing the 1986 budget, additional cuts were made to department budgets and fund transfers were identified, in order to create a new $3 million reserve. These budget reductions actually served two important purposes. In addition to making the money available to be placed in the new reserve, ongoing operations were reduced, resulting in a lower level of services in that year. Hopefully when Council hits the crunch in 1987 monies from this new reserve will fund transition/investment programs such as productivity improvements or organization consolidation costs.

Then the city would reap the maximum benefits of spending one-time resources on one-time items while continuing to control the ongoing cost of municipal services.

EXPENDITURE CONTROLS

The annual budget development process is the major but not the only means to control the city's expenditures. During the course of the year the budget office and finance department use other tools to manage expenditures, after the budget has been approved. It should be noted that these additional controls are vehemently disliked and resisted by the departments, who believe they have just run the gauntlet to get their budgets only to turn around and find that they do not have total discretion in their expenditure. Therefore these tools require specific Council and administrative approval before being used. As explained in the following paragraphs, techniques used include appropriation control, imposing a selective hiring freeze, internal service fund pricing for services, and strict control of any mid-year budget adjustments.

Appropriation Control

The final products of the budget development process are a series of appropriation ordinances passed by the City Council, authorizing department operating and project budgets for the year by expenditure code categories. To meet the line managers' need for some degree of flexibility and performance accountability, the city does not appropriate by detailed line item for the 200 separate budgets programs, or for the over 200 Community Development and CIP annual project authorizations. But to meet the need for expenditure control, appropriations are made at aggregate expenditure code levels for similar line items, down to the division level within the larger city departments. For example, department employee salaries, leaves with pay, longevity, and retirement lump sum payments are grouped into one expense code category and appropriated as a single dollar total for each division within a department. During the year, if unexpected position vacancies occur, freeing up money in a personnel services account, a division cannot use the money to purchase other items. Nonpersonnel costs such as additional printing, gasoline, and rents cannot be taken from personnel services accounts and the accounts and audits staff of the Finance Department closely monitor vouchers for this very reason. The nonpersonnel expense items such as contracts or supplies are appropriated as an aggregate dollar amount to the divisions for those types of expenses only.

Similarly, unexpected savings in nonpersonnel budget items cannot be used by the division to hire additional employees over the number already budgeted in the personnel services account. A forced savings accumulates for recapture at the city wide level at the end of the year, due to appropriation restrictions.

TWO BUDGET DIRECTORS VIEW "TARGET BASE BUDGETING"

Al Desilet, Budget Officer, City of Tampa, Florida:

I started the TBB method in Tampa in 1979. It works well for us both in planning resource allocation and in tax reduction. In the past seven years the millage rate has gone down from 9.7 to 4.42 mills per $1,000, a 54% reduction.

By using the TBB "Service Levels" concept, a modification of Zero Based Budgeting, we have been able to reduce total city positions from 5,000 to 4,100 over the same time period.

We have also been able to reallocate money from operations to capital improvements. Between 1980 and 1986, our Operations budget dropped from 86% to 59% of our budget, while Capital Improvements rose from 14% to 41%.

For TBB to work best you should be able to project revenues six months to one year in advance, as accurately as possible. Then you assign a target budget to each department, with a 2% "holdback" that departments can later get, in competition, if they fully justify it. This way you can tell a department it has $40 million in basic service money; you don't get a department request for $55 million, and then have to cut it back.

If you can't make accurate predictions, set a low target for each department, giving yourself plenty of margin.

Ellen Davenport, Budget Officer, Hampton, Virginia:

We used TBB for the first time this year. We started by giving each department two target figures: Target 1, representing an average 5% decrease below last year's budget; and Target 2, the same budget level as last year plus a small increase for inflation and merit pay.

We created Target 1 because of fears of federal grant cut-backs. We also allowed departments to budget a third level, asking for everything they wanted.

(continued)

Our new system for making revenue estimates is just being implemented, so for this year we simply used last year's budget figures,
after factoring out one-time expenditures and anticipated losses,
such as federal Revenue Sharing. We did not include the Capital
budget in the system this year. We are not in the cutback mode, so we
did not have any of the problems associated with that process.

I visited Cincinnati to learn the system. We had one problem with
implementation: two departments initially did not comply with the
new process. One turned in a padded Target request; another simply turned in its own high budget using its own figures and format.
Under guidance, however, both did comply with the new system.

In evaluating our new TBB system, we found it successful. We got a
lot of positive feedback from departments; they said that, in contrast
to the old process, where requests were cut back without understandable reasons, the new method gave them a much better idea of
what they were going to get. We plan to continue the TBB system.

—Edward C. Hayes

The city has over one hundred separate funds, required by the governmental fund accounting procedure to keep separate records of receipts and disbursements depending upon the sources of revenue. For
example, money received from water bill payments is accounted for
separately from income tax or golf greens fees. About 15 of the operating funds are set up annually with direct authorization through Council
appropriations. All other budgets are controlled at the administrative
level. But Council has the authority to appropriate budgets in all other
funds if they so choose. Symbolic of the severity of coming budget constraints and the value of expenditure control through appropriation,
Council has taken action to appropriate in 1986 two more funds never
before controlled by Council at that level.

Not everyone agrees with the concept of creating savings and carrying
this total forward to the next year. Department directors want to use the
money to get more done, and taxpayers would prefer that instead of
increasing the city's savings account a tax rebate could be granted. But in
response to similar criticism in New York city, that city's budget director
recently offered this comment in a letter to the *The New York Times:*

We all want higher levels of essential city services. But our hard-won recovery from
the fiscal crisis is due in no small part to our ability to restrain spending until we can
pay for the services we are increasing. We have worked hard to avoid a 'boom and

bust' cycle in city budgeting and service levels. It is extremely disruptive to spend every nickel we can scrape together in one year, only to have to retrench when revenues fall short of projections, or we are hit with new spending mandates by the courts or other levels of government. . . . New Yorkers can be sure we will continue the prudent financial management that has brought this city four years of genuinely balanced budgets, investment-grade ratings for our notes and bonds, and steady improvements in city services.[7]

Selective Hiring Freeze

In the personnel services area, which comprises over 82% of the total operating budget, savings goals are met by imposing a selective hiring freeze. Instead of automatic authorization to fill a budgeted position when it becomes vacant, a department director must get a reauthorization in the form of an exemption from the hiring freeze. The exemption request must identify whether the vacancy is in a high or low priority program, and whether it will be filled by transfer or hiring someone not currently employed by the city, as well as cost and budget information. Generally, departments do not request an exemption for every vacancy as it occurs, so on one level the freeze is self-enforced. Few exemption requests for critical services have been denied, but the delay caused by the request process itself acts to save money. As described in the sections about central fringe accounts and appropriation restrictions on personnel services budgets, savings from the vacancies accumulates in two places and becomes part of the next year's beginning balance.

This mechanism is used to translate attrition into savings, but just as important, it will minimize future layoffs by reducing the size of the workforce. Obviously the hiring freeze cannot be without exception because attrition occurs in any program and random reduction is not acceptable in high priority programs. Eventually the budget office staff plans to replace the hiring freeze with department staffing plans, whereby departments use combinations of attrition, program consolidation, and internal reassignments to meet staff reduction goals. This would reduce the random nature of the impact to program performance, reduce the red tape involved in the exemption request process, and give managers flexibility to meet performance criteria as well as to address budget constraints.

Internal Service Fund Pricing

In the philosophy of program budgeting, each program covers the costs to produce the services to achieve the program goals, such as salaries and supplies. The purchase of gasoline, cited previously, provides an example. The municipal garage buys all the city's gas and in turn "sells" it to the programs at the pumps. The price paid at the city pumps is the contract price paid by the garage (plus a 5% handling fee), but as discussed earlier, the contract price is by no means fixed. The budget office can cut program gasoline budgets to reflect the price reduction experienced at any time during the budget process, but what if the price of gas drops further after the budget is finalized? Another option available to the budget office is to require the garage to continue to charge the programs at the budgeted price. Then the municipal garage can accumulate any surplus resulting from subsequent contract price reductions and return it in lump sum form to the funds charged, to become part of the carry forward fund balances instead of being used as a windfall funding by the individual departments.

Control of Mid-Year Adjustments

No plan is perfect, and the annual budget for planned expenditures is no exception. The people preparing the budget will never be able to anticipate every expenditure need or shift in costs. As a practical matter, Cincinnati has a specific administrative regulation that outlines the procedure departments must follow to request any budget adjustment during the fiscal year. Departments are instructed to first attempt to accommodate any unexpected expense by adjusting activities to reduce subsequent costs, or in effect "eat" the new expense. However if an adjustment is absolutely necessary, the department must make its case to the budget officer, whose first response will be to help identify alternative ways which the department can use to absorb the expense. The objective here is to absorb all costs and maintain budgets, to increase budgets rarely, and then only in extraordinary circumstances. The budget office will initiate downward adjustments, but strictly control any upward adjustments.

One useful release valve to strict budget control that both the departments and the budget office rely on is an accounting adjustment procedure performed at the end of each year by the finance department. Even when departments make a good case for a midyear budget adjustment, the budget office may approve it for future action in the final transfer ordinance instead of preparing an ordinance or series of adjusting ordinances through the year. By year's end the need for a budget increase identified earlier may not materialize or may be offset by other expenses coming in under budget. If the need for adjustment persists until the end of the year, it is made and explained to Council in the final transfer ordinance process, which is viewed more as a housekeeping action than as a budget adjustment. Again note that the next year's budget targets will be based on the departments' original approved budgets, not on the adjusted actual expenditures.

IMPLEMENTING TARGET-BASE BUDGETING

1. Estimate Resources
   Forecast your anticipated resources for the new Fiscal Year.

2. Determine how much or what percentage of resources will be set aside for Hold Back (discretionary money).

3. Determine Departmental Targets
   Departmental targets can be calculated on resources approved for base funding. Adjustments to the target may include:

   a. Deletion of any known one-time expenditures from previous year's budget (such as a new police cruiser, or temporary positions which have achieved one-time objectives).
   b. Items that are legally required (e.g., court ordered building renovations).
   c. Additions or deletions based on legislative mandates.

4. Develop the Target Base Budget

   a. Departments Develop a Target Budget (Service Level One)
      Departments include all services which can be provided within assigned allocation.
   b. Departments Develop Service Level Two Budget
      This section contains those services currently offered which are not continued in the target base; and new service program requests.

5. Take Budget to Appropriate Legislative Authority
   The budget submitted includes both the services that are included in the base budget (Level One) and those that cannot be accommodated (Level Two). Appropriate hearings are held and the final determination of which levels of services will be funded is made.

CONCLUSION: TARGET BASE BUDGETING AND BUDGET CONTROL

Control is a basic tenet of budgeting. This is especially true in public budgeting where the taxpayer wants assurances that public money is not mishandled. Cincinnati follows a well-documented budget process with informed citizen input. Expenditures are maintained within consistent accounting principles and practices, and as a result, the city has been able to adjust its inflation-corrected budget *downward* over the past 15 years (see Table 1). Together these practices constitute real control, and are the building blocks for the management and planning aspects of budgeting outlined by Schick (see p. 161, this chapter).

It is careful management and planning which identify, and sometimes increase, the resources available to the city. Control is not the knee-jerk budget office response of "no" to budget requests. It is not the creation of a tangled bureaucracy to prevent line managers from getting the job done. It is the attitude that careful use of existing resources will result in programs using money efficiently to achieve the goals of the city. It is setting criteria, consistently applied to all departments and activities to insure credibility of the dollars and cents information, and fairness in allocation.

Management and planning are control accessories; often the three concepts are difficult to separate in practical application. In order for control to be accepted in the organization, it is very important that the policies and intent which produced the control criteria in the first place are articulated and communicated for all city staff. Regulations followed to the letter may be viewed as red tape—and if written without department input, or if misunderstood by the line staff, are too much red tape. It is not control for control's sake, but control for the sake of maximizing good management (efficiency) and meeting public needs (effectiveness) that is important.

Control through good management is evidenced in the saying of the Cincinnati budget office staff, that the real work for the office is not during the nine month budget preparation, hearings, and approval cycle. Rather the real budget management work is in the "breathing space" between budget cycles. Organizational studies and recommendations are made seeking productivity improvements, assessing service privatization alternatives, attempting to streamline administrative procedures, pushing to consolidate departments, comparing the investment returns of capital projects, and so on.

Finally, in public budgeting it is the citizens and City Council whose oversight provides the ultimate control. But to operate effectively, Council and citizens need in place, in city hall, a budgeting method that really works, and this is the case with TBB, which has allowed Cincinnati to continue adequate services, reduce real-dollar costs, adjust to federal grants cuts, and avoid tax increases.

ACKNOWLEDGMENT

The author wishes to thank Ms. Julie Horne, Management Analyst for the Office of Research, Evaluation, and Budget, City of Cincinnati, for assistance in preparing this chapter.

NOTES AND REFERENCES

1. See Thomas W. Wenz and Ann P. Nolan, "Target Base Budgeting," *Public Budgeting and Finance*, 2, 2 (Summer 1982): 88–91. For an illustration of municipal Zero Base Budgeting, as used in Phoenix, see Charles E. Hill and Terry Sharp, "Zero Based Budgeting: A Practical Application," *Governmental Finance* (March 1983): 13–18.

2. See comments by the Budget Officers of Tampa and Hampton on p. 171, this chapter. Thunder Bay tried TBB for one year, but then replaced the City Manager who was the moving force behind it, and has discontinued the method.

3. Allen Schick, "Macro-Budgetary Adaptations to Fiscal Stress in Industrialized Democracies," *Public Administration Review*, 46, 2 (March/April 1986): 124.

4. Allen Schick, "The Road to PPB: The Stages of Budget Reform," *Public Administration Review*, 26, 4 (December 1966): 243–258.

5. Unfortunately the term "discretionary" implied that these budget items were unnecessary luxuries or special services for a select clientelle. To avoid this confusion the City of Tampa calls these funds "the Mayor's hold-back", as described on p. 25 of this article. Eventually the public, city employees, and City Council in Cincinnati learned that discretionary requests represented real cuts in the levels of municipal services citizens expected in Cincinnati.

6. In practical zero-base budgeting, budgets are not necessarily built from scratch, but presented as packages of alternative spending levels. Often the packages represent pre-set cuts or increases in increments such as five or ten percent of the current budget. The increments in target-base budgeting are not pre-set at a specific percentage level. Rather, they are determined by the nature and size of each discretionary request.

7. Alair A. Townsend, "How a Surplus Kept the Balances," Letter to the Editor, *New York Times* (July 25, 1984).

Chapter 9

METHODS IMPROVEMENT AND WORK MEASUREMENT:
INDUSTRIAL ENGINEERING FOR LOCAL GOVERNMENT

Edward C. Hayes

SUMMARY. Two of Industrial Engineering's major foci, Methods Improvement (work simplification) and Work Measurement, sometimes combined with Preventive Maintenance and Scheduling, provide the greatest source of outright cash savings of any method in this book. Overcoming the problems associated with the early years of time measurement, local jurisdictions have developed a wide variety of approaches to the subject, including in-house teaching of measurement/simplification techniques to government employees.

HOW LONG SHOULD IT TAKE
TO MOW THE PARK?

Before Frederick Winslow Taylor's development of methods[1] which have become today's Industrial Engineering (IE), managers could report how long it took to complete tasks, but they could not say how long it *should* take. With Taylor, and the hundreds of writers[2] and still more

179

hundreds of local government IE projects[3] in work measurement and simplification that have occurred since then, that question can be answered for any task in any department. This chapter will outline these methods and their application.

METHODS IMPROVEMENT 1:
THE WORK DISTRIBUTION CHART

It is worse than a waste of time to measure required times for tasks that are unneeded. A basic objective of any Industrial Engineering analysis is to determine what part of the work process should be kept, what should be abolished or reordered, or combined with others, and which might be contracted out.[4] In his original focus on individual work motions, Taylor called, in step two, for *eliminating* unnecessary motions, and most texts on industrial engineering suggest the same early objective.

To achieve this purpose a *work (time) distribution chart* is a useful tool. A work distribution chart shows, for example, what percent of employees' work time is devoted to each of the tasks (work steps) of any activity or program.

One method for gathering time data for a Work Distribution Chart is called "Work Sampling."[5] A work sampling form is shown in Figure 1. By taking a sufficient number of work sample observations, the analyst can arrive at a close approximation of the actual amounts of time spent by each employee on each task, as shown in Figure 2. Having the organization down on paper this way allows the analyst to probe for common errors in staffing and procedures:

- *Misguided efforts.* Too much time may be put on tasks with little or secondary priority, having little impact on the main objectives of the program.
- *Poor or non-existent scheduling.* When employees are shifted too rapidly from one task to another, they are unable to get any one job done correctly. Or, lacking any advance schedule of the week's work, wasteful trips back and forth occur.
- *Inadequate staffing patterns.* Employees who are assigned unchallenging tasks will get bored, make mistakes, produce less, or quit. Lack of backup staffing during vacations can cause crises. Undertrained people will produce poor results.
- *Too many actors.* Too many people, and too many staff hours, may be assigned to the same task.

Work sampling of *Jonesville Vehicle Maint. Parts Room*

Observer: _____ Date _____

Random Times of Observation

Employee	8:30	9:01	10:30	11:51	1:50	3:21	4:38
1 Banes	1	3	1	5	10	2	2
2 Jackson	3	1	7	1	1	7	2
3 O'Dell	4	4	4	3	2	4	4
4 Washington	4	4	8	4	4	8	8
5 Dangelo	1	1	3	9	10	3	1
6 Bauer	4	6	4	5	6	9	3
7 Hernandez	8	8	8	3	8	9	8

Tasks	1	Review orders, specs	9	Update records
	2	Compare vendor prices	10	Idle, away
	3	Computer entry		
	4	Distribute parts to mechanics		
	5	Order parts		
	6	Discard old tires		
	7	Administration		
	8	Stock parts		

Principles of sampling: Break down the department work into work processes; or further, into tasks. Choose sampling times based on randomization and stratification. Using Table of Random Numbers, choose the exact time of day to make observations (above example uses 7 times); stratify, by choosing exact days over a period of 30 days.

Using the Supervisor: The supervisor is a logical data gatherer. He or she has knowledge of the work and employees' work habits; by doing the study, the supervisor is simply systematizing what he does already. No new personnel need be introduced; supervisor will accept the results of his own study, and can make a good estimate of total amounts of time spent on each work process or task.

Figure 1. Data Collection Form For Supervisors Using "Work Sampling" Technique

A detailed Work Distribution Chart appears in Figure 3. As an alternative to work sampling, this chart has been established by asking employees to keep a record of their own times for each task. This personal time card should be kept for a minimum of one week, and preferably for two to four weeks. Data gathered in this way may have an error factor of

Work process/task	Total manhours	% total	Parts Mgr	Jack	Wash	O'Del	Dang	Bauer	Hernan
New Vehicle Parts Purchases									
Review orders, specifications		10	10	20					
Compare vendor prices		12	5	10					
Select vendor, place order		6		8		7			
New Vehicle Parts Distribution									
Receive, stock parts		17			5			5	
Distribute parts to mech's		24			20	15		15	18
Tire Control									
Receive, stock tires		3					15		18
Distribute tires to mech's		2					16		
Discard old tires		2					9		
Inventory Maintenance									
Update computer records		5		2					
Order new parts		2	5			3		1	4
Rebuilt Parts Control									
Receive, stock parts		3							
Distribute parts		7			15	15		19	
Administration & Miscellaneous		7	20						
TOTAL MAN HOURS PER WEEK	280	100%	40	40	40	40	40	40	40

Adapted from: George T. Washnis, *Productivity Improvement Handbook for State and Local Government* (New York: John Wiley & Sons 1980) p. 207

Figure 2. Work Distribution Chart, City Vehicle Maintenance Parts Room

Activity	Hrs	*Employee* John English Supervisor Grade: $15/hr Tasks	Hrs	*Employee* Nancy Roberts Grounds Keeper II Grade: $10/hr Tasks	Hrs	*Employee* Andy Mason Grounds Keeper I Grade: $7/hr Tasks	Hrs	Total hours	Percentage
1. Turf Maintenance		1 7 gang mower 2 3 Edger 4 Fertilizing 5 6		1 7 gang mower 2 Triplex mower 3 Edger 4 5 6		1 2 Triplex mower 3 4 Fertilizing 5 Litter pick-up 6			
2. Tree Maintenance		7 8 9 10		7 Tree pruning 8 9 10		7 Tree pruning 8 Aeration 9 10			
3. Playground Repair		11 12 13		11 Install 12 13		11 Paint fence 12 13			
4. Equipment Repair		14 7 Gang Repair 15		14 7 gang repair 15		14 Triplex prev m. 15			
5. Administration		16 Planning 17 Inspecting 18 Training 19		16 17 18 19		16 17 18 19			
6. Special projects		20 Graffiti remov 21 Tourn. prep 22 23		20 Graffiti remov 21 Tourn. prep 22 23		20 Graf. removal 21 Tourn. prep 22 23			
Total hours	120		40		40		40	120	100

Figure 3. Alternative Format, Work Distribution Chart, Grounds Maintenance

183

	Highly skilled	Less skilled	Trainee
Very important			
Less important			
Least important			
Administration			

To use the chart in analysis, collect and fill in correct times for all tasks, using work sampling or employee's own time card. Then ask the following questions:

1. Looking from left to right ("horizontal analysis"), ask: Do people with similar job-skills specialize, or spend the same amounts of time on the same tasks? Do production counts compare favorably based on hours charged to task? If someone goes on vacation, can another do his/her tasks?

2. Looking up and down ("vertical analysis"), ask: Are highly skilled employees spending their time on the difficult/important tasks? With the exception of administration, highly skilled employees should be spending their time on tasks at the top of the chart.

3. Looking at the chart as a whole, ask: Can the number of people doing one task be reduced (specialization)? Can skills useable in one task be applied in another, calling for a transfer of assignments?

The Six Questions of Table 1 (who, what, where, and so forth) can be tried out on each entry in the Work Distribution chart. The list of possible questions raised against the chart is limited only by the analyst's imagination, knowledge of the work, and creativity.

Figure 4. Using the Work Distribution Chart for Analysis

20%. The analyst rolls up the self-kept time cards, and aggregates them into a Work Distribution Chart. The great advantage of employee-kept time measures is that all possibility of resentment against an outside time analyst is closed off.

METHODS IMPROVEMENT 2: FLOWCHARTS

There are two broad kinds of flow chart. The first, the *process flow chart*, follows the movement of a document, material, or part from its inception to final disposition. For this traditional IE flowchart the following symbols are employed:

○   represents an act which creates, changes, adds, or deletes to the work substance or process

▭   represents transportation or movement

▢   represents an inspection, examination, or verification for completeness or accuracy

◻   represents a delay in the work process

≳   represents destruction of an item or substance

▽   represents storage or final disposition

Using these symbols, a flowchart is shown in Figure 5 for check collection and deposit in a city utilities department. In developing process flow charts the analyst must be sure that the flow chart shows *actual* procedures, not hypothetical ones. An Operations Manual can be consulted but only as a first approximation. The real process must be checked and validated with supervisors and employees, the people who supervise and perform the work itself.

A "skeletalized" process flow chart is helpful in presenting the work process with clarity (see Figure 6). A *program flow chart,* which is the second kind of flow chart, focuses on broad program elements or modules. A module may include one or twenty worksteps or more, as illustrated in Figure 7.

Figure 7 shows a prototypical flow chart suitable for any local government department. For a General Services department, Track I describes several work modules (broad tasks): (1) clean golf course public toilets; (2) maintain fairways; (3) maintain putting greens; (4) maintain club house grounds; and (5) maintain entrance grounds. Track II could refer to road resurfacing, curb replacement, and pothole patching. For Social Services, Track I's modules include: (1) intake; (2) counseling; (3) basic training; (4) advanced training; and (5) job placement. Track II could be another social service program, or the same program with quicker (more employable) students.

For the analyst, the broad program flowchart offers a real opportunity to shuffle staff hours between different modules, "balancing" the workload against achievement of stated objectives for the overall program and modules.[6]

METHODS IMPROVEMENT 3: "SIX HONEST, SERVING MEN"

Although there is no magic way to improve/simplify work methods, the analyst has a series of six questions that are standard procedure (see

FLOW PROCESS CHART

Page ___ of ___

Activity _Check entry BATCH_____　　Man ____ or Material ____

Chart Starts_____　　Charted by_____

Chart Ends_____　　Date_____

	Details of method	operat'n / transp't / inspect / delay / storage	dist.ft.	qty.	time	Notes
1	Open envelope	●⇨□D▽				
2	remove bill/check	●⇨□D▽				
3	inspect: bill = check?	O⇨■D▽				
4	If does: Sort to 3 stacks	●⇨□D▽				
5	enter amounts	●⇨□D▽				
6	batch checks	●⇨□D▽				
7	deposit checks	O➡□D▽				
8	destroy envelopes	O⇨□D▽			⧦	
1	If not: determine error	●⇨□D▽				
2	enter documentation	●⇨□D▽				
3	store for super	O⇨□D▼				
		O⇨□D▽				

Summary :		
	Operations....... No. __13__	Time __36 min__
Total distance traveled ____ feet	Transportations.. No. __1__	Time __4 min__
	Inspections...... No. __1__	Time __12 min__
	Delays.......... No. __0__	Time
	Storage........ No. __1__	Time __8 min__

Figure 5.　Process Flow Chart

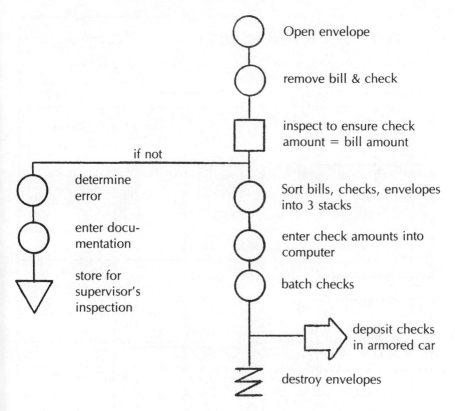

Figure 6. Flowchart, Bill Receiving Unit
City Utilities Department

Table 1). There are many formats for introducing Methods Improvement, and applying the six questions. A short list would include:

1. The formal process used in Value Engineering, steps 1 through 3:
    Information Gathering, Creative Development of Alternatives
    (brainstorming), and Refinement. The full process, outlined in
    Chapter 7, includes both a trained session leader and any number
    of employees.
2. The trained Industrial Engineering consultant who leads a small
    group of employees of any rank who have been tested for aptitude
    and who will become the team of computer/work management
    technicians operating the new system.
3. The individual supervisor, or hourly employee chosen by the de-

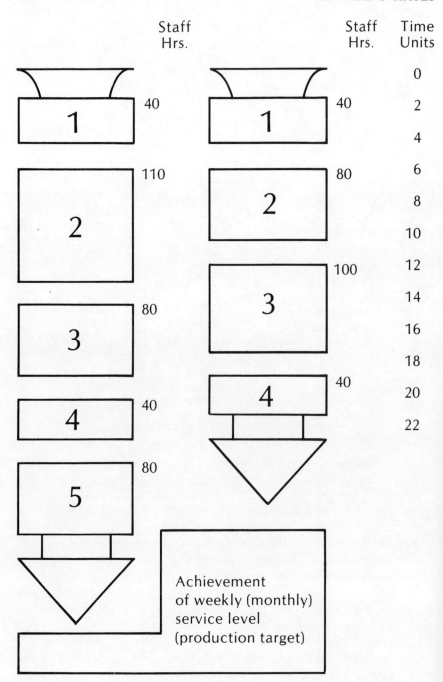

Figure 7.   Program Flowchart.

Table 1. "Six Honest, Serving Men":
Main Questions and Answers For Work Simplification

	Questions	Answers
What?	What is being done?	A precise description of
	What happens to the material, the	results/outcomes.
	product, the client?	Increase the results.
Why?	Why is it done?	Determine the relation of work-
	Why are certain modules used?	process to objectives.
	Why are certain workprocesses and	Determine workstep interdepen-
	motions used?	dency.
	Why is this process even needed?	Determine feasbility of discarding
		process entirely.
When?	When in the whole process is it	Determine present sequencing.
	done?	Change sequencing to increase re-
		sults.
How?	How is it done?	Simplify, recombine, eliminate work-
	How *exactly* is each process or task	steps.
	accomplished?	
Where?	Where is it done (location)?	Bring materials/workers into
	Where in the workprocess?	proximity.
	Where, on the physicalunit, does the	Eliminate trips; decentralize
	worker direct his energy?	operations.
		Improve ergonomics.
Who?	Who is doing the work?	Assign the non-over-qualified.
	Who *should* be (skill level)?	Eliminate unneeded personnel.
	Who does what exact workstep?	

Source: List of questions taken, with modifications, from Delmar W. Karger and Franklin A. Bayha, *Engineered Work Measurement*, 3rd ed (New York: Industrial Press, 1977), p. 34. The title of the table comes from Rudyard Kipling: "I kept six honest serving men / They taught me all I knew / Their names are What and Why and When / And How and Where and Who"; see Rudyard Kipling, *Just So Stories* (London: MacMillan and Company, 1902).

partment head, who takes inside or outside training and returns to work on programs designated by the department. This is a method used by Los Angeles County (see page 201, this chapter).

4. The outside consultant who establishes a project with top management and extends this down through the ranks. This "traditional" method can be made too "top down" and lose vital management support.

5. The wholly in-house study performed by staff with the Industrial Engineering degree. This was the recent scenario in Dade County, whose chief of Management Analysis is a Professional Engineer (PE).

6. Employee input sessions. This can include the standard suggestion box; staff meeting discussions, workgroup discussions, or

special Roundtables. Japanese auto plants, with Quality Circles, try to get over 100 suggestions per employee per year.

7. Any combination of the above. The "right format" is whatever is right for a particular local jurisdiction.

WORK SCHEDULING AND PREVENTIVE MAINTENANCE

Work Scheduling (WS)[7] and Preventive Maintenance (PM)[8] are subdivisions of methods improvement. They are such important subdivisions that they are here given separate treatment.[9]

The theory of WS and PM is to create a monthly production schedule that a workcrew or department can follow without fail. This may seem an inconsequential achievement, but in fact accurate service and production scheduling is considered by some to be the key to workforce productivity improvement.[10] Preventive Maintenance contributes to this, by insuring that vehicle downtime is minimized, reducing disruptions and people standing around idle for hours–or days. This allows WS/PM to achieve its objective: to reduce "demand work" (emergency work) to less than 20% of all worktime, and increase "scheduled work" to 80% *and more*.

The results of this can be dramatic. A significant part of the savings outlined in Table 2 can be attributed to WS/PM, an integral part of Work Management.

WORK MEASUREMENT: THE OTHER HALF OF THE LOAF

There are five traditional ways to estimate and measure the time required to perform work.[11] Beginning with the simplest, these are:

1. *Historical estimates.* This is a relatively easy method because it requires no measurement techniques. Existing historical data are used. Staffing patterns and total staff hours divided by the total work unit output give a broad idea of department or program efficiency. This method is particularly appropriate when there are no fine motions to be measured, or when the work is performed intermittently.

2. *Technical estimates.* The supervisor and the employee both have perspectives on the amount of time used to perform any task. Their opinions offer a viable starting point. Supervisors and motivated employees can offer useful insight into the proper (standard) time for tasks.

Like historical estimates, technical estimates require no measurement techniques.

3. *Work sampling.* For work sampling, the analyst makes a series of random, spot observations, to record simply what the employee is doing or not doing at the time of the observation. This is the simplest work measurement technique. The results of one day's observations in a vehicle parts department is shown in Figure 1.

In Figure 8, 147 observations are noted. Reliability of data increases sharply with 200 observations or more, and in the private sector, 5,000

Observing & Recording Form					
DATE:				PAGE:____OF____	

Total Number of Observations

JHt LHt Jttt Jttt Jttt Jttt Jttt Jttt Jttt Jttt
Jttt Jttt Jttt Jttt Jttt Jttt Jttt Jttt Jttt
Jttt Jttt Jttt Jttt Jttt Jttt Jttt Jttt
Jttt Jttt ll

DELAYS

Personal	Idle	Waiting	Instruction	Telephone	Telephone
				Business	Personal
₩₩ ///	₩₩ ₩₩	₩₩ /	₩₩ //	₩₩ ₩₩	//
Absent	Other	Walking			
//					

Figure 8.   Work Sampling Form Showing Work,
Idle, and Away Observations

Source: Los Angeles County Application (Work Simplification) Training Course, *Work SMART* (Los Angeles: LRT Group Inc., 1986), p. 20

observations are not uncommon.[12] This number of observations in the public sector would be a "textbook example."

4. *Work-Idle-Away Study.*   For this study the analyst may watch a particular employee for a length of time. Using up to three stopwatches, which may be kept in-pocket and out of sight, the observer looks up every two minutes and records, on the appropriate watch, whether the employee was at work, idle, or away. "Idle" does not imply loafing, and "away" may mean performing necessary work. The data, in short, do not give ultimate answers; but they yield a useable benchmark through an accepted method.

5. *Time Studies.*   For this method the analyst measures, with watch or other measuring device, the exact amount of time necessary to perform a certain movement or task. Unlike work sampling, in which observations may be hours apart, or work-idle-away studies in which observations may be seconds apart, Time Studies are continuous and aim at a precise answer the first time out. Any of several instruments may be used: a stopwatch, of which three kinds are available; a wristwatch, for cruder measures; a special motion picture camera with frame counter and multiple speed settings; a tape recorder; a 35mm or Polaroid camera; a video camera; or a strip chart recorder. Time studies are the method usually associated with Industrial Engineering. Taylor himself used the stopwatch, having learned this method from the Frenchman M. Coulomb who employed it around 1760.[13]

HOW LONG *SHOULD* IT TAKE? DEVELOPING AN "ENGINEERED" TIME

After the time studies have been done, the next step is to *determine existing (actual) ratios.* There are at least three of primary importance: utilization of time (applied time); the performance ratio; and the percentage of effectiveness. *Time utilization* is determined by the formula

$$\frac{\text{work (applied) time}}{\text{available time}} \times 100 =$$

where applied time is time actually working, and available time is 40 hours minus set-up/clean-up.

The *performance ratio* is determined by the formula

$$\frac{\text{man hours expended}}{\text{work units produced}} =$$

where "work units" refers to any convenient unit of output, such as clients served, warrants processed, or miles of pipeline maintained.

The *percentage of effectiveness* is determined by the ratio

$$\frac{\text{standard man-hours}}{\text{actual man-hours}} \times 100 =$$

where "standard man hours" are hours that have been determined appropriate for this job in this setting.[14]

An "engineered time" is a standard time developed for City X, showing how long a job should take using a specified method, under specified conditions, working at a normal pace by a qualified employee.[15] The formula (ratio) for establishing an engineered time standard is

$$\frac{\text{working man hours} \times \text{effort} \times \text{allowance factors}}{\text{work units}}$$

where "work units" are any convenient unit of measure of output, such as lineal feet of curb replaced, clients served, and so forth.

In developing an engineered (appropriate) time for Department D in City X, the analyst goes through several stages, which include: (1) measurement of existing times (previously described); (2) reference to Standard Data, yielding a written definition of a standard time; (3) reference to Predetermined Time Systems; and (4) reference to Pacing and other Allowance Factors.

Predetermined Time Systems

Over the past 75 years standard times for every basic movement in industrial manufacturing and office work has had a standard (appropriate) time developed.[16] These measure very minute motions, in subfractions of a second called Measured Time Units (TMUs). 1 TMU equals 0.00001 hours; 1 hour equals 100,000 TMUs; one *second* contains 27.8 TMUs.

An analysis of MTM-1, measuring TMUs for the workstep "Replace page in 3-ring binder," is shown in Figure 9. In the columns "left hand motion" and "right hand motions" are codes (starting R7A), which refer to the exact description of that motion contained in a published MTM-1 database. The entire operation requires 577.8 TMUs, or just under 21 seconds. Another predetermined time system, MOST (Maynard Operations Sequence Technique) aggregates elemental movements and reduces the amount of time required to develop an engineered time.[17]

MTM-1 ANALYSIS					VALIDATION

MTM ASSOCIATION FOR STANDARDS AND RESEARCH

ELEMENT TITLE: Replace page in 3-ring binder
STARTS: Get binder from shelf at left
INCLUDES: Get binder, open cover, locate correct page, open rings, replace old sheet, close rings, Aside binder to shelf
ENDS:

ANALYST:
DATE:

LEFT HAND DESCRIPTION	F	LH MOTION	TMU	RH MOTION	F	RIGHT HAND DESCRIPTION
1. GET BINDER - OPEN COVER						
Reach to binder		R30B	25.8			
Grasp binder		G1A	2.0			
Move to desk		M30B	24.3			
Release		RL1	2.0			
Reach to cover		R7B	9.3			
Grasp edge		G1A	2.0			
Open cover'		M16B	15.8			
Release		RL1	2.0			
			83.2			
2. LOCATE CORRECT PAGE						
			14.6	EF	2	Read first page data
Reach to edge	3	R3D	21.9			
Grasp	3	G1B	10.5			
Move up	3	M4B	20.7			
Regrasp		G2	—			
			43.8	EF	2×3	Identify pages
Move pages back		M8B	10.6			
Release		RL1	2.0			
Reach to hold		R8B	10.1	R4B		To edge of page
Grasp		G5	0.0	G5		Contact
			8.0	MfB	4	Slide back up
Contact	3	G5	0.0	RL2	4	Release
Move	3	MfB	7.5	R1B	3	To corner
			0.0	G5	3	Contact
Regrasp pages		G2	5.6			
			87.6	EF	4×3	Identify pages
Move pages back		M8B	10.6			
Release		RL1	2.0			
			255.5			

Figure 9. MTM–1 Analysis*

Note: *This chart is approximately half the total calculation sheet, which includes a total of 56 worksteps and 577 TMU's.

Source: MTM Association brochure.

	MOST-calculation		Code		I₁O₁6₀₁3₄₄₀5

Area **COLLECTIONS**
Date **12/7/77**
Sign. **A.M.G.**
Page **1/1**

Activity **ASSEMBLE CHECKS IN INSIDE COLLECTIONS**
Conditions

No.	Method	No.	Sequence Model	Fr	TMU
1	GET CHECK AND NOTICE	1	A₁ B₀ G₁ A₁ B₀ P₀ A₀	3	90
2	REMOVE AND ASIDE	2	(A₀) B₀ G₁ A₁ B₀ P₁ A₀	3	90
	PAPER CLIP	3	(A₀) B₀ G₀ A₁ B₀ P₁ A₀	3	60
		4	(A₀) B₀ G₁ A₁ B₀ P₀ A₀	3	60
3	PLACE CHECK AND NOTICE	5	A₁ B₀ G₃ (A₁ B₀ P₁) A₀	3	120
	ON DESK	6	A₀ B₀ G₀ A₁ B₀ P₁ A₀	3	60
		7	A₁ B₀ G₁ A₁ B₀ (P₁) A₀	3	90
4	PICK UP FORM	9	(A₀) B₀ G₁ A₁ B₀ P₁ A₀	3	90
5	REMOVE CARBON AND	10	A₁ B₀ G₁ A₁ B₀ P₃ A₀	3	180
	ASIDE	11	A₀ B₀ G₀ A₁ B₀ P₁ A₀	3	60
6	PLACE NOTICE ON DESK	12	A₁ B₀ G₁ A₁ B₀ P₁ A₀		40
7	PLACE TOP COPY OF				Tot 1,090
	NOTICE ON CHECK				
8	GET CHECK AND NOTICE				
	AND STAPLE				
9	GET COPIES OF NOTICE	8	A₀ B₀ G₁ A₁ B₀ P₁ M₃ A₁ B₀ P₀ A₀	3	810
	AND PLACE WITH CHECK				
10	GET AND PLACE PAPER				
	CLIP ON NOTICE				
11	ASIDE PAPERS				
12	THROW AWAY CARBONS				

TIME = **.6540** minutes (min.)   **1090**

Copyright: Maynard 1974 M101 - REV. 1

Figure 10. A "MOST®" Calculation Sheet*

Note: *The MOST predetermined time system aggregates motions into larger worksteps and TMU blocks, compared with MTM–1 (see Figure 7). Here, 12 worksteps use 1,090 TMUs; in Figure 7, 56 worksteps use only 577 TMUs. MOST Computer Systems represent the state-of-the-art in computerized time measurement.

Source: Kjell B. Zandin, *MOST Work Measurement Systems* (New York: Marcel Dekker, 1980), p. 196. Reprinted by permission.

195

The Use of "Standard Data"

Local government managers are primarily interested in the amount of time required to mow an acre of grass, vacuum 10 square feet of rug, empty a wastebasket, issue one building permit, and other "macro" workprocesses or tasks. TMUs are too finite. Standard Data provide the times for these "macro" processes. The standard is described first in TMUs (elemental times) that are aggregated into a standard time for the macro process. The most important of these standard data sources is Universal Standard Data, proprietary to H.B. Maynard and Company.

Pacing: How Fast Is Normal?

When industrial engineers estimate "pace" (a process which is called "levelling"), they are "measuring the effort expended on any task—the

HAROLD B. MAYNARD was pioneer in Predetermined Time Systems. Starting with an Engineering degree from Cornell, he began work with Westinghouse Electric, then travelled and served as a consultant. He is co-author of Methods Time Measurement system (MTM), which has been translated into most languages, and a co-founder of the MTM Association. He founded and served as editor in chief of the H.B. Maynard Industrial Engineering Handbook, still a preeminent reference work, and cited frequently in this chapter. Mr. Maynard contributed to the leading engineering journals, and won many awards, including the Gilbreth Medal and an honorary Doctor of Laws from the University of Miami. His company, H.B. Maynard and Co., Inc. (Philadelphia), is still one of the largest of all industrial engineering firms that serve the local public sector.

Source: Permission to reprint photo by MTM Association, Los Angeles, California.

drive of the worker to expend his energy."[18] There are six defined levels of effort, from "poor effort" (kills time, resents suggestions) to "excessive effort" (extends his pace to an unreasonable limit; could not maintain pace through the day). A total of fifty-seven criteria are used to define these six effort levels.[19] A "standard time" is based on the third defined effort level, "average effort." For many motions, the films provided by the Society for the Advancement of Management (SAM) provide graphic illustrations of average pace, above average pace, and below average pace.

Allowance Factors

Besides pacing, IE provides for seven "allowance factors" to be taken into account when establishing engineered times. The first three are Fatigue, Delay, and Personal Requirements. In addition allowances may be made for the monotony of a repetitive job, and for good safety procedures in the work routine, including the wearing of protective clothing.[20] Allowance is also made for varying levels of skill of workers, and while an engineered time can be based on any skill level, the usual skill level for a standard time is "Average Skill."[21]

PUTTING IT TOGETHER:
EXPLOITATION OR SCIENTIFIC MANAGEMENT?

The great fear among some managers is that Work Measurement will lead to speed up. A thorough search of literature, including queries to AFSCME, the nation's largest public employee union, produced no evidence that this has in fact been the result of any Industrial Engineering project in any city. If a manager wants to engage in speedup, he does not have to call in a man with a watch, and most public managers are not inclined in this direction. Indeed, the careful measurements of a trained industrial engineer and the use of allowance factors provides data of considerable help in defending the interests of employees.

The emphasis of IE on ergonomics illustrates this last point. Ergonomics studies how the work environment can be fitted to the mental and physical requirements of the employee. Given its predisposition to study fatigue and other allowance factors, and its long concern with office and plant layout to maximize objectives, industrial engineering is the only discipline that can answer the questions of ergonomics scientifically, and has already developed a literature on the subject.[22]

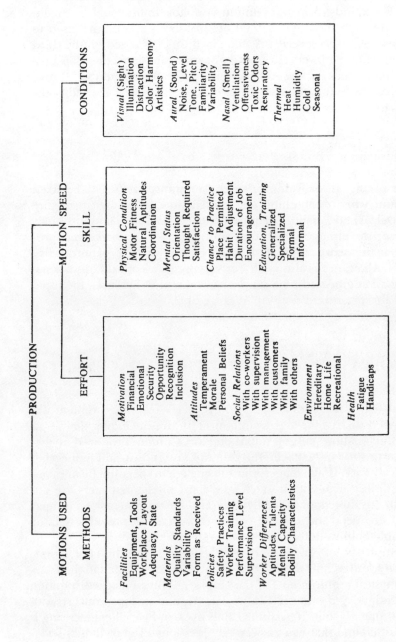

Figure 11. Variables Determining Productive Output

Source: Delmar W. Karger and Franklin H. Bayha, *Engineered Work Measurement*, 4th ed. (New York: Industrial Press, 1987), p. 19. Reprinted with permission.

198

AN APPLICATION:
WORK MANAGEMENT IN SCOTTSDALE, ARIZONA AND MIDLAND, TEXAS

Engineered times, plus work scheduling, plus preventive maintenance, plus a computerized data system equals Work Management. This program establishes engineered times for tasks performed by any work crew, such as custodial or parks maintenance; establishes schedules for crews, so that 90% of tasks are completed on schedule, not "on demand"; sets up a preventive maintenance (PM) program to enhance the scheduling effort; and caps it off with a computerized MIS (Management Information System) centered on the Work Order form. The Work Order triggers task activity.

In Midland, Texas the Parks Department installed Work Management in 1980 and watched its employee productivity percentage rise from 46% to between 80% and 90% in 1987.

Productivity in the Parks Maintenance Department in Scottsdale, Arizona rose from a base rate of just under 50% in 1981 to between 90% and 115% in 1987.[23] Under the Work Management system, Scottsdale saved some $353,000 in the first year (see Table 2). Manpower needs were reduced by almost one-third (eleven positions). Redundant employees were rotated to other departments, not fired.[24]

"APPLIED TIME" IN VISALIA, CALIFORNIA

Industrial engineering has been applied in the context of a productivity program in Visalia, California. The city's new program began in its General Services Department in 1982. The Department includes divisions for public transit (city buses), solid waste collection, and fleet management. As a whole the department was suffering from severe turnover problems, low output, and an annual deficit sometimes reaching $45,000.

The new program had several features:

1. "Applied time" would be the key measure of department productivity. In the city bus and garbage truck divisions, applied time meant the percent of hours vehicles were up and running; in all divisions, it meant the percent of the eight hour day that employees actually spent working.
2. The new manager told the employees that if productivity could not be raised, the department would start contracting out by 1985.

Table 2.   Savings From Work Management in Nine Cities, 1975–1984

Government Unit	Annual Savings*		
	Projected	Actual	Fee
Oklahoma City School District	450,000	815,000	251,000
City of Scottsdale, Arizona Municipal Utilities and Parks Maintenance	300,000	352,960	104,000
City of Midland, Texas Street, Park, Water, Sewer and Traffic Maintenance	531,000	628,466	215,000
City of Tacoma, Washington Street Maintenance	400,000	729,000	134,000
City of Lawton, Oklahoma Street Maintenance	150,000	165,000	65,000
City of Costa Mesa, California Leisure Services Public Services	150,000 175,000	165,000 122,450	65,000 92,000
ABC Unified School District Maintenance Custodial	155,000 455,000	151,000 617,000	49,000 137,500
City of Gardena, California Engineering, Street Maintenance & Parks	194,000	376,000	65,000
City of Montebello, California Parks Maintenance Street Maintenance	142,000	268,000	66,500
Total Average Return on Investment, First Year: 3.5 to 1		4,379,000	1,246,500

Note: *Savings can be taken either as outright cash savings, or as an equivalent amount of service increase.
Source: Kapner, Wolfberg & Associates, Van Nuys, California.

3.   The new manager promised that 80% of all management decisions would be made in weekly all-department meetings, where
employees could evaluate the week's progress.

The new program was met with a combination of skepticism and fear—
that jobs would disappear in three years. The new manager was willing
to support requests for equipment, but was not willing to ask for additional money. New equipment had to be financed out of the existing
budget.

Dramatic changes took place. To find the money for needed new
equipment, the employees focused on energy costs, and in a year-and-a-

half had saved 30% of such costs, applying the difference to equipment. The employees themselves drew up the equipment list.

By 1987, applied time has risen to over 90%. The deficit is history, and the fear of contracting away jobs is past. Garbage trucks and street sweepers are on-line 97% of the time. A truck that breaks down reduces department applied time, and as one worker put it, "come backs are a no-no here."

THE DOWNSIDE:
WHY LOCAL GOVERNMENTS
DISCONTINUE WORK MEASUREMENT

Not all work measurement programs endure. From a random sampling of both cities and consultants, here are the main reasons for discontinuation:

1. Lack of top management support. Turnover of management often brings a new manager unfamiliar with work measurement and time standards. He simply discontinues the process.
2. Failure of the consultant to give credit to managers. Without feeling that "they are responsible for the success," managers do not buy into the program.
3. Failure of the consultant to offer continuous follow-up service in the first year. This is crucial for smaller jurisdictions which are unlikely to have any trained IE staff on board.

WORK SIMPLIFICATION
IN LOS ANGELES COUNTY

Los Angeles County has used work measurement since the 1960s. Putting programs on time standards continued in the 1970s. A significant number of these programs were discontinued, as new work procedures required all-new time measurements and staff were not always eager to respond. Proposition 13 then radically reduced the amount of money for time measurement, and the county faced a problem.

Its response was to broaden its approach, to include both in-house training in work simplification *and* low-cost contracted industrial engineers. For managers who wish to hire professional IE consultants, the county maintains two master contracts with outside employment agencies whose rosters include industrial engineers. For departments that prefer to remain in-house, it has established a training program with the following elements:

1. Analyst-trainees are rank and file employees from any department whose manager has assigned the trainee.
2. Courses last only 40 hours, in classes of four hours each. The first three hours teach basic Industrial Engineering techniques, including work sampling, levelling, problem analysis, and development of alternatives. The last hour of each class deals specifically with students' special projects.
3. Instead of stressing work measurement and sophisticated reporting systems, the classes focus on work simplification.
4. The program is sensitive to the potential costs of any solution. The class SMART manual includes pages from the county auditor's handbook, showing how to estimate unit costs. Any solution must have a justifiable Return on Investment (ROI).
5. A key question for any proposed solution is taken from Value Analysis: Is it worth it?

Any graduate of the county's program receives the title of "Systems and Work Measurement Analyst 1." As of 1987, ten of the county's 54 departments had used this in-house program.[25]

CONCLUSION:
THE MANY CONTEXTS OF
INDUSTRIAL ENGINEERING

What city managers should remember about Industrial Engineering is its ultimate flexibility. The many methods of IE can be combined in any number of ways with approaches and programs that suit the individual department and program. Scottsdale uses IE in its Organization Development program. Dade County (Miami) undertook a broad Productivity Improvement Program (PIP) using Work Sampling as one of ten elements in 1984. Los Angeles County has stressed work simplification and simple employee-kept time cards, in the context of a broadscale in-house education program whose purpose is to make the workforce itself aware of the value of IE methods. This latter objective may be the key to successful implementation, and retention, of IE programs. Keeping in mind the Japanese success in making the workforce itself expert in productivity methods and relying on its input, cities can always "start easy" with the education of their own employees. At the same time, nothing is more convincing than a professional work measurement project to which management is committed and which shows a high return on investment in the first year.

APPENDIX:
PROFESSIONAL INDUSTRIAL ENGINEERING ASSOCIATIONS, PUBLICATIONS, AND CONSULTANTS

Professional Associations

Institute of Electrical and Electronics Engineers (IEEE)
IEEE Service Center
445 Hoes Lane
Piscataway, NJ 00854
(212–705–7900)
Publication: *IEEE Transactions On Engineering Management*
(quarterly)

Institute of Industrial Engineers (IIE)
25 Technology Park/Atlanta
Norcross, GA 30092
(404–449–0460)
Publications: *Industrial Engineering* (monthly)
Transactions of Annual Conference
Industrial Management (bi-monthly)
The Engineering Economist (quarterly)
IIE Transactions: Industrial Engineering Research and Development (quarterly)

MTM Association for Standards and Research
1601 Broadway
Fair Lawn NY 07410
(210–791–7720)

Consultants In Public Sector Industrial Engineering

Kapner, Wolfberg and Associates Inc.
7120 Hayvenhurst Ave.
Van Nuys, CA 91406
(213–781–8851)

Management and Communication Consultants
PO Box 14372
Oklahoma City, OK 73113
(405–751–4077)
        or
125 Pearl Avenue
San Carlos CA 94070
(415–594–0198)

H.B. Maynard and Company Inc.
235 Alpha Drive
Pittsburgh, PA 15238
(412–963–8100)
        or
Maynard Management Institute
2250 East Imperial Highway
Suite 252
El Segundo, CA 90245
(213–640–1739)

M.E. Mundel and Associates
Management Consulting
821 Loxford Terrace
Silver Spring, MD 20901
(301–593–2397)

ACKNOWLEDGMENTS

For assistance in preparing this chapter, the author gratefully acknowledges the assistance of the following: William M. Aiken, the late Chairman of H.B. Maynard and Co., Inc.; John Gee, Office of the CAO, Los Angeles County; Sylvan L. Kapner, President, Kapner, Wolfberg and Associates, Van Nuys, California; Perry S. Shimanoff, President, Management Communication Consultants, San Carlos, California; Charles E. Lopez, editor, Institute of Industrial Engineers, Norcross, Georgia; and Alan Kapanicas, City of Scottsdale.

NOTES AND REFERENCES

1.   "Step 1: Divide the work of a man performing any job into simple elementary movements. Step 2: Pick out all useless movements and discard them." The whole method is outlined by Taylor, *Transactions of the American Society of Mechanical Engineers (ASME)*, 34 (1912): 1199–1200. Taylor's main text still repays the modern reader: Frederick Winslow Taylor, *Principles of Scientific Management* (New York and London: Harper & Brothers Publishers). Taylor in historical context can be read in Samual Haber, *Efficiency and Uplift. Scientific Management In the Progressive Era, 1890–1920* (University of Chicago Press, 1964).

2. Two major handbooks summarize current methods of Industrial Engineering (IE). Duane Geitgey, editor in chief, H.B. Maynard's *Industrial Engineering Handbook*, 4th ed. (New York: McGraw-Hill, 1988); and Gavriel Salvendy, ed., *Handbook of Industrial Engineering* (New York: Wiley, 1982). For publications of major engineering societies see Appendix.

3. The H.B. Maynard Company of Pittsburgh, Pennsylvania has conducted over 100 Work Management programs with local government. Several of the Big 8 accounting firms, and many smaller independent consultants, do work measurement and methods simplification; see Appendix.

4. Methods Improvement, also called "Work Simplification," is described by Salvendy, "Methods Engineering," in *Handbook of Industrial Engineering*, pp. 1.11–1.43; and by Geitgey, "Methods Engineering," in *Industrial Engineering Handbook*. See also Chief Administrative Office, County of Los Angeles, *Work SMART* (1986); Patricia Haynes et al., "Industrial Engineering Techniques," in *Productivity Handbook for State and Local Government*, ed. George J. Washnis (New York: Wiley, 1980), pp. 206–213; and Delmar W. Karger and Franklin H. Bayha, *Engineered Work Measurement*, 3rd ed. (New York: Industrial Press, 1977), pp. 33–49.

5. For exposition of Work Sampling methods, see pp. 191–192, this chapter.

6. The module flow chart is most useful as a staffing tool during the planning phase. By using objectives as the criteria for deciding staff time, money can be saved and justification for time studies established. For example, if a golf course has low priority, then a planning decision can be made to reduce staff hours on upkeep. Contrarily, if the city's objective is to increase play (and revenues, to make the course attractive to sell to a private owner), then more staff hours can be assigned, and justification made for measuring exact times, because this has become a more expensive item.

7. With Work Scheduling, managers fill out production schedules—who will be doing what jobs, when—for a week, or a month, ahead of time.

8. With Preventive Maintenance, repairs are made according to a calendar, not when breakdowns occur. After 25,000 miles, for example, all hoses on patrol car engines are replaced; after 10,000 miles, all spark plugs; after 1,000 hours, all compressors. This insures that equipment does not break down and helps maintain a rigorous Work Schedule.

9. See Edward H. Hartman, ed., *Maintenance Management* (Norcross, GA: Institute of Industrial Engineers, 1987); and Sylvan L. Kapner, "Maintenance Management," in *Industrial Engineering Handbook*, 2nd ed., ed. H.B. Maynard (New York: McGraw-Hill), pp. 7.50–7.64.

10. "The absence of systematic work planning and scheduling is prevalent throughout government organizations. It is perhaps the greatest opportunity for productivity improvement." National Commission on Productivity and Work Quality, *So Mr. Mayor, You Want To Improve Productivity* . . . (Washington, D.C.: U.S. Government Printing Office, 1974), p. 22.

11. For detailed expositions of Work Measurement methods see Geitgey, "Work Measurement," in *Industrial Engineering Handbook;* Richard L. Shell, ed., *Work Measurement: Principles and Practice* (Norcross, GA: Institute of Industrial Engineers, 1986); William S. Oakes, ed., *Developing Work Standards* (Norcross, GA: Institute of Industrial Engineers, 1985); Delmar W. Karger and Franklyn H. Bayha, *Engineered Work Measurement*, 4th ed. (New York: Industrial Press, 1987); and U.S. Army Management Engineering Training Agency, *Work Measurement* (Washington, D.C.: U.S. Government Printing Office, 1971).

12. See W.J. Richardson and Eleanor S. Pape, "Work Sampling," in Salvendy, *Handbook of Industrial Engineering*, Chapter 4, Section 6.

13. Karger and Bayha, *Engineered Work Measurement*, p. 91.

14. The formuli for performance ratio and percentage of effectiveness are from Don-

ald R. Herzog, *Industrial Engineering Methods and Controls* (Reston, VA: Prentice-Hall/Reston Publishing, 1985), p. 349.

15. *Ibid.*, p. 329.

16. There are several Predetermined Time Systems, each a somewhat different method of measuring discrete movements, including MTM 1, MTM 2, MTM 3, and MTM-C. Others include MTA (Motion-Time Analysis), Work Factor, and MTS (Motion Time Standards). Another system, MIL Std 1567A, while not a predetermined time system, is a requirement of the U.S. Department of Defense, which mandates military equipment suppliers to validate costs with an acceptable work measurement system.

17. "MOST is far simpler in application than MTM, requiring only 1 to 2% of the time that MTM requires, but giving comparable results in terms of methods description and accuracy of standards." Letter to the author from the late William M. Aiken, a former Chairman of the Board, H.B. Maynard and Company, Inc. (October 8, 1984). For a full analysis of MOST see Kjell B. Zandin, *MOST Work Measurement Systems* (New York: Marcell Dekker, 1980); and Ronald A. Soncini, "Raising Clerical Productivity With MOST Clerical Computerized Systems," in *Success Stories in Productivity*, ed. Jerry L. Hamlin (Norcross, GA: Institute of Industrial Engineers, 1985), p. 172.

18. Karger and Bayha, *Engineered Work Measurement*, p. 76.

19. *Ibid.*, pp. 76–77.

20. See *Ibid.*, Chapter 6, "Allowance and Variance Factors"; and Herzog, *Industrial Engineering Methods and Controls*, pp. 329–335.

21. The criteria for "Average Skill" are: (1) self confident; (2) proficient at the work; (3) coordinates mind and hand reasonably well; and (4) appears to be fully trained and therefore knows the job. Source: Karger and Bayha, *Engineered Work Measurement*, 3rd ed. (1977), pp. 74–75.

22. See David C. Alexander and B. Mustafa Pulat, *Industrial Ergonomics: A Practitioner's Guide* (Norcross, GA: Institute of Industrial Engineers, 1985).

23. In Scottsdale's system of measurement, the term "performance" is used in place of productivity. A performance rating of 100% is normal, based on engineered times. City of Scottsdale, "Work Management Guide for Parks Maintenance" (1986), p. 9.

24. Edward C. Hayes, "In Pursuit of Productivity: Scottsdale, Arizona," *National Civic Review* (September 1984): pp. 273–278.

25. Mr. John Gee, Productivity Unit, Chief Administrative Office, County of Los Angeles, Interview (May 29, 1987).

PART III

TOWARD THE SELF-FINANCED CITY

Chapter 10

THE ENTREPRENEURIAL CITY MANAGER

Ted A. Gaebler

SUMMARY. The entrepreneurial manager represents a new synthesis of old and new public management practices: new, in that city staff is encouraged to "think entrepreneurially", to cut costs, to find new sources of revenue including the sale of city services or purchase of profitable businesses; old, in encouraging private sector economic development, economic growth, and greater workforce productivity. It is a fluid concept, coined in the 1980s, with a wide spectrum of practices varying from city to city. At its best, it calls on cities to run themselves more like private businesses, to adopt certain practices from the private sector that can reduce the cost and scope of government.

THE ENTREPRENEURIAL MANAGER: WHAT KIND OF DUCK?

A small but growing number of cities share a conscious attitude of being "entrepreneurially managed." At first glance the meaning of this designation is not clear, for it includes several puzzling combinations of practices and attitudes:

- The entrepreneurial manager believes in maximizing economic development and reducing government rules and red tape. Yet he does not carry the "give away city hall" attitude.

- In some cities the entrepreneurial manager believes in having the city itself become an investor in private, for-profit corporations, taking the same risks and sharing in profits like any other investor. Yet its practitioners disclaim any socialist philosophy or intent.

- The entrepreneurial manager urges his departments to cut certain services and staff, contract out, and use volunteers. Yet entrepreneurialism is not simply a new phrase for the old chestnut Alternative Service Delivery.

- Entrepreneurial management calls for charging fees for city services, and sees this as desirable wherever possible. Yet it does not identify with the established body of theory that calls for systematic charging of fees for public (city) goods, Public Choice.[1]

The simplest way to begin understanding it is to look at several examples.

Fairfield, California

When Proposition 13 passed in 1978, Fairfield (population 64,400), to cover its share of the costs of a major shopping mall development, asked for and gained an equity position in the mall. This now guarantees to the city a percentage share of mall cash flow of between 10 and 17% in perpetuity. Since 1980 Fairfield has also built, and leased at a profit to the federal government, a federal postoffice. It has also become a partner in a regional hydroelectric power venture, and built a $1.2 million cogeneration plant which provides heat and power to civic center buildings at a city-estimated annual savings of $120,000.[2]

Visalia, California

In my own city during my tenure as manager we both went into business (described on p. 223) and went out of business. We gave the library to the county, the ambulances to private hospitals, day care to churches and the junior college, historic preservation to a private non-profit group, recycling to another private non-profit group, city public relations activities to the chamber of commerce (who charge a fee for their service), and animal control to the humane society. We bought and then sold a minor league baseball franchise, and gave a theatre to the private sector. ICMA publications call this "loadshedding"; we preferred the business term, "divestment." Why provide a service if someone else can and wants to?

Saint Paul, Minnesota

Saint Paul (population 266,500) called in the RAND Corporation to provide an entrepreneurial blueprint for the city in the early 1980s. The final report called on the city to turn its Division of Traffic and Lighting, and its Municipal Athletic Facility, into self-styled "Revenue Centers." These were to be largely self-supporting, and the final report offered several suggestions to this end. It also suggested a systematic examination of all real costs of all operations, including depreciation costs and fringe benefit expenses, and a relaxing of the rules of Civil Service to allow top management greater entrepreneurial flexibility (see p. 225).[3]

The Report is a useful document as an illustration of how an entrepreneurial city should run. In fact Saint Paul has barely begun to implement these reforms. No "Revenue Centers" have been created. But two new funds have been established to help make services more self-supporting, using the expedient of grouping some revenue-producing programs with some "pure cost" programs.[4] The Police and Fire Departments have been aggressive in marketing their services to surrounding small cities, and the city has installed a bubble canopy over its sports stadium, allowing year-round useage of the facility for paying events.[5]

THE ELEMENTS OF
ENTREPRENEURIAL PUBLIC MANAGEMENT

The previously described examples, which look at only a fraction of what is called entrepreneurial activity, make clear that entrepreneurial management is a complex phenomenon. No single definition could be agreed on even by its practitioners. It is practice-oriented, representing a pragmatic response to the revenue deficits of the past decade. Its devotees have not taken time to spin a consistent theory; perhaps they could not, because entrepreneurialism leads both in the direction of reducing government services and costs, and at the same time, in the direction of expanding government's role to include private investments, selling assets and services, and raising user fees. This complexity and contreity of practice is both frustrating and intriguing. Yet a very rough program for entrepreneurialism could be drawn up as a series of strategic injunctions:

1. Encourage the private sector, by providing a stable fiscal environment, an adequate infrastructure, and a pro-business attitude. Perhaps the cardinal objective for entrepreneurial cities is to build

the private sector, thereby guaranteeing adequate revenues
through taxation.

2. Create public/private ventures. This means in the first instance
    engaging public and private leaders in joint planning of the city's
    economic growth over the long term, using strategic economic
    planning and projections. The city and its business leaders must
    enhance each other's efforts using the same vision of the city's
    future.

3. Foster an "entrepreneurial attitude" among managers and em-
    ployees. This requires, first, that cities *redefine their role* from that
    of service provider to that of *service referral or brokerage*. It requires
    city employees to start thinking like businessmen: treating city
    money as though it were their own, building cash reserves, look-
    ing twice at projects that are not self-financing, and generally
    being "bottom line oriented."

4. Reduce program costs and variety. The entrepreneurial manager
    can choose freely from a variety of techniques: acting as a referral
    service to groups needing services, rather than providing the ser-
    vice; reducing demand, most often by raising user fees; di-
    vestiture of existing programs and capital stock; employing alter-
    native service mechanisms, including contracting out and
    contracting in, volunteers, and franchises.

5. Tailor service levels and tax rates to neighborhood need and
    useage levels.

6. Act as private lender, investor, and vendor of services. In this role,
    cities may take an equity position in private investments; buy
    whole for-profit businesses; or improve the financial status of ex-
    isting city-owned enterprises to increase revenues.

7. Create an entrepreneurial government structure, budget and per-
    sonnel system.

How have these elements of entrepreneurialism been implemented, and
how well have they worked? What criticisms can be made of all this?

ENCOURAGING THE PRIVATE SECTOR

American cities have sponsored campaigns to attract outside private
investors, even to the point of giving away land and buildings, throughout much of this century. In contrast the entrepreneurial cities and some
states are working towards a broader understanding of government's
proper role in economic development. This includes four elements: (1)
Maximizing the total wealth of the community, not simply focusing on

immediate business expansion; (2) Eliminating barriers to competition, especially government-created monopolies; (3) Creating a stable fiscal environment by keeping taxes low and bond ratings high; and (4) Providing adequate infrastructure, together with a vibrant downtown and healthy neighborhoods, to hold and attract business.

Maximizing The Total Wealth of the Community

At first blush this seems commonsense; but in fact, maximizing community wealth means that jobs are not the only or major short-term economic objective.[6] Boston, for example, has focused for over a decade on nurturing small, high-tech companies rather than trying to recruit big employers. As a result, Boston has not had over 3.5% unemployment in any recession in the past decade, even in 1978 and from 1981 to 1982, when unemployment reached 10% in Chicago and 15% in Detroit.

The real wealth of a community includes many things: the skills level of its workforce; the potential for growth of its industries; the quality of its neighborhoods and downtown; the level of development of its transportation and communications facilities; and the quality of its schools, from kindergarten through graduate bio-physics, to name just a few. It is not simply the dollar value of public and private sector output, although this is the easiest single measure of *output* as opposed to wealth.

GLENDALE, ARIZONA'S "GROSS CITY PRODUCT" (GCP)

The City of Glendale, Arizona has established a Gross City Product (GCP) measure of total production of goods and services. Developed jointly by Arizona State University and the city's Department of Strategic Planning, the measure is modelled after the Gross National Product (GNP) measure of the federal government, and the Gross State Product (GSP) measure, the latter developed by Arizona State University for the State of Arizona in 1984.

The new Gross City Product allows the city to make comparisons with both the state and national economies, according to Dr. Lee McPheters of the ASU Bureau of Business and Economic Research. It can be adjusted for inflation.

Sources: *Public Management,* 68, 7 (July 1986): 2; and Larry Stevenson, Department of Strategic Planning, City of Glendale, "Glendale Gross City Product and Main Economic Indicators. Summary Report" (April 1986).

From another angle, the real wealth of a city consists of the *degree of opportunity available to people of all social strata,* including opportunities for entrepreneurial development of private business. The entrepreneurial manager can maximize wealth thus defined by implementing the steps shown in the inset titled "Maximizing the Wealth of Cities."

MAXIMIZING THE WEALTH OF CITIES

1. Minimize special tax favors for select companies; provide low citywide taxes for all
2. Maintain high Moody ratings (at least A); follow GAAP; forbid speculative investments of reserves
3. Promote a favorable attitude toward business by city departments; show that the city is willing to go out of its way to help business start, expand, and relocate
4. Spend money on good schools and labor force training
5. Maintain neighborhood economic and residential viability and an attractive downtown; rely on the private sector for housing and cultural investment, for neighborhood facilities including parks and other amenities, and private citizen security programs and patrols.
6. Maintain fully adequate infrastructure: bridges, roads, sewage treatment, water. Encourage low-cost electricity supply
7. Focus efforts on helping *existing* businesses to expand, instead of disproportionate efforts on national advertising
8. Create Economic Zones to put jobs in place of unemployment. Foster new-business incubator facilities and quasi-public consulting help for new and expanding companies. Encourage venture capitalists (see Chapter 11, "Enterprise Zones: An Alternative To Federal Aid?").

Remove Barriers to Competition

In addition the entrepreneurial manager of the 1990s has his or her work cut out for him in removing the publically-created monopolies of the past two decades. In New York City a medallion costs $30,000 to operate a taxi. The number of cabs is limited and fares are high. In Washington, D.C., by contrast, a licence costs around $200 including insurance, and the rider can go over 20 blocks for around $2.00. Cabs are plentiful. The list in the inset titled "Encouraging State and Local Entrepreneurs" is a starting point for action.

ENCOURAGING STATE AND LOCAL ENTREPRENEURS

1. Limit the power of cities to grant monopolies to cable TV companies. Require the phasing out of monopoly cable franchises over time.
2. Eliminate the power of local government to grant monopolies to cab companies or to limit the number of cabs through exhorbitant fees.
3. Establish programs for Urban Homesteading that allow low-income private citizens to become owners of their own, or rental, housing.
4. Establish a "one stop" permitting and assistance method for new or expanding businesses.
5. Four or five times a year, hold meetings in the neighborhoods between your Department of City Development and neighborhood businessmen; bring charts and information; answer all questions on zoning, parking, and whatever else businessmen need to know.[7]
6. Eliminate state-level licensing requirements that act as barriers to entry.
7. Identify and modify or eliminate state and local regulations that make service provision difficult in health and day care.

Source: Based on Roger Vaughan *et al., The Wealth of States* (Washington, D.C.: Council of State Planning Agencies, Hall of the States, 1984), p. 60 *et. passim.*

Create A Stable Fiscal Environment

Many cities still provide a free tax ride for relocating companies. Tampa, Florida, for example, offers substantial "tax incentives" to attract private investors. Yet the city also offers some of the lowest taxes of any Florida city, a condition that encourages growth and relocation as much as any exceptionalist policy.[8] States that offer lower taxes seem clearly to increase their growth rates. Even Minnesota, governed by the liberal Farmer-Labor party, has been assiduously lowering its taxes in recent years to encourage investment. This may be "supply side economics" without benefit of clergy. The important point is that it seems to work.

Ironically, the tax-cutting measures of the 1970s such as Propositions 13 and 2½, which were bemoaned when passed, seem to have stimulated strong economic development. California, scene of the "Prop 13 deba-

Table 1. Income, Sales, Property Taxes, and Economic
Growth in States, 1970–1980

Growth Category	Income Tax/ Capita	Sales Tax/ Capita	Property Tax/Capita	All Taxes/ Capita
High growth states	$117.94	238.35	228.13	846.15
Medium growth states	303.26	223.13	238.04	987.52
Low growth states	265.69	222.11	363.56	1,066.33

Note: Figures for tax amounts are averages for the states within the category, weighted by population,
based on 1979–80 Department of Commerce data.

Source: Richard K. Vedder, "Rich States, Poor States: How High Taxes Inhibit Growth," *Journal of
Contemporary Studies,* 5, 4(Fall 1982): 19–32.

cle," leads all states in job development, having created over 2 million
new jobs between 1980 and 1985, an increase of 14.8%. University of
Massachusetts professor Ralph Whitehead Jr., advisor to liberal Massachusetts Governor Michael S. Dukakis, argues that the 17.6% reduction in taxes in Massachusetts between 1975 and 1978, caused largely by
Proposition 2½, actually helped. "Without Prop 2½ we would be on our
way to becoming a banana republic," he has stated.[9]

Provide Adequate Infrastructure

The focus on adequate infrastructure cuts two ways. On the one hand,
it is increasingly common for cities to demand that the developer include, at his expense, such amenities as streets (in residential areas),
street lights, libraries, parks, and water and sewer pipes. In California, a
leader in developer-paid amenities, the city and developer negotiate the
best deal each can make, a very entrepreneurial process. In Houston the
businessmen in the city's growing west side recently financed and con-
structed their own four-lane divided highway.[10]

When the city or county cannot afford to build or replace infrastructure, the private sector can do the job. With $500 billion of state and
local infrastructure coming due over the next decade this "privatization"
trend will necessarily increase, both because many infrastructure projects can be run as enterprises, and because the private sector can act so
much more quickly than government.[11] Auburn, Alabama (population
28,500) called in the private engineering firm of Metcalf and Eddy to
design, finance, and construct its new 5.4 MGD wastewater plant. From
the beginning of work in November 1984 to the first day of operation in
December 1985 required only 13 months,[12] an impossible schedule for
the public sector. (For examples of privatized and contracted services,
see Chapter 5.)

CREATE PUBLIC/PRIVATE VENTURES

In addition to helping entrepreneurs the entrepreneurial manager must foster a working partnership with the private sector. As City Manager of Visalia I joined the city's chamber of commerce. The creation of business incubators, redeveloping downtown, and any of the major projects sponsored by cities in recent years have been partnerships of some kind.[13] Job training in most cities is now under the overall guidance of local Private Industry Councils (PIC). Many school programs, including Adopt-A-School and combination business-education parks, have featured extensive private sector involvement.

The key to success in this area is the *cultivation of non-specific, long term relations with the business community*. Mayor Michael Boyle of Omaha, speaking at a conference on entrepreneurialism in 1984, stated the prime requisite. "I guess the key is that mayors who have been successful have decided to let the business community in," he said. "[The business community] has to feel comfortable in the city; they have to feel they are part of it."

Omaha's small business incubator is an example of what the mayor meant. The incubator was created in large part by private efforts. The mayor noted: "It really began with personal calls, personal relationships, bringing the business people to the office to have lunch. . . . I turned those relationships into dollars. When the time came, I was able to pick up the phone and put together some pretty substantial donations from the private sector." A grand total of no less than $2 million was raised for this purpose. "It's a very long, tedious process that requires personal relationships with the corporate leadership," said Boyle. "But it leads to good things."[14]

PUBLIC/PRIVATE PARTNERSHIPS IN BOSTON:
A SYSTEMMATIC METHOD OF PROBLEM SOLVING?

Boston is among the leaders of cities which have used public/private partnerships. Five years ago the leaders of the city's manufacturing, financial, and insurance industries, known as "The Vault," signed "The Boston Compact" with the city's School Department. Business promised to provide jobs to graduating city public school graduates, in exchange for improvement in student attendance, drop out rates, and reading and math scores. By 1986 between 350 and 400 Boston firms have signed the Compact, and in 1985 placed 800 graduates in permanent jobs and provided 2,500 summer jobs. So far the School Department has not significantly improved drop out rates or academic scores. *(continued)*

In a second Compact program, Boston businesses have put up a $5 million endowment, including a $1 million grant from New England Mutual Life. With it the city has established the Action Center for Educational Services and Scholarships to help every Boston high school graduate to find scholarship money for college. When existing scholarship sources fail, the Center, through its endowment, guarantees financial aid to every city graduate who wants to attend college.

In a third program, about 90% completed in 1987, the Boston Housing Partnership assists community organizations in the rehabilitation of abandoned and deteriorated multi-family buildings. Some 700 units will be rehabilitated this way, at a total development cost of $1.3 million.

In addition, the Housing Partnership's director Robert Whittlesley has stated that private business support enabled the Partnership to provide umbrella financing for neighborhood Community Development Corporations (CDCs) when those organizations themselves were unable to significantly improve neighborhood housing. The support has also led the State of Massachusetts to float a $22 million housing bond issue, and has created a channel to federal mortgage agencies.

Sources: Boston *Globe.* JFK School of Government, Harvard University, *Profiles in Innovation* (September 1986), p. 24.

FOSTER AN "ENTREPRENEURIAL ATTITUDE"

The entrepreneurial attitude is the antagonist of the bureaucratic mentality. It draws on Webster's definition of the term, "Doing things a new way," to be creative and unorthodox in approaching problems. Perhaps the most important requirement of this new attitude is the willingness of city officialdom to redefine their role. Instead of providing every service that is demanded by every constituency, the traditional model that requires the city to be "all things to all people," cities need to ask themselves the question put by Steve Garman, recent manager of Pensacola Florida: "What business are we in?" What services do we *want* to provide? And instead of providing all services to all citizens, cities should look at themselves primarily as brokers of services: providing some, and referring to the private sector, both profit and nonprofit, for others. Is there a need for low income housing in City X? The city cannot provide all poor people with a house or apartment, and federal funds are drying up. But it can maintain a file on innovative programs in low-income home ownership that work elsewhere—such as Marin County, California's shared housing—and help local churches and foundations get involved. Professor Ted Kolderie has expressed this exactly: cities are not responsible for providing all services, but for seeing to it that services are provided by some entity—private, semiprivate, another level of government—and for bringing citizen and provider together.[15]

"Thinking entrepreneurially" also means demanding that your department heads and program managers treat the money they are spending as their own. As manager of Visalia, California I told my mangers: "When you are deciding what to spend money on, ask yourself: 'If it were my money, would I spend it?' If the answer to that is no, then your decision is already made."

Thinking entrepreneurially also means asking your department heads

---

MARKETING CITY SERVICES IN GARDENA, CALIFORNIA

On the instructions of its city council, the Human Services Department in the City of Gardena, California (population 50,000) developed the following services packages:

1. *The [Troubled] Employee Assistance Program (EAP).* This program provides diagnosis and referral to appropriate mental health counseling centers, for company employees whose personal habits, including drug abuse, interfere with their on-job performance.
2. *ESL In The Factory.* On a cost-plus basis, employers pay for credentialed city staff to instruct non-English speaking immigrant workers in vocational English. Classes are on-site.
3. *Computerized Child Care Referral.* For a fee, the city uses its computer to match employees from enrolled companies with licensed facilities, based on the particular needs of parent and child.
4. *Supervisory Training.* Many small and medium sized companies lack the resources to provide training for their supervisors, many of whom were good technical workers promoted to supervisor level without formal management training. The Human Services Department has developed training curricula for local companies and provides facilitators to conduct the workshops for a fee.

Source: Frank Benest, "Gardena's Approach to Entrepreneurship," *Western City Magazine,* 62, 9 (September 1986): 27.

to inventory their programs and services, and identify those which can be sold to raise revenue for the department. It means requiring that the department director be responsible not only for spending money, but to some extent, for finding ways of obtaining it. This was the good purpose St. Paul had in mind in calling for Revenue Centers. This is what Pensacola did when city manager Steve Garman called for an inventory of all city services which could be sold for income, and enterprises for which user fees should be raised.[16] It remains a part of operations in Visalia.

And it is espoused by the City of Long Beach, whose manager considers each department a "revenue center," and who recently completed an inventory of its services to see which can be sold to private customers. Long Beach found that the information and research services generated by its library are of such value to local business that it has started to make a small charge for these services. The renting of video, film, and audio tapes is identical to the private video rental market, and the Library now charges a small fee for such rentals. Branch libraries now charge for use of meeting rooms. The Library considered but rejected any fees for circulation of books or magazines.[17]

The whole purpose of management is to solve problems. That is what entrepreneurial management is all about: getting the creative juices to flow, thinking in nontraditional ways, cutting across traditional notions of what is public, private, and personal. It is vital to get managers to think as owners; to invest them with the sense of personal responsibility and motivation that managers in private firms are supposed to exhibit. Part of this new mind-set comes through rewarding managers and employees abundantly for cost-saving, revenue-enhancing ideas (see p. 226). Part of it is in the language that is used to identify city functions. If the word "department" is replaced with the phrase "Profit Center" or "Revenue Center" then the concept of ownership comes alive. In Visalia the city manager's "state of the city" report is called the "Report to the Shareholders"—the voters. The City Council is the Board of Directors and the city manager is the Chief Executive Officer. In 1984 we ended the year with a surplus. As city manager, I proposed that this money be refunded to the shareholders as a dividend payment, making Visalia the first city in America to make a proposal in these terms. Language is important. When you call the city a business corporation, that rings a bell with taxpayers and businessmen. It is a language they understand and it pays dividends.

REDUCE LIABILITIES, COSTS, AND DEMANDS

Cities need to adopt cost accounting and lifecycle costing, to follow GAAP principles scrupulously, and improve their financial management practices. However, prior to this, a set of terms must be agreed on that allow public officials to really understand what costs them money and what does not. Cities carry physical assets like buildings and watermains on their books as assets. They are assets only if the city decides to sell them and realize income—a rarity. Until such time, the physical plant— mains, valves, meters—are a drain on the city's revenue. Only the sale of water is an asset, and this may or may not cover the operating/replacement expenses. It is crucial to note that most cities do not have their books arranged to make this central fact easily determinable.

To remedy this cities should go through their programs and capital stock and divide them into "net gainers" and "net losers." "Net gainers" are programs that yield more in revenue than they cost; "net losers" are programs that are a drain on finances. New developments that require

---

QUESTIONS CITIES SHOULD ASK BEFORE UNDERTAKING
NEW OR EXPANDED SERVICES OR FUNCTIONS

1. What will the program cost, in direct and indirect expenses?
2. What follow-on expenses will be required in subsequent years?
3. What expectations and constituency groups will be created to demand future action?
4. How much staff time and council meeting time will be necessary to properly manage the activity?
5. What is the probability of the program generating net revenues?
6. Can the program or activity be an asset to some other group, if not to city government?
7. Will the city reduce financial risk by divesting the program?
8. What can the city do to maximize the asset potential of the program?

Source: Steve Garman, "The Terminal City," *State and Local Government Review* (Winter 1983): 37

---

more in outlays than they yield in revenues should be gone into cautiously or not at all. New housing developments in which the city pays all infrastructure and for which anticipated taxes will not cover investment and repair costs are the most important example.

Reducing costs has been discussed earlier in this chapter, and other chapters deal with major techniques for doing this. But there is one area of cost reduction which needs examination: the total cost of salaries and fringe benefits. As distinct from personnel practices (discussed on p. 224, this chapter), wage and fringe benefits are a subject in themselves.

They constitute the largest single source of expense for any corporation, public or private. Revising the very generous retirement funding formulas that cities have adopted over the past two decades would be a useful starting point. Cities can even forego their traditional pension systems and instead open up IRAs for *new* employees. Over 30 years, an IRA which pays an annual rate of 8% will be worth well over half a million dollars. Automatic cost-of-living escalators in wage agreements are among the biggest causes of rising costs. Automatic increases for completing six months employment, or linking pay to levels of other departments (as in police-fire parity) are practices that can be corrected locally. Of course all of this dovetails with the need to pay employees big bonuses, of 15% regardless of the dollar amount, for all suggestions which result in savings.

Reducing service demand can be done several ways. One way is conservation, and the most typical form of conservation is in energy useage. How well this can pay off is illustrated by the city of Seattle which, in 1977, considered investing in two atomic energy plants to assure the city of an adequate energy supply into the 1990s. While this move was being studied, the City Council commissioned a full study by an outside consultant on city energy needs. Based on the consultant's report, the Council ruled out investment in energy plants, and began an aggressive program of citywide energy conservation. Today, the city has an energy surplus.[18]

Conservation among citizens is equally important. In northern California the Pacific Gas and Electric Company pays cash to cities that can persuade their citizens to reduce electricity consumption during peak demand hours.[19] Fire departments that buy carloads of sprinkler systems, and pass them along to consumers at no markup, are probably saving the city money. Vaccinations against illness eliminates public and private hospitalization costs.

Underlying demand management is the shift *away from the supply mentality*. Landfills provide an illustration. In California some 65% of all county landfills will be filled to capacity by the year 1996. The supply mentality would argue that California is running out of capacity and should invest in more landfills. The demand management psychology argues that California has *too much waste*, and looks at ways of reducing the volume. These ways include trash-to-energy plants, recycling, composting, and reducing the amount of waste generated by homes and businesses.[20]

"Targeting" service delivery levels and tax rates is another important technique in reducing costs and approaching the ideal of payment-for-service. Robert Biller argues that cities should not provide the same level of service to every neighborhood. Some areas will require two or more garbage pickups per week, some only one. Some neighborhoods, and especially downtown, use an enormous amount of electricity for lighting, while some use distinctly less. Some neighborhoods may want less street sweeping and more recreation. Biller argues that each neighborhood should get what it needs or "demands" via surveys.[21]

A form of neighborhood targeted tax rates can be created by the formation of "improvement districts," a common expedient in Los Angeles and San Diego and cities across the country. A geographically-defined area taxes itself for a special benefit used by residents of that area—a park, a road or culvert or overpass, or upgraded water pipes. An improvement district is a useful halfbreed, somewhere between a pure tax and a user fee.

THE CITY AS "PRIVATE" INVESTOR

The entrepreneurial model's sharpest break with tradition is its willingness to allow cities to invest in income-producing businesses. Fairfield pioneered this in California, stepping in as an investor in an enormous regional shopping center in the 1970s, taking the risks like any other investor, and in the 1980s receiving up to 15% of the center's profits.[22] In Visalia we set up nonprofit corporations to act as entrepreneurs for public housing, and to bring a major private hotel to the city. Sarasota Springs, New York (population 24,000) created a community hotel corporation and built 750 new hotel and motel rooms for the city, in an operation financed by a local bank and managed jointly with the city.[23]

In York, Pennsylvania (population 50,000) the mayor has established the York City Industrial Park (YCIP), in which the city is a co-development partner with the York County Industrial Authority, thereby sharing the risks and profits between city and developer. The city receives profits from any land sales and plows these profits back into other economic activities.[24]

In Visalia, when a group of private developers building a local industrial park needed to sell part of their land, the city bought it, put in improvements, and sold it for a profit of $600,000.[25]

Of course certain cities have run utilities and other enterprises at a profit. Palo Alto, California (population 56,400) and Traverse City, Michigan (population 18,000) both own the city electric utility, as does Lansing, Michigan (population 128,500).

In the South it is more common for cities to own utilities. Pensacola, Florida divides its enterprises into four categories:

1. Profitable activities;
2. Marginally profitable activities;

3. Activities structured to break even only; and
4. Activities which can partially, but not completely, support themselves.

The city sold its wastewater utility to a nonprofit private authority but continues to own the Port facility, the city airport, and the city gas utility. The Airport and the gas utility operate at a profit, and the profits are used to provide other city services. Some $7 million a year comes to the city through such profits.

Palm Springs, California (population 32,000) recently floated a $6.5 million bond issue to build a cogeneration project which will supply 100% of the city government's heating requirements and 87% of its cooling requirements. Some 40% of the project's power output will be sold to Southern California Edison.[26]

Prophetstown, Illinois (population 4,100) recently sold $70,000 worth of stock to its own citizens to create a for-profit economic development corporation. This corporation plans to purchase two small manufacturing firms and a for-profit service firm.[27]

The attitude of the entrepreneurial cities on private profit-making is expressed by Visalia's John Biane, head of the city's real estate program: "Other cities do a project and see what the expense is. We do a project and figure how much money we can make."[28]

Both cities and states have acted as *venture capitalists*. Some 20 states have put up a total of $280 million in venture capital for new, usually smaller businesses. Cedar Rapids (population 110,000), Ithaca, New York (population 29,000) and New Haven, Connecticut (population 126,000) all have venture capital pools, in which the city directly supplants the private venture capital banks.[29]

AN ENTREPRENEURIAL GOVERNMENT STRUCTURE AND PRACTICE

If cities are going to be truly entrepreneurial they must give top management the freedom to hire and fire key staff with some degree of freedom. That means loosening up encrusted Civil Service and personnel rules, and this is not easy. In St. Paul, following the RAND study of 1984, the city passed a new Charter, redesigned the city personnel department, and tried to loosen up Civil Service Commission rules.[30] Yet implementation of significant change has not been easy. The mayor today has only slightly more freedom in choosing administrators than he did before the IPA study recommendations.

Visalia has taken a somewhat different tack, establishing an Employee

RECOMMENDED CIVIL SERVICE CHANGES FOR ST. PAUL

In addition to tne RAND study (see p. 211) St. Paul hired the Institute for Public Administration (IPA) to examine and make recommendations on "modernizing" the city's venerable personnel/civil service system. After a survey that went to all city and school board employees (and which yielded a 50% return rate) and a series of background papers on various aspects of possible reforms, IPA recommended the following as ways to make St. Paul's system more "entrepreneurial":

1. *Accountability of the Chief Personnel Officer.* This person was formerly covered by Civil Service. IPA recommended that the Mayor appoint the Personnel Director for a fixed term and oversee personnel administration. The Civil Service Commission should be an appeals board only
2. *Job Titles and Salary Grades.* Reduce the number of job titles. Currently the city has 800 job titles for 4,200 employees.
3. *Recruitment and Appointment of Employees.* Instead of simply choosing among the top three on civil service exams, choose from among the top ten; use an oral exam, and training and experience, as employment criteria.
4. *Managers.* Exempt more managerial positions from the classified service; provide managers with more in-service training.
5. *Performance Appraisal.* Employees and supervisors should jointly establish rating criteria, with a system of tasks and standards more job-related and tied to organizational goals.

With a few modifications these recommendations were accepted by the Mayor and the City Council. The most significant aspect of this process was the amount of participation by employees and the public, which led to a "resounding consensus" around the recommendations.

Source: George Latimer and Linda K. Carlisle, "Personnel Modernization in St. Paul: A Model for Participation and Consensus Building," *National Civic Review,* 74, 8 (September 1985): 365–371.

Development Program to help talented people move up the ranks regardless of where they start. Carol Cairns was a youth development officer for the Police Department when she signed up. In 1986 she was running the city's Human Resources Department. Two other department heads have come from—surprise—the police force, and when the airport manager left, his secretary got the job.[31]

Visalia has a strong reward system. If an employee comes up with ideas that make or save money for the city, he or she keeps 15% of the savings, with no cap on the total figure. This is more generous than most public bonus programs, and approaches "gainsharing" programs in the private sector.

Perhaps the most important contribution that Visalia has made to entrepreneurial government procedures is its budgeting system. Because the city is in an expansion mode[32] the city manager sets each departments' budget based on a formula: last year's amount, plus the percent of population increase, plus one-half of the rise in the consumer price index. There are no exceptions. If the police department wants new cruisers, it has to generate the savings from annual appropriations based on this formula. In Visalia this has resulted in the Police Department finding ways to stretch the usefulness of its cruisers from three to five years. Department heads cannot come to the city manager and say "I need more money for the same level of service." They have to make do with what they get. If new methods result in consistent savings, the city ultimately will take that money back. Visalia calls this "Expenditure Control Budgeting," and in 1982, after five years of the system, I was able to take back $1.9 million in savings from departments that no longer needed the funds.

CRITIQUE: DO ENTREPRENEURIAL CITIES GO TOO FAR?

California columnist Ed Salzman has called entrepreneurial city management "urban socialism."[33] In becoming investors and venture capitalists the entrepreneurial city is of course risking city assets. So far, in Visalia and elsewhere, the investments have been winners. In San Jose, California however, the result recently was not so agreeable. In 1984 the city Finance Department invested a substantial portion of the city's investment portfolio in long-term, high risk bonds and lost, causing the city to lose an alleged $60 million and costing the city Finance Officer his job. Cities are not trained investors, and they may not all have such surefire investments as a regional shopping center in a Sunbelt city.

The fact of "leveraging investments," which works to the city's advantage when the economy is going up, works just as strongly to its disadvantage when the economy is on the decline. A recession could cause investments that were once paying cities 15% of the net to start losing money, just at a time when the same recession is cutting city tax revenues.[34] Since the early 1980s, when "entrepreneurialism" has been on the rise in American cities, the economy has also been on a prolonged rise. The test of the city-as-investor will occur when the next, inevitable business recession hits. A city with no "capitalist investments" might end up in a much better financial position.

CONCLUSION: WHAT'S LEFT?

Granting the just-stated criticism, there are all the other aspects of entrepreneurialism that constitute real improvements in city management practices. The effort to make managers creative; to get employees thinking like owners, to be more productive; taking inventory of the city's real financial "gainers" and "losers"; the lowering of the barriers between the public and private sectors, with all-out encouragement of the private sector in creative ways; requiring that major budget increases come out of increased productivity: putting all these elements together, the resulting total package is a strong net plus for city management. In efforts to revamp Civil Service, while met with continued resistance, the entrepreneurial cities are pointing to the single most important area for economizing.

What is left is a model, the entrepreneurial model, for city management. Its very essence is to shatter tradition and to bring financial realities into the center of public management. It is happening in many different ways and at different speeds across the country. The good news is that it is happening, and that, in an era of dwindling free federal aid, it offers the single most useful model for city management in the coming decade.

ACKNOWLEDGMENTS

The author wishes to thank in particular Dr. Carl Bellone of Cal State Hayward, and Mr. David Osborne of Dedham, Massachusetts for their assistance in locating material for this article.

NOTES AND REFERENCES

1. See the periodical *Public Choice* (Virginia Polytechnic Institute, Center for the Study of Public Choice, Blacksburg). See also James M. Buchanan and Gordon Tullock, *The Calculus of Consent* (Ann Arbor: University of Michigan Press, 1962); and James M. Buchanan and H. Geofrey Brennan, *The Reason of Rules: Constitutional Political Economy* (Cambridge: Cambridge University Press, 1985).

2. B. Gale Wilson, "The Entrepreneurial Municipal Strategy," *Public Management*

(April 1983): 11; and Ben Merritt, "B. Gale Wilson, Fairfield's City Manager," *Public Management* (August 1986): 18.

3.   Kevin Neels and Michael Caggiano, *The Entrepreneurial City: Innovations in Finance and Management for Saint Paul* (Santa Monica, CA: RAND, 1984), 135 pp.

4.   The Parking and Transit Fund, for example, includes five programs, including Parking Meter Collections (a revenue earner) and the self-supporting Parking Enforcement unit. Source: Speech of Mayor George Latimer to City Council (August 14, 1986), p. 6.

5.   Peter Hames, Saint Paul City Manager's Office, Interview (November 1986).

6.   See Roger Vaughan *et al.*, *The Wealth of States. Policies For a Dynamic Economy* (Washington, D.C.: Council of State Planning Agencies, 1984). This short volume is a succinct exposition of this expanded concept of creating wealth. The chapters are entitled: Creating Wealth. Traditional Views on Economic Development. The Entrepreneurial Environment. Investing in Innovation. Investing in Human Capital. Investing in Public Capital. Strategy.

7.   City of Milwaukee, Department of City Development, Interview (November 1986). This is the technique pioneered by Milwaukee.

8.   See Robert Duckworth *et al.*, *The Entrepreneurial American City* (Washington, D.C.: Partners for Liveable Places and HUD, 1986) and National Council of State Legislatures, *Taxation of Business by American State and Local Governments* (Denver, CO: NCSL, 1986).

9.   "Top Growth States Have Tax Sense," *Insight* (October 27, 1986), p. 51.

10. Thomas Hazlett, "They Built Their Own Highway," *Reason Magazine* 15, 7 (November 1983), pp. 22–30.

11. See David M. Saltiel and Steven N. Avruch, "A Review of the State Privatization Statutes," *Privatization Review*, 2, 4 (Fall 1986): 30–50. The *Review*, an excellent quarterly update by practicing experts, is published by The Privatization Council, Inc., of Washington, D.C.

12. Mr. Doug Watkins, City Manager, City of Auburn, Alabama, Interview (June 1986).

13. Useful volumes on public/private partnerships include: Barbara H. Moore, ed., *The Entrepreneur In Local Government* (Washington, D.C.: International City Management Association, 1983); Committee for Economic Development, *Public Private Partnerships: An Opportunity for Urban Communities* (New York: CED, 1982); John J. Kirlin and Anne M. Kirlin, *Public Choices, Private Resources* (Sacramento, CA: Cal-Tax, 1982); Gary E. Stout and Joseph E. Vitt, *Public Incentives and Financing Techniques for CoDevelopment* (Washington, D.C.: Urban Land Institute, 1982); E.S. Savas, *Privatizing the Public Sector* (Chatham, NJ: Chatham House, 1982); Verne Johnson and Ted Kolderie, "Public Private Partnerships: Useful but Sterile," *Foundation News* (March/April 1984), pp. 29–33. *National Civic Review* (November 1983): entire issue on public/private partnerships.

For a fascinating and useful examination of such partnerships back to our earliest history see Terry L. Cooper, "The Public Private Continuum: Interdependence in a Democratic Society," *Public Budgeting & Finance* 5, 3 (Autumn 1985): 99–115.

14. United States Conference of Mayors, *Entrepreneurship in Cities: The Mayor's Role* (Washington, D.C.: USCM, 1984), pp. 23–24.

15. Ted Kolderie, "Let's Not Say Privatization," *Urban Resources*, 2, 4 (Summer 1985): 11.

16. Steve Garman, "The Terminal [Dying] City," *State and Local Government Review* (Winter 1983), pp. 32–37. Mr. Garman is former City Manager of Pensacola, Florida.

17. Long Beach Library Director of Public Services, Interview (December 1986).

18. Mr. Larry Gunn, City of Seattle Conservation Program, Interview (December 1986).

19. League of California Cities, *Alternative Service Delivery Project* (Sacramento: Author, 1984), p. 51.

20. Norman R. King, "Pricing Policies and the Economics of Demand Management," *Western City Magazine* (October 1982); Carl Bellone, "Public Entrepreneurship: New Role Expectations For Local Government," *Urban Analysis*, vol. 9 (London: Gordon & Breach Science Publications Ltd., 1985). Employing demand management for waste is suggested in California State Waste Management Board, *A Comprehensive Plan for Management of Nonhazardous Waste in California* (Sacramento: CSWMB, 1985), Appendix B.

21. Robert Biller, "Turning Conflicts Into Challenges," *Public Management*, 64, 1 (January 1982): 2–4.

22. See Wilson, "The Entrepreneurial Municipal Strategy."

23. See Duckworth et al., *The Entrepreneurial American City*, p. 42.

24. *Ibid.*, p. 11.

25. David Osborne, "The Most Entrepreneurial City in America," *Inc* (September 1985), pp. 54–61.

26. Duckworth *et al.*, *The Entrepreneurial American City*, p. 22.

27. *Ibid.*, p. 40.

28. Osborne, "The Most Entrepreneurial City in America," p. 56.

29. Duckworth *et al.*, *The Entrepreneurial American City*, pp. 33–34.

30. Ann Marie Walsh, Executive Director, Institute for Public Administration (New York City), Interview (December 1986).

31. Osborne, "The Most Entrepreneurial City in America," p. 56.

32. For budget management in the reduction phase, see Chapters 4 and 8, this volume.

33. Ed Salzman, "Personal Perspective," *California Journal* (1982): 310.

34. The author is indebted to Mr. Rob Munson for this point.

Chapter 11

ENTERPRISE ZONES:
AN ALTERNATIVE TO FEDERAL AID?

Edward C. Hayes

SUMMARY. Enterprise Zones (henceforth Zones) offer a radical *potential* departure from the usual welfare-cum-demolition programs for the inner city. As originally envisaged, they were to be like free trade zones, with taxes and regulations drastically rolled back allowing the private sector to build permanent jobs for low income people. This article looks at the original theory, at the history of federal programs, and at the original theory of Zones. It then examines the major provisions of state/local Zone programs, and their evolution into fairly traditional tax-incentive programs. It concludes by looking at the issues associated with the Zones strategy: Has the original, and most potent, vision of Zones been abandoned too soon? Have Zones, as they have evolved, been effective? And the payoff question: do Zones, or could Zones of any model, serve as a substitute for federal welfare and grants in aid?

ENTERPRISE ZONES: THE POLICY SETTING

Prior to Enterprise Zones the federal government had two broad approaches to the poverty of the inner city. The most familiar, because it has been so expanded in the past two decades, is the welfare approach: putting money into the poor's pocket, and the landlord's pocket; food into refrigerators; and money into the accounts of local governments to pay for poverty program administration. All of these objectives, begun in the New Deal and expanded in the Great Society and since, have taken form as programs: Aid to Families with Dependent Children (AFDC), Section 8 housing supplements, food stamps and milk for pregnant mothers (WIC), General Revenue Sharing. Between 1964 and 1989 the cost of these welfare programs, symbolized in the 1960s by the Office of Economic Opportunity, amounted cumulatively to billions of dollars, A Marshall Plan for the cities which exceeded the $14 billion real Marshall Plan to Europe by many times, but with less results.

The second federal approach to urban poverty, which began in the 1930s and has analogues today, has been the demolition and rebuilding of physically deteriorated parts of the city. It began as slum clearance with the public housing act of the late 1930s; was strengthened by the Housing Act of 1949, which promised "a decent dwelling in a suitable living environment for every American"; and was forwarded by the urban renewal of the 1950s and 1960s. The Model Cities legislation and programs of the late 1960s and 1970s continued massive demolition activities, with large land price writedowns and resale to private businesses or residential contractors. Land was cleared, and in the bulk of projects through the early 1970s, demolition of low-income housing units took place with no provision for new quarters for residents. This resulted in mass displacement, overcrowding, and the creation of more tawdry conditions at the rim of the cleared areas.[1]

These two approaches had opposite impacts on the poor. With its massive transfer payments to low-income recipients, the federal government was kind. In its slum clearance projects it was often ruthless. Cleared land frequently remained as vacant lots for anywhere from one year to five years. Former residents, displaced and doubled up with relatives, could return to the site of their old building, gaze in wonder at the weeds, and draw their own conclusions about the arcane notion "policy implementation."

The failures of both approaches have been noted and debated frequently. It has been argued that the more welfare was given, the more the poor lost their will to work, leading to a spiral downward.[2] That thesis was disputed, but the vast demolition of housing and "ghetto" businesses is not subject to debate. In places like Oakland, where some 8,900 housing units were demolished between 1955 and 1970,[3] the poverty-level housing stock was radically reduced, laying the groundwork for housing problems of the poor, now called "the homeless," in the 1980s. Nationwide, tens of thousands of small businesses were eliminated. Oakland never kept count. In the large urban redevelopment project in the Kenwood-Hyde Park section of Chicago, 641 businesses were in the area before redevelopment in the 1960s. Of these, only 233 survived disruption.[4] Blocks of commercial structures, including some buildings in first class condition, were torn down and replaced with condominiums, removing the old local businesses and local sources of employment.

Finally, the HUD-sponsored and funded public housing projects often became the slums they intended to replace, filled with crime and rapid physical decay.[5]

The outcry from middle-class critics and newly-created local poverty leaders against bulldozing policies moved Washington to its most recent approach, the Community Development Block (CDBG) program. The CDBG program put an end to mass bulldozing, and created policy boards staffed in part by local residents. Under President Carter, as Chapter 1 indicates (see especially Figure 1) the amount of grants of all kinds, while continuing to increase in absolute size, began a pronounced drop as a percent of local government income.

The Reagan administration entered Washington in 1980 with an intellectual rationale for greater cuts developed by a host of supply-side writers, who argued that the way to help the poor was by tax cuts, capital formation, and job creation, not transfer payments and welfare. Charles Murray's *Losing Ground,* published in 1984, while hotly contested, strengthened the Reagan administration critique of welfare by arguing that, in the late 1970s, as transfer payments to the poor skyrocketed the number of poor actually increased.[6] Policy oriented research by the Heritage Foundation examined the theory and track record of Enterprise Zones, and Free Trade Zones in England and around the world, and made applications to the United States.[7]

The yin and yang of British enterprise zone theory was the *reduction of government taxes and regulations in the zone economy* to effect a *more rapid rate of capital formation* and growth in overall economic activity. The models looked at by Professor Peter Hall, the architect of the British program, were Singapore, Hong Kong, and the free trade zones in ports around the world, all the epitome of unregulated capitalism. The absence of taxes and regulations in these areas is as well known as the fact of their rapid growth and full employment. Hall and his Heritage Foundation interpreters argued that radical deregulation, getting government out of the way, would allow "freed capitalism" to go to work creating jobs in poverty areas in the Western world.[8]

In Singapore and Hong Kong the entire apparatus of the Administrative State is nonexistent. To follow the Hong Kong example literally in the United States might have meant any or all of the following:

Regulatory intervention: *Deregulation:* eliminate minimum wage laws, building codes, environmental quality requirements, occupational health and safety laws.

     Tax changes: *Tax reduction/elimination:* sales tax; corporate
                       income, capital gains, and property tax.

It is the *absence* of such regulations, and in Free Trade Zones, the complete *absence* of taxes, that makes these economic units flourish.

THE CENTRAL QUESTION

The program that was originally talked about by Heritage, conservative groups, and some Congressmen before any legislation was introduced, was based on the original conception of Enterprise Zones—Enterprise Zones$_1$, so to speak. The initial idea in 1980 and 1981 was to fashion a Great Alternative to the Great Society: in place of federal grants and outright cash assistance, the new federal program would be the "privatization" model, according to which taxes and regulations of all kinds would be reduced in selected low-income areas of American cities—or, in a phrase, Supply Side for the ghetto. The liberals, so the argument went, had had fifteen years of massive federal aid programs, and still the slums persisted and poverty grew; it was now time to let the private sector have its shot.

PROPOSED FEDERAL LEGISLATION: KEMP-GARCIA, 1982 AND SINCE

The first federal legislation advocating Zones was introduced by two New York Congressmen of opposite political stripe, conservative Republican Jack Kemp and liberal Democrat Robert Garcia. Introduced as the "Enterprise Zone Tax Act" in 1982, the bill provided for large tax rollbacks and for the creation of foreign trade zones. It did not make it out of Democratic-controlled House Committees, although it had, remarkably, the support of the liberal urban lobbies, including the National League of Cities. But what it, and its 1983 successor bill, failed to do was anything real about deregulation; it took back in one sentence what it gave in another, marking the progress of thinking from Enterprise Zones$_1$ to Enterprise Zones$_2$:

- *Tax Relief:* Elimination of all federal capital gains taxes on investment within Zones. An additional investment tax credit for investment within Zones, equally 5% for personal property and 10% for new construction. The bill insured that Industrial Development Bonds (IDBs) would continue in Zones. In addition, an employer credit was provided, giving employers credit for hiring disadvantaged workers. The credit was equal to *50% of the worker's wage for three years.*

- *Personal Tax Relief:* Provides for an employee personal income tax credit for wages earned, equal to 5% or more of income.
- *Foreign Trade Zones:* Whenever possible and desired, foreign trade zones should be established within enterprise zones.
- *Regulatory Relief: State and local governments may together apply for the modification of Federal regulations if such modification is in the public interest, will not overturn a statutory requirement, and will not present a risk to health, safety, or the environment. Accordingly, there is no change proposed in minimum wage.*[9]

Enterprise Zones$_2$ represented a huge retreat from the Peter Hall model, turning Zones into a tax incentives program. This is their essential configuration at the state level today. This still would have been a significant program, because the federal government is capable of offering huge rebates if it is of a mind. But again the Democratic House refused to pass a bill. For the 1986–87 session, therefore, Zone advocates introduced legislation which represented a marked departure: tax rollbacks were scaled back or dropped completely so that some kind of bill could be passed and HUD could designate 100 federal Zones. Even so, the bill failed to clear the House Ways and Means Committee.[10]

As a result of this failure, state Enterprise Zones are the only Zones in existence. It must be admitted that, without federal tax incentives, and without either federal deregulation or much state or local deregulation, the Enterprise Zone$_1$ idea cannot be put to a full and fair test. Nevertheless twenty-seven states, plus the District of Columbia, have designated Zones in 734 local jurisdictions (cities or counties), and it is the job of the remainder of this chapter to examine how well state-designated Enterprise Zones have done their job.

ENTERPRISE ZONES AT THE STATE LEVEL

The failure of federal Zone legislation has had one peculiarly beneficial result: a burst of creative energy at the state level. The variety of state approaches, and their tailored quality for local situations, demonstrates how powerful the mechanism of federalism can be when the federal government gives the state and local levels room to run.

What are the programs and policies of these Zones, and do sub-numerals 1 or 2 apply? In Table 1 we see the broad difference between the privatisation model of Zones, and the way Zones at the state level have actually developed.

In general state Zones have dropped the original Peter Hall "freed enterprise" definition almost entirely. Instead they have developed En-

Table 1.   Enterprise Zone Models: Privatization (Enterprize Zones₁) and
Public/Private Venture (Enterprise Zone₂) Models

Broad Approach	Policies and Programs	Model
1. Regulatory intervention	*Deregulation:* eliminate minimum wage laws, building codes, environmental quality laws, occupational and safety laws.	Privatization
2. Tax Changes	*Tax Elimination:* Sales tax, property tax, corporate income and capital gains tax. *Tax reduction:* sales tax, property tax, corporate income and capital gains tax.	Privatization
3. Grants and Loans	*Grants and loans:* CDBG, EDA, UDAG, SBA programs, reimbursements for on-job training (JTPA), public financing of infrastructure, housing, community facilities.	Public/Private Ventures

Source: Very broadly modified from chart by Richard A. Whitman and Deborah K. Belasich, "Implementing and Evaluating a State Enterprise Zone Program," Paper delivered at the April 1986 ASPA Conference, Anaheim.

terprise Zones₂ in which existing regulatory legislation at the state and local level is left almost entirely intact. The notion of privatization has been replaced by the concept of public/private partnerships between the state and local governments, on the one hand, and the private sector, on the other. The entire picture which emerges is that of an enhanced, traditional state or local economic development program, featuring a combination of tax incentives and economic inducements such as assembled land, new infrastructure, and tax credits for hiring the poor—all programs which were in place before Enterprise Zones. At the heart of state Zone programs are *tax credits* and *sales tax exemptions* for businesses locating or expanding within Zones.

Of all the "policies" advanced by Zones, tax incentives are the most numerous, and the most effective. The conclusion, drawn by both the National Conference of State Legislatures and the Urban Institute, that Enterprise Zones are primarily tax-incentive programs, is fully justified. An examination of all incentives offered by four states through 1986 shows the centrality of tax incentives in Zone programs (see Table 3).

Table 2. Types of State Enterprise Zone Incentives Available to Firms Located Within a Zone

Type of Incentive	Available			Not Available	Missing Cases
	Statewide Before EZ Program	New for EZ Only	New Statewide		
Below Market Loans	12	2	0	4	0
Tax Credits for Business Investment	4	7	1	5	1
Income Tax Credits for Employers	5	9	0	3	1
Sales Tax Exemption	2	10	0	5	1
Public Work Grants	8	1	1	6	2
Job Training	15	0	0	2	1
Tax Increment Financing	8	0	3	5	2
Deregulatory Action	0	8	0	8	2

Source: Roy E. Green and Michael A. Brintnall, "State Enterprise Zone Programs: Variations in Structure and Coverage," paper presented at the 1986 ASPA Conference, Anaheim, California (April 1986).

237

Table 3.   Deregulatory, Tax and Grant/Loan Incentives
           for Enterprise Zones in Four States

Connecticut

Deregulation	Negligible
Tax Changes	50% reduction in State corporate business tax for 10 years, provided that 30% of the firm's employees are zone or city residents or JTPA eligible municipal residents
	Assessments fixed over a 7-year period for new or improved residential or commercial/retail projects
	Purchase of replacement parts for manufacturing machinery are exempt from sales tax
	80% real and personal property tax abatements for new manufacturing projects
Grants and Loans	Employment Training Vouchers
	$1,000 provided to manufacturers for each new job created, provided that 30% of new hires are zone residents or JTPA-eligible municipal residents

California (Nolan Act)

Deregulation	One shop permit process; potential Environmental Impact relief
Tax Changes	Tax credits for hiring disadvantaged individuals; 50% of qualified wages in year 1 down to 10% of qualified wages in year 5, zero after year 6.
	Tax credit for employees, of 5%, up to total credit of $450; reduced for each dollar in wages over $9,000
	Carryover of net operating loss for up to 15 years
Grants and Loans	Existing state, local programs

Florida

Deregulation	Negligible
Tax Incentives	Corporate income tax credit equal to 25% of first $1,500 in monthly wages of new employees, for 12 months; employees must reside in zone.
	A credit against the corporate income tax for new or expanded businesses, equal to 96% of the school portion of ad valorem taxes levied. Credit can be claimed for 10 years up to maximum of $50,000 annually. Effective January 1981–December 1986.
	A 50% credit on Florida income tax for donations to local community development projects. Must be made through an eligible agency such as a community development corporation or community action program. Annual amount of credit limited to

Table 3.   (Continued)

	$200,000 per firm; statewide limit $3 million. Unused credits may be carried forward up to five years.
	Local governments authorized to use
	• economic development sales tax exemption • Industrial Revenue Bonds (IRBs) • Tax increment financing.
Grants and Loans	Interest free, 15-year loans to Community Development Corporations (CDCs).

Illinois
(partial listing only)

Deregulation	Authority granted for cities or counties to modify local ordinances and regulations dealing with zoning, licensing, building codes, rent, and price controls.
Tax Incentives	Individuals and corporations may deduct from their adjusted gross income an amount equal to the dividends paid by a corporation that conducts substantially all its business in a Zone,
	State income tax credit of 5% is allowed for investment in qualified property servicing an enterprise zone by a business locating or expanding in an enterprise zone. Since 1985, a carry forward of 5% is allowed for unused credit for tax years ending after December 31, 1985.
	Financial instututions may deduct from their gross income for state income tax purposes the total amount of interest income from loans to a taxpayer, to the extent that the loan is secured by investment tax credit eligible property.
	Any taxing district may order the county clerk to abate any portion of its taxes on real property located within an enterprise zone. The amount may not exceed the amount attributable to improvements, renovation, or rehabilitation of existing improvements.
Grants and Loans	Authority for the Illinois Industrial Development Authority to loan up to $100 million to new or expanding businesses.

Source: U.S. Department of Housing and Urban Development, *Enterprise Zone Update*, (March 1986).

THE FATE OF "DEREGULATION"

As previously shown the first Kemp-Garcia act abandoned any effort to maintain deregulation, the key concept in Enterprise Zones[1]. Perhaps more important, President Reagan's own proposed Zone legislation introduced in 1983 had language effectively curtailing any significant rollback of federal regulations. This signalled that Enterprise Zones$_1$, with vast tax rollbacks, and wholesale reduction or elimination of national environmental, wage, and health regulations was a dead letter from the start in Washington.

At the state level there are seventeen states that in their Zone acts, mention regulatory relief, and at least four of these states call for sharp cutbacks. Kentucky's law raises great expectations

Section 10
(1) In order to carry out the purposes of this Act, any administrative body which promulgates administrative regulations . . . may, by regulation, exempt designated enterprise zones from the provisions of any regulation, in whole or in part, promulgated by that administrative body.

only to dash them in the next sentence:

(2) Enterprise Zones shall not be exempted from the provisions of any regulation, if such exemption endangers the health and safety of the citizens of the Commonwealth.

Kentucky's law relates only to state regulations. Louisiana's goes further, authorizing the Louisiana Department of Commerce "to supercede certain specified local regulations and ordinances which may serve to discourage economic development within the enterprise zone" (section 1785).[11] This is among the strongest of any deregulatory language in state Zone legislation; yet in practice, it has meant only that localities review their regulations. They have not had to give up control.[12] Despite the fact that 17 states have some deregulatory provisions in their Zone laws, of which at least four are strongly worded, no state or local regulation or ordinance has been repealed or overruled against local authority wishes as a result of Zones.

PURPOSES AND CHARACTERISTICS OF STATE ENTERPRISE ZONES

In deciding the criteria for designating Zones, state legislation is wrestling with the basic question of why Zones exist. Are they there to encourage rehabilitation of neighborhoods, *sans* bulldozers? Then the criteria for selection would stress neighborhood housing condition and commercial decay. Are they in existence to create economic development per se, without targeting these jobs to the low-income? Then simple investment, without targeted hiring requirements, would be in order. Or are Zones there to provide jobs to poor people, living in poor neighborhoods? Then selection criteria would stress the percent of poverty and unemployment in an area, and give incentives based on the percent of hires from the local poor.

The Brintnall and Green survey shows clearly that in establishing Zones, states have come down on the side of creating jobs and economic development, as opposed to neighborhood revitalization. All 17 states they surveyed listed "Job Creation" as a purpose of Zones; 14 listed "Industrial growth" and "Create new business" as purposes. Only 8 listed "Revitalization of the inner city," and only 4 listed "Neighborhood/housing" as purposes.[13]

This difference becomes clear when individual states are examined. Four states, including Florida and Pennsylvania, consider the condition of housing stock in any proposed Zone. Indiana, Maryland, New Jersey, and Virginia require that a Zone have "sustained high levels of unemployment" for twelve or more months. At least five states, including Arkansas, Connecticut, Louisiana, New Jersey, and Ohio consider the percent of Zone residents on welfare as a criterion for Zone designation. Another nine states have requirements for a minimum number of Zone residents living in poverty. Another nine, including Tennessee and Texas, require that a certain percent of the Zone population be "below a median income level."

In short, every state lists some kind of poverty indicator as a requirement for Zone designation; neighborhood revitalization is of secondary importance; jobs and industrial development are the main focus. Most Zones do require that a certain percent of jobs created be targeted to Zone residents. Creating assembled land packages and the use of the wrecking ball has been a minor Zone activity.

Zones: Limited in Number

Technically there are 1,997 designated Zones in 27 states plus the District of Columbia in early 1988. Another eight states have passed Zone legislation but have not as yet designated any Zone.[14]

This total number of Zones is deceptively large for two reasons. First, well over half the 1,997 Zones are "noncompetitively designated"; that is, the state simply declared certain areas to be Enterprise Zones, based on poverty indicators. Local communities did not mount any campaign to gain Zone designation, unlike the process in competitive Zones, where local jurisdictions have to demonstrate need and push for action. As a result, the noncompetitive Zones are, often, simply shells. Three states alone, whose Zones are all noncompetitive, account for well over half of all the Zones nationwide: Louisiana, 1,029 Zones; Kansas, 160 Zones; and Arkansas, 374 Zones. These three total 1,563 Zones, or 78% of all the Zones in the country.[15]

Second, many Zones are located within the same city or county, with a single city or county "marketing" and administering them. For this reason HUD looks at the *number of local jurisdictions*—cities or counties—as a more meaningful number than the simple 1,997 Zone total figure. As of January 1988 there were 734 local jurisdictions (cities or counties) that had Zones.

Limited Benefits, Small Staffs

Benefits in Zones are capped. Most states set limits to Zone duration, and to the duration of benefits to specific companies. Tax incentives are modest; paybacks from some firms are mandated; and local tax relief is often required before state tax relief can be considered.[16] California's Zone administrators estimate that California state tax incentives can add at most from 5 to 10% in net income, and these gains would be likely only for the larger firms whose state taxes are large.[17]

Finally, staffing of Zone programs is minimal. The HUD review of ten state programs found that Zone programs were often administered by existing agencies, typically Departments of Economic Development or Commerce; and that in eleven of eighteen states for which the question was asked, the State Coordinator was the only person working on Zone programs. In five of these states the coordinator only worked part time.[18] Clearly, even if Zones are adjudged a total failure, they would have been a very inexpensive failure; and in fact such an easy conclusion is not justified.

DO ENTERPRISE ZONES[2] CREATE JOBS AND INVESTMENT?

Because the main intention of Zones is to create economic development, and provide jobs to low-income people, the question arises: Do they?

The aggregate data supplied by HUD on state Zone performance is substantial. It shows that through early 1985 Zones had created or saved some 80,000 jobs, and that $3 billion of capital investment had occured in Zone areas.[19] By 1987 HUD figures showed 113,000 new jobs in Zones, and another 67,400 jobs saved by Zone programs that prevented relocation or bankruptcy. The total of new and saved jobs was, then, 180,400 over approximately three years.[20] A close-up look at the process in the state of Missouri gives an idea of how Zones operate.[21]

Missouri: An Illustration

In Missouri, state Zone legislation allows for 28 Zones. Each must have an unemployment rate of at least 1.5 times the state rate, and at least

65% of Zone residents must earn less than 80% of state median family income. Like many Southern states, Missouri has as many rural as urban Zones.[22]

How has Missouri's Enterprise Zone legislation worked in practice? HUD literature reports many successes, of which the following is typical. In 1983 the rural county in which the City of Macon (population 5,800) is located had a countywide unemployment rate of 32% and was about to lose two major employers, Banquet Foods and Toastmaster Co. In response, the city fathers went to the state and succeeded in having the state designate the Macon County Enterprise Zone. The city also got a state grant to improve the sewer system. In HUD's report, these changes induced Banquet Foods to stay and invest an additional $1.5 million in plant and equipment. The company retained 200 workers and hired an additional 150. Toastmaster also stayed, retaining 400 workers and shortly thereafter added another 250 employees as the result of a $2 million dollar new investment. According to the Director of the Missouri Department of Economic Development, the county's overall labor force had increased by 1,000 by 1986, while the Macon unemployment rate had dropped to 6%, a roaring success.

The Midtown Zone in downtown St. Louis experienced a 30.5% decrease in population between 1970 and 1980, together with an exodus of business and jobs, leading city fathers to seek and get Zone status from the state. Engineering Air Systems Company, which produces defense-related products, took over a large empty warehouse in the new Zone, refurbished it, and now employs 70 assemblers who were formerly classified as "difficult to employ" owing to a lack of job skills.

"Without the help of the city and state through the Enterprise Zone program it is doubtful that we could have expanded," according to Mike Shanahan, the President of Engineering Air. "We started with five or six people, grew to 70, and have promoted some into our other operations."

The MidTown Zone has also attracted a $3.1 million medical laboratory, a joint venture of St. Louis University Hospitals and American Bio-Sciences Laboratories. Expected payroll is eighty five people. Vulcan Manufacturing Company, which designs and manufacturers safety windows and steel furniture, has also invested. Vulcan began with fourteen people in 1984, and the next year reached fifty employees including twenty Vietnam veterans. In 1986 it was expected to reach 100.

How Much Growth In Zones Is Because Of Zones?

In 1987, an extensive article on Enterprise Zones was published in *Business Facilities*.[23] Using data gathered by her own state-by-state investigation, as well as information from the Washington, D.C.-based American Association of Enterprise Zones, the author concludes that only 4%

to 12% of new firms inside Zones came as a result of Zone activity, and that only 10% of firms preexisting in Zones have had an increase in economic activity because of Zone programs. The total of jobs created in Zones (113,000) and jobs saved (67,400) is 180,400. If 12% of these are the result of Zone activity, then over three years Zones have created or saved 21,650 jobs, or about 7,000 jobs per year over three years. If 4% are the result of Zone activity, then Zones are responsible for creating/saving only some 2,400 jobs per year.

Although the total number of jobs created/saved is confirmed with HUD, the percent due to Zone activity is subject to debate. The *Business Facilities'* figures are only one, and at present the only, such published estimate. Many states do not gather centralized data on Zone results, a fact that makes it difficult to draw any hard and fast conclusions. And, because Zone marketing programs interact with existing economic development and redevelopment programs, it is not easy to apportion blame or praise among competing agencies. It is possible that Zone "promotion" is responsible for a higher total of jobs than the figures here given; and it is certain that, whatever the numbers, the jobs which have been created or saved are located in those urban and rural areas where there is a crying need.

At the same time it should be observed that, if the *Business Facilities'* figures are close to correct, then about seven out of every eight jobs created in Zones were created by the unaided activity of the private market. In the first quarter of 1987, the private sector as a whole generated 1.6 million new jobs, or *17,750 new jobs every twenty-four hours*[24]— over twice as many jobs in *one day* as Zones create and save in an entire year.

EVALUATING ZONES

There are several important issues in dealing with Zones, of which the following are most pressing.

Changing Subnumerals:
Would Deregulation Make Any Difference?

As the foregoing has made clear, the original Peter Hall conception of Zones, as free enterprise islands in the sea of the Administrative State, has been sacked at the state, local and national levels. But does this matter? Would "radical deregulation" make any difference, in terms of fostering the entrepreneurial spirit, and creating rapid development of new businesses, new investment, and new jobs?

There is evidence and argument on both sides. Economist Walter

Williams argues that deregulation could make the *whole* difference for young, unemployed minorities, and points to the mass of licensing requirements for professions, largely at the state level, as bottlenecks to entrepreneurial development. To Williams, the high cost of taxicab medallions is a prime reason that entry into the taxi industry is limited and fares high. In New York, a medallion costs $30,000, and just to get in the cab costs $1.50; in Washington, D.C., a cab license is $200, and you can ride across an entire "zone" of the District for a flat $2.00.[25] Williams, joined by several economists at the CATO Institute and the Heritage Foundation, conservative "think tanks" in the nation's capital, argue that minimum wage makes it more difficult for teenagers to land their first jobs and get started on career job ladders. They believe that the black teenager unemployment rate of over 40% in center cities is due, in part, to minimum wage. A $2.00 wage would encourage employers to hire an inexperienced youth.[26]

On the other hand, the State of Connecticut, while preparing its own Zone legislation, appointed a special Commission to look into licensing and regulatory policies of state and local government to "determine the extent to which such policies restrict the development of entrepreneurial activities." The Commission concluded that such policies were not a significant barrier to economic development, but were in fact reasonable and necessary to protect the public.[27]

Yet the proponents of Enterprise Zones$_1$ are strengthened by the general evidence of successful deregulation which has been taking place at the federal level in trucking, airlines, and telecommunications.[28] Moreover the only scientific testing of the cost of deregulation has proved positive. In the early 1980s HUD undertook an Affordable Housing Demonstration in three cities. In Phoenix, a builder who was allowed to save money on reduced processing times, through lesser requirements, and who followed "some building practices not normally allowed in Phoenix," built a new subdivision of 255 units at an overall saving of $1,360,047, or $8,039 per unit. Of this, $2,198 was attributed to the reduction in processing time alone. A saving of $5,663 was shown in Mesa County, Colorado, including $3,000 attributable to higher densities. Savings were also shown in Elkhart County, Indiana.[29]

An illustration of how housing codes inhibit housing starts—and hence help reduce the supply, and raise the price, of housing—comes from Harris County (Houston). With a fraction of the population of the city of Houston, Harris County, which has *no zoning or building codes*, builds 77% of the housing in the county, and often has the highest number of housing starts of any county in the nation.[30]

At the same time, opinion surveys of businessmen consistently show that local businessmen do not express much concern about local regulations. A survey conducted by the National Federation of Independent Business, an organization which generally opposes Zones, found that local inspection, the ease of obtaining licenses and permits, and local zoning ranked near the bottom of a list of 25 problems faced by urban small business.[31] And a survey of businessmen in Cleveland showed that only 16 percent thought that building codes were a detriment to their expansion.[32]

Yet the evidence which denies the importance of deregulation is based largely on opinion; the arguments that support deregulation—the evidence from federal deregulation, the observable price of a taxi ride in Washington, D.C., the HUD deregulated home construction demonstration—are all based on tangible experience. Of course, the current majority in Congress, and on the House Ways and Means Committee where federal Zone legislation has met its Waterloo for the past five years, realises that without nationally-designated, partially-deregulated Zones, there can be no nationwide deregulatory evidence to point to, and it seems unlikely that either the Committee or the House will allow a test of a model that might prove successful. Without that larger national demonstration, and the massive tax abatements that only the federal government can grant, Zones will be limited to small programs that create several thousand jobs, nationally, in any year. Given that level of performance, Zones can not be an alternative to federal grants; in fact, Zones will continue to depend on those very grants (UDAG, CDBG, SBA) for some of their programs.

Are Enterprise Zones$_2$ Effective?

Taking Zones as they are presently designed, are they effective, or at least cost-effective, in reducing poverty, encouraging investment, and placing jobs in the inner city?[33]

Because Zones are largely tax abatement programs, the evidence from the long history of such programs helps frame the question accurately.[34] In the literature on urban economics there is argument against the efficacy of tax abatements from both liberal and conservative economists.[35] Yet the factual evidence suggests that tax levels and tax abatements *are* one factor looked at, altogether with site location, labor costs, and general government attitude towards business, when companies make decisions on location and relocation.[36] Southern states have been luring business to the South for decades with a combination of cheap labor rates (and no unions), prebuilt facilities, and low taxes. "Operation Bootstrap," the radical tax-reduction program for companies willing to invest in Puerto Rico after World War II, resulted in a mass migration of capital to the island, essentially shaping its current economic base.[37] The

CETA/JTPA federal job training programs, which offered both training money to employers and tax credits of up to $1,500 for two years for hiring and training an entry-level worker, were extremely popular with *very small* employers having under ten employees. For them, the small incentives offered by state programs will prove significant.

In certain cases, then, Zone programs and enthusiasm will make a difference, as the case studies from Missouri showed. By relaxing the building code and taking a nick off local taxes, Chicago Zone administrators were able to keep the big Spiegel company in Chicago—a small story in the grand scope of history, perhaps, but a headline story to the company's several hundred employees. The difference between Zones and, for example, Operation Bootstrap is in the size of impact. Billions of dollars went straight to Puerto Rico, because of billion dollar tax rebates. Zones have small tax incentives and even smaller cash resources. In the Zone in Norwalk, Connecticut, the Zone claims to have kept or created over 2,000 jobs, yet total employment in the Zone has dropped.[38] Zones are effective, but only within the limit of their resources.

The Other Issues:
Constitutionality, Piracy, Marginality

Questions have been raised about the constitutionality of Zone practices. In particular it has been suggested that Zones, by reducing taxes for Company A inside the Zone, but not reducing taxes for Company B just outside it, may be guilty of violating the Equal Protection and privileges and immunities clauses of the Constitution; and that, in reserving jobs for the neighborhood poor, Zones run afoul of the same objections that EEO "quotas" encounter.[39] Yet, if this is the case, it can also be said that no court of law has yet made such a decision at any level of government. Like the case against EEO, there is, as the poet wrote, "much argument; but ever I came out through that same door / Wherein I went."

It has been argued that Zones will "pirate" companies away from areas that need them; or that unscrupulous operators will set up business just because of the lure of tax credits. While this has undoubtedly occurred in isolated instances, HUD officials report that it is not a significant problem.[40]

What seems a more significant problem is that the small credits and cash outlays of Zone programs are most likely to attract not only small business, but *marginal* business. These are the kind that need $1,000 tax rebates for hiring the poor, but who suffer from (1) lack of capital, (2) lack of marketing expertise, and (3) lack of real management competence. The SBA's stereotype as a "handholder" to small companies that become semi-permanent wards of the agency is only partly stereotype. If a company is solid, the low wages and nonunion atmosphere of many inner city locations would, like the South, be sufficient inducement. It is with this in mind that Zones should keep the brakes on "incubator" projects.

CONCLUSION: A FREE TRADE ZONE IN SOUTH BRONX?

Zones have four things going for them. First, they are inexpensive, and do not involve the federal government. Second, they help to pull together the disparate state and local programs that all aim at economic development; as an overall rubric and motivator they have already proven beneficial. Thirdly, Zones don't bulldoze. And finally, they create an interest and enthusiasm that is disproportionate to any resources in Zone programs. Connecticut found that the prestige of being an Enterprise Zone "often generated a kind of psychological boost encouraging investments", according to the report of the Connecticut Department of Economic Development in December 1985. The very fact that over 700 local jurisdictions, and over half the states, have created Zones without Federal aid says something in itself.

And yes, it would be very interesting if New York State could summon up the enthusiasm to declare the South Bronx, the worst slum in America, a Free Trade Zone. Just once. Just to see.

NOTES AND REFERENCES

1. For the most forceful statement, see Martin Anderson, *The Federal Bulldozer: A Critical Analysis of Urban Renewal, 1949–62* (Cambridge, MA: MIT Press, 1964). See also Peter H. Rossi and Robert A. Dentler, *The Politics of Urban Renewal: The Chicago Findings* (New York: The Free Press of Glencoe, 1961).
2. Charles Murray, *Losing Ground. American Social Policy 1950–1980* (New York: Basic Books, 1984). For a summary critique of Murray see Juan Williams, "Liberal Thinkers Rally in Defense of 'Great Society'," *Washington Post* (May 28, 1985), p. A–4; and Murray, "*Losing Ground* Two Years Later," *The CATO Journal*, 6, 1 (Spring/Summer 1986): 19–30.
3. Edward Hayes, *Power Politics and Urban Policy: Oakland, California* (New York: McGraw-Hill, 1972), pp. 116–117.
4. See Rossi, *Urban Renewal: The Record and the Controversy;* and Brian J.L. Berry, Sandra J. Parsons, and Rutherford H. Platt, *The Impact of Urban Renewal on Small Business, The Hyde Park-Kenwood Case* (Chicago: Center for Urban Studies, University of Chicago, 1968), p. xiv.
5. See Herbert J. Gans, "The Failure of Urban Renewal," in *Urban Renewal: People, Politics, and Planning*, ed. Bellush and Hausknecht (Garden City, NY: Doubleday Anchor, 1967), p. 467; Martin Mayer, *The Builders* (New York: Norton, 1978), p. 191; and John C.

Egan et al., *Housing And Public Policy* (Washington, D.C.: American Enterprise Institute/Ballinger, 1981), pp. 14–19.

6. Charles Murray, *Losing Ground,* pp. 56–68, esp. p. 57, Figure 4.1.

7. Stuart M. Butler, *Enterprise Zones: Greenlining The Inner City* (New York: Universe Books, 1981).

8. See David Hardison, "From Ideology to Incrementalism: The Concept of Urban Enterprise Zones in Great Britain and the United States" (Princeton, NJ: Princeton Urban and Regional Research Center, 1981).

9. Office of Congressman Jack Kemp, "The Enterprise Zone Employment and Development Act. Brief Description," Mimeo (February 1, 1983); emphasis added.

10. *Insight* (May 19, 1986).

11. As quoted in Stephen D. Gold, "State Urban Enterprise Zones: A Policy Overview," a report prepared under contract with the U.S. Department of Housing and Urban Development (Washington, D.C.: National Conference of State Legislatures, July 1982), p. 16.

12. *Ibid.,* p. 16.

13. Roy E. Green and Michael A. Brintnall, "State Enterprise Zone Programs: Variations In Structure and Coverage. A Preliminary Survey Report," a paper presented for ASPA convention (April 16, 1986), p. 17a, Table 1.

14. The information in this and the next two paragraphs comes from HUD's office for Enterprise Zones.

15. Until December 1986, Florida had 136 noncompetitive Zones. Unhappy with the results, Florida let all its Zones lapse on December 31, 1986, and since then has designated 30 competitive Zones.

16. Ronald E. Jones, "State-Designated Enterprise Zones: A Summary of Ten Case Studies" (Washington, D.C.: U.S. Department of Housing and Urban Development, 1986), p. 5.

17. Richard Whitman and Deborah Belasich, "Implementing and Evaluating a State Enterprise Zone Program," a paper prepared for the ASPA convention (April 16, 1986). This paper, expressing personal views, was written by the director of the California State enterprise zone program.

18. Jones, "State Designated Enterprise Zones," p. 4.

19. Lee L. Verstandig, former Undersecretary of HUD for Enterprise Zones, Letter to the author (May 13, 1986).

20. Dora Hatras, "Enterprise Zones," *Business Facilities,* 20, 5 (May 1987). These figures were confirmed by the author with HUD.

21. For a review of Zones in five states through 1986, including Missouri, see Edward C. Hayes, "From Rags to Riches," *American City and County,* 101, 11(November 1986): 64–72.

22. The information on Missouri's experience on this and following pages comes from: Office of Program Analysis and Evaluation, U.S. Department of Housing and Urban Development (HUD), *State Designated Enterprise Zones: Ten Cases Studies* (Washington, D.C., August 1986), pp. 103–138.

23. Dora Hatras, "Enterprise Zones."

24. U.S. Department of Commerce, Bureau of Economic Analysis, "Economic Indicators," *Survey of Current Business,* 67, 5 (May 1987), p. S–10.

25. Walter Williams, *The State Against Blacks* (New York: McGraw-Hill, 1982), p. 56.

26. *Ibid.,* p. 79; Thomas Rustici, "A Public Choice View of The Minimum Wage," *The CATO Journal,* 5, 1 (Spring–Summer 1985): 103–132.

27. Steven Gold, "State Urban Enterprise Zones," p. 26. See also Marc Bendick, Jr., and David W. Rasmussen, "Enterprise Zones and Inner-City Economic Revitalization," in *Reagan and the Cities,* ed. George E. Peterson and Carol W. Lewis (Washington, D.C.: Urban Institute Press, 1986), p. 105.

28. See Robert W. Poole, Jr., *Instead of Regulation. Alternatives To Federal Regulatory Agencies* (Lexington, MA: Lexington Books, 1982, 1987).

29. U.S. Department of Housing and Urban Development, "The Affordable Housing Demonstration. Mesa County, Colorado" (Washington, D.C.: HUD, January 1984), pp. iii, 9–11. See HUD reports with the same date for Elkhart, Indiana and Phoenix, Arizona. See also *Reducing the Development Costs of Housing: Actions for State and Local Government* (Washington, D.C.: Urban Land Institute, 1979), the Proceedings of a HUD conference on housing costs.

30. Dick Bjornseth, "No Code Comfort," *Reason*, 15, 3 (June 1983), pp. 43–47.

31. Quoted *Enterprise Zones—1982*, Hearings before the U.S. Senate, Committee on Finance, 97th Congress, 2nd sess. (April 21, 1982), p. 212.

32. *Ibid.*, p. 433.

33. For an overall defense of Zones, see David Stoesz, "The Case for Community Enterprise Zones," *Urban and Social Change Review*, 18, 2 (Summer 1985). For a critical assessment see Susan A. Jones, "Urban Enterprise Zones: How Have The Panaceas Panned Out?," *Economic Development Commentary*, 10, 2 (Summer 1986). See also Susan A. Jones, Allen R. Marshall and Glen E. Weisbrod, *Business Impacts of State Enterprise Zones* (Cambridge, MA: Cambridge Systematics, 1985).

34. Surrey, Stanley S., "Tax Incentives as a Device for Implementing Government Policy: A Comparison with Direct Government Expenditures," *Harvard Law Review* (December 1979), pp. 705–738; and Roger Schmenner, "City Taxes and Industry Location" (New York: National Bureau of Economic Research, 1971).

35. The "entrepreneurial management" style of city management generally prefers low citywide tax rates as opposed to rebates for a special class or selected businesses. See Chapter 10, "The Entrepreneurial City Manager," esp. p. 9.

36. See the seminal volume by Victor Fuchs, *Changes in the Location of Manufacturing in the United States Since 1929* (New Haven: Yale University Press, 1962); and George Sternlieb et al., *Tax Subsidies and Housing Investment* (New Brunswick, NJ: Rutgers, The Center For Urban Policy Research, 1976).

37. See, despite its title, Edward Humberger, "The Enterprise Zone Fallacy," *Journal of Community Action* (September/October 1981): 20–28.

38. Cait Murphy, "Connecticut. EZ Does It," *Policy Review*, 36 (Spring 1986): 67.

39. See Michael Allen Wolf, "Potential Legal Pitfalls Facing State and Local Enterprise Zones," a paper delivered at the April 1986 ASPA Conference, Anaheim, California (reprinted in *Urban Law and Policy* [1986]). Available from HUD USER, P.O. Box 280, Germantown, MD 20874.

40. Panel presentation by Michael Savage, Director, HUD Zone Program, at the 1986 ASPA conference, Anaheim, California (April 1986).

PART IV

THE HIDDEN WEALTH OF CITIES

Chapter 12

PRODUCTIVITY AND LOCAL GOVERNMENT POLICY

Edward C. Hayes

SUMMARY. In their efforts to increase productivity cities would be aided by the adoption of a "Productivity Policy." This chapter outlines four elements of such a policy, how a unit can be established to administer it, and how it can be implemented to avoid miscommunication. A new, prestigious national award for productivity is advocated; the present practice of the cities of Scottsdale, Arizona and Sunnyvale, California point the way.

THE "PRODUCTIVITY POLICY"

Cities should consider adopting a Productivity Policy, to *focus attention on the subject of costs and productivity,* just as federal incomes policy, family policy, and many others focus attention on national problems.

In recent years federal domestic policy debates have been preludes to expensive federal programs. A Productivity Policy debate at the munici-pal level might, if it resulted in the institution of a comprehensive pro-ductivity program (as advocated in Chapter 6), lead to initially higher costs. However, such a policy should focus on reducing costs, and in the near term the only cost is the time required to debate and devise the policy's content.

There are four principles that could form the basis of such a policy:

1. Make wage and salary increases partially dependent on productivity increases.
2. Commit to Least Cost Methods (LCMs).
3. Establish two budgetary measures: (a) cost-per-unit of service, and (b) cost-per citizen, for whole government and each department.
4. Instill a "productivity consciousness" into all levels of the workforce.

TIE WAGE INCREASES PARTIALLY TO PRODUCTIVITY INCREASES

Managers' pay in the city of Phoenix has depended on productivity improvements since the 1970s. A productivity clause was written into the contracts of New York City sanitation workers during New York's fiscal crisis of the mid-1970s. The clause reminded both the public and the workforce that pay increases *have to come from somewhere,* and the only real options are productivity increases or tax increases. After the fiscal crisis passed, however, the clause was dropped and most of the back pay foregone by the sanitation workers as a result of the clause was paid out.

COMMIT TO LEAST COST METHODS (LCMs)

The methods outlined in this book make a good starting point; but there are many books with many more good ideas and methods. All of these methods have been known for a long time, and practiced in a few cities; yet on the whole, cities have been slow to adopt, and fully implement, the range of techniques which are available to them, and those that do implement often reverse themselves. Probably half the cities that have timed jobs, using industrial engineering methods, have partially or wholly abandoned the effort in the past decade.

To make productivity happen, there must be a commitment to make it happen. The purpose of debating and forming a policy is to create that commitment, from the Council level to management and down through the ranks. "Least Cost Methods" may sometimes mean hard choices, such as the choice to reduce or reassign staff, and this can cause indefinite delays in taking action. In the private sector, Detroit resisted for ten years the trend to robots, with the result that Japan has outproduced us in automobiles. Government productivity can only increase if elected officials, managers, and all employees are ready to adopt whatever bet-ter methods are available, while mitigating any difficult consequences.

In Scottsdale the City Council required early on that no one lose his job as a result of the new Work Management program[1] (see Chapter 9 for a description), and has followed that requirement since its adoption six years ago. When redundancies occur, people are transferred to other programs. When programs are contracted out, job loss may again occur. Yet a policy of transfer, and of requiring the new private service pro-vider to give city employees the first crack at employment in the private sector, can soften the consequences. In its May 1985 study of the impact of Los Angeles' County's contracting out program, the consulting firm of Deloitte, Haskins and Sells found that of the 1,002 employees affected by the program, only 9 were laid off and not rehired, while 204 received a promotion.[2]

ESTABLISH COST-PER-UNIT AND COST-PER-CITIZEN GOALS

Scottsdale reports overall city costs in a way that brings government home to every employee and citizen. It is a figure showing the cost of government per citizen, and is derived by dividing the total number of city residents into the total cost of city government for that year. Cost-per-citizen is also required for every department; departments are called Cost Centers. Cities that have a higher cost per citizen than neighboring cities might hesitate at this. So might older, larger cities with higher costs. But a good manager, whose commitment is to improved perfor-mance, will push hard for such a measure regardless of city, knowing that with it in place he will have leverage over several desirable objec-tives: bringing private investment to the city, persuading Council to look hard at costs, auditing department performance, and appealing to the private sector for resources to help keep costs in line.

Scottsdale now requires that every department (cost center) use cost-per-citizen as a measure of department performance. The Organiza-tional Development Unit, for example, is budgeted at $262,000. With Scottsdale's population at 115,000, this yields a cost-per-citizen of $2.27. By requiring this measure the city ensures that every department man-ager is aware of *how much his department costs citizens.*

The City of Sunnyvale, California uses a budget system, and parallel cost-accounting system, that also helps focus attention on costs. The Sunnyvale budget reports, among other things, both "service units" and "unit costs." Service units are defined for every department, and include such things as miles of pipeline laid and number of emergency runs.

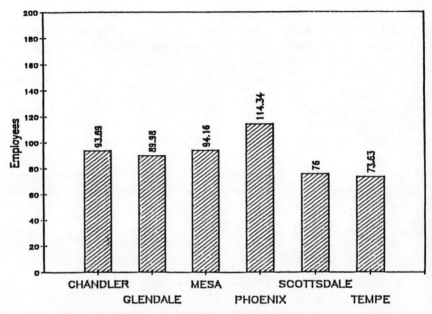

Figure 1.   City of Scottsdale: Comparison of Employees
Per Ten Thousand Citizens For Selected Cities, FY 1984/85

Source: City of Scottsdale.

This takes the Program Budget one step further by breaking programs
down into, first, tasks, and second, service units for each task, giving a
very fine measure of control.[3]

Sunnyvale is also unique in reporting both time and dollar measures
of productivity in graphic form. Two charts, like those shown in Figure
2, show whether productivity is rising or falling in every program area.
Together, the Sunnyvale budget format makes it easy for employees and
citizens to see whether the city's productivity level is trending up or
down.

DEVELOPING A PRODUCTIVITY
CONSCIOUSNESS—AND WILLINGNESS

Consciousness without willingness is futile. In developing both, the following pages will draw together several points touched on but not elabo-
rated in earlier chapters.

Table 1. Performance Budget Format

Task	Definition of Units	Total Number of Units	Unit Cost	Total Number of Task Hours	Total Task Cost
Program 165: Fire Services.	Objective: Emergency Responses Under 4 Minutes, 90% of Runs				
1651 Respond to Fires	Responses	700	266.81	4,250	186,766
1652 Maintain Equipment	Work Hours*	12,500	28.00	12,500	350,000
Program 275: Accounting.	Objective: Process Invoices Within 3 Days, 90% of Time				
2751 Process Invoices	Number of Checks Paid	28,000	5.18	8,900	145,040
2752 Audit Invoices	Work Hours*	572	14.33	572	8,196
Program 345: Storm Drain Maintenance.	Objective: Maintain Grates at Cost of $300 per Grate				
3451 Repair Grates	Number of Repairs	14	298.00	60	4,172
3452 Flush Storm Lines	Lineal Feet	4,000	.59	100	2,365
3453 Inspect Discharges	Inspections	20	71.89	60	1,437

Note: *Whereas "work hours" are not a unit of output, the units of output for some tasks are so diverse that the use of work hours is the only practicable system.

Source: Adapted from *Resource Allocation Plan* [Budget], City of Sunnyvale.

257

Program 275: Accounting

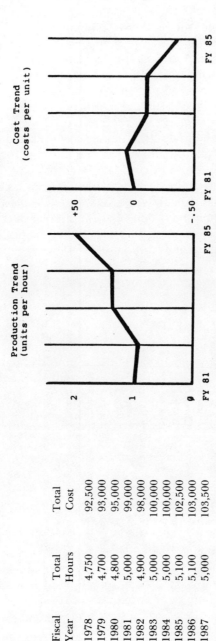

Production Trend
(units per hour)

Cost Trend
(costs per unit)

Fiscal Year	Total Hours	Total Cost
1978	4,750	92,500
1979	4,700	93,000
1980	4,800	95,000
1981	5,000	99,000
1982	4,900	98,000
1983	5,000	100,000
1984	5,000	100,000
1985	5,100	102,500
1986	5,100	103,000
1987	5,000	103,500

What These Charts Show: The left chart shows the number of production units produced in one hour in Accounting. "Units" include file transactions, checks cut, and all department tasks. The right chart shows the cost of producing one unit.

The Advantage of This Reporting Format: These charts show productivity; traditional budget figures show only expenditure totals. For illustration, charts this page show costs-per-unit have dropped by 50%, and production per hour has *doubled*, a dramatic (if fanciful) improvement. This shows on the charts, while the left-hand columns reflect only a slow increase in overall costs, due to inflationary pressures. Only the performance budget format allows the tracking of productivity.

Source: Adapted from *Resource Allocation Plan* [Budget], City of Sunnyvale.

Figure 2. Performance Budgeting Trend Charts (Schematic)

258

Creating Performance Objectives, Measures, and Standards

This method, first described in Chapter 6, can be viewed both as a technique, and as a way of raising employee understanding—and willingness—about productivity. As a method of developing employee willingness it is of prime value, for it gives both management and hourly workers the chance to look at their own performance and understand just what the concepts productivity, efficiency, and effectiveness are all about. Whether this is done by an outside consultant, as Scottsdale did in Parks Maintenance, or by a process of internal discussion led by employees, the educational benefits are great.

As a technique, the use of objectives and measures is square one in productivity management, and allows managers to evaluate both departmental and personnel performance.[4] In Scottsdale, in addition to showing costs-per-citizen, each department must develop additional performance measures, showing *what* is to be achieved, any *special conditions* for achievement, and a *measurable standard* of achievement. For example, the city's daytime police patrols' objectives include the familiar one: "Will respond to emergency calls within four minutes, 90% of the time." Having measurable objectives established *by the departments own employees* in every department gives the message to employees and gives management a means of control.

Pay for Performance At All Levels

Scottsdale is one of the few municipalities in the country that has adopted pay-for-performance not just at the management level but for every level of employee.[5] The advantages of this system are:

1. It involves employees in setting their own performance objectives and standards.
2. It carefully sets up standards for performance in advance of evaluation reviews.
3. It provides flexibility in administration.
4. It provides supervisors with the means to clearly determine performance, and to adjust pay up or down accordingly.

Although pay-for-performance at the management level is occasionally used among cities (and is an old story in the private sector), putting the *entire* workforce on this footing is a rarity in public management. Its great strength lies in its compelling of all employees to realize that their real job is to *perform well*. With its flexibility in setting objectives (see box,

Using COMSTAR, Scottsdale's departments can receive and transmit data directly, including performance and all budget data. Research time and paperwork are reduced.

below) performance can be defined as cost-control and productivity wherever appropriate.

In addition to Pay for Performance, Scottsdale offers cash bonuses to employees at all ranks for outstanding performance. The city recently paid a $200 bonus to an alert secretary, who realized the city was being deliberately double-billed; and another $200 to each of two detectives who performed a brilliant apprehension of criminals. And the city is now preparing to institute Gain Sharing, similar to the Scanlon Plan, whereby up to 4% of a department's cash savings from productivity improvements is rebated to employees as salary.

Workforce Involvement In Setting Objectives

Without workforce involvement in setting objectives, and employee cooperation in setting new objectives and time standards, any policy aimed at cost control will be hampered. Scottsdale has included employees at all levels in determining time standards throughout its Work Management programs.

GOALS, KEY RESULTS AREAS, AND STANDARDS
FOR A HUMAN SERVICES DIRECTOR
For Use in Performance Pay System

Major Goal

To direct the activities of recreational centers, the senior center, and the support services program, so as to use resources effectively and efficiently while developing good community support and enhancing the image of the City of Scottsdale.

1. *Key Result Area:*   Develop program budgets that enable staff to do their jobs and are acceptable to department head.
   Performance Standards: There is competent performance when:
   a. the program budgets are submitted on time;
   b. all data is accumulated and presented so as to be easily understood and justified;
   c. department head makes no major revisions; and
   d. program managers support the budget as their own.

2. *Key Result Area:*   Improve communications with the Human Services program, to enable employees to be more effective
   Performance Standards: There is competent performance when:
   a. regular staff meetings are established;
   b. a means is developed for staff to share ideas and program activities; and
   c. the director regularly visits program sites to view programs and performance.

3. *Key Result Area:*   Develop the skills of Human Services staff.
   Performance Standards: There is competent performance when:
   a. performance plans are developed for all staff; and
   b. a training program is presented quarterly by the Human Services Director.

It is important for management to realize that no matter how benign its motives, whatever it does will be seen by its employees through the employees' perspective, and that may be dramatically different from management's. The box on the following page illustrates how such differing perspectives operate. The only certain way to prevent such differences from interfering with the productive functioning of the city is for the workforce to be "included in" in designing the objectives and standards of each department. Regular department meetings and special Roundtables are forums for inviting this participation. Sensitizing all

MISCOMMUNICATION:
THE "PERSPECTIVES PHENOMENON"

When you give someone as assignment, *will* it get done? Or *might* it
get done? How the manager (boss) and the employee see the assignment—their perspectives—play a major role.

Consider the following examples of how different perspectives color
performance and on-job personal relationships:

Department Head	Supervisor
I wish he'd shape up his crew and get 'em to work on time.	We're having our best month ever—we've cut tardiness by 10%!
Manager	
Jones has a really bad attitude. He doesn't like me or the job, and it shows.	**Employee**
	The boss doesn't really care how much I do.
Fire Chief	**Employee**
We've had two people almost die *after* our EMT got there. Something's wrong.	We still don't have the right training. It's not my fault.
Manager	**Employee**
Hm, she's had three hours and only finished 2 data batches. How can she be so (deleted) slow?	This is the best job I ever did for Accounting. They'll love the new format.

Underlying these differences in perception are at least five broad
elements, including: authority/lack of authority; higher/lower level
of expectation; more/less familiarity with work process; need to
"look good" to different stakeholders; and needs for recognition
and control.

personnel to the "perspectives phenomenon" can be done, at the outset,
by a session with a consultant trained in this field.

THE ORGANIZATION

The bureaucracy needed to carry out Production Policy activities need
not be bureaucratic. Scottsdale has long had a unit devoted to improving
management skills and department productivity. Today it is called the
Organizational Development Unit (OD Unit). It provides studies and in-

---

What We Believe
City of SCOTTSDALE, ARIZONA

The quality of life in the City of Scottsdale depends upon the partnership between citizens, elected officials and us, the employees of the City.

We can make the difference between a good organization
and an excellent one.

Management is committed to certain expectations
that we all can share.
They are:

WE ARE THE BEST SOURCES OF INFORMATION

**about the City. Even if we don't always have an answer,
we know where to get it.**

WE ARE COST-CONSCIOUS

**We are expected to spend taxpayer dollars wisely and effectively
for the benefit of all.**

WE SUPPORT CITY POLICY

and uphold the values of the democratic process.

WE PLAN FOR ACCOMPLISHMENT

**and stay "ahead" of our problems. We seek out challenges
and recognize that to get better we must
accept the risks associated with change.**

WE DO RIGHT BY OUR PEOPLE

**Citizens and fellow employees are treated with the dignity, respect
and fairness to which all human beings are entitled.
Individualism is valued and respected.**

WE DO RIGHT BY OURSELVES

**Our individual physical and mental health are the foundation of a
sound government and a well-run organization.**

We are proud of the City of Scottsdale, its leadership and the citizens we serve.
Through teamwork, understanding and dedication to these principles of action, we
can prove ourselves worthy.

Roy R. Pederson, City Manager

Figure 3.

house training in Work management, staffing evaluation, position request reviews, methods improvement, and organization assessment. It is charged with fostering commitment to the values and responsibilities listed in the City's "What We Believe" statement. The entire Scottsdale OD unit is neither large nor expensive. The unit is comprised of only seven people, including the director and secretary, and in 1987 cost $262,000, only one-third of one percent of the city operating budget of $77 million.

OD units, sometimes called evaluation units or management services programs, seem only to exist in cities of over half a million. Scottsdale, a city of around 115,000, is living proof that smaller cities can afford such a unit; or if a city is under 25,000, special training can be given to department heads to perform their own OD analysis. Savings from a successful productivity program, such as contracting out or Work Management, could easily pay for a whole OD unit. Scottsdale saved $350,000 in the first year of its Work Management program in just one city division, far more than the city's annual OD unit cost. New Jersey has had a Productivity Investment Program off and on for fifteen years. In this, the state treasury funded the program the first year, but thereafter all income to the fund had to be realized from cash savings realized by program innovations.[6] Such a method seems feasible at the local level.

THE PRIZE

A national award to local governments that excel in productivity and cost control would help enormously. There are numerous awards offered now, at the state level, and at the national level by professional organizations, including the National Civic League. But nowhere is there a prestigious national group that puts a loving cup in the arms of a city that has done the most for controlling costs. Without this kind of recognition, interest in the subject will grow slowly. A prize could be offered by a professional management group, a productivity center, a university, or a national newspaper. Because cities are endeavoring to reward employees' efforts in productivity, shouldn't cities' efforts be rewarded— and encouraged?

CONCLUSION: PRODUCTIVITY AND
THE CULTURE OF EMPLOYMENT

Without a Productivity Policy, the methods outlined in this volume for improving methods and tapping cities' "hidden wealth" will face tough sledding. The Productivity Policy is the first order of business for cities serious about productivity and cost containment.

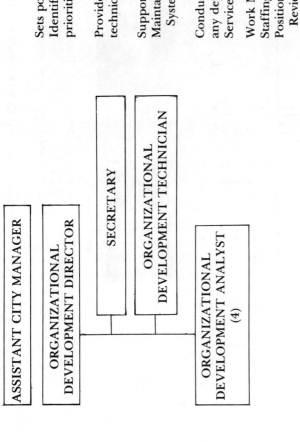

ASSISTANT CITY MANAGER

ORGANIZATIONAL
DEVELOPMENT DIRECTOR
— Sets policy
Identifies projects
prioritizes projects

SECRETARY
— Provides clerical,
technical support

ORGANIZATIONAL
DEVELOPMENT TECHNICIAN
— Supports OD Analysts
Maintains Work Management
System

ORGANIZATIONAL
DEVELOPMENT ANALYST
(4)
— Conduct projects for
any department.
Services include:

Work Management
Staffing Evaluations
Position Request
Reviews
Methods Improvements
Organization Assessment
Employee Involvement
Conflict Resolution

Total budget for unit, 1987–88: $262,000
Unit staff: 7

Figure 4. Organizational Chart: Scottsdale Organizational Development Unit

Source: City of Scottsdale, "Organizational Development in the City of Scottsdale" (1987), p. 4

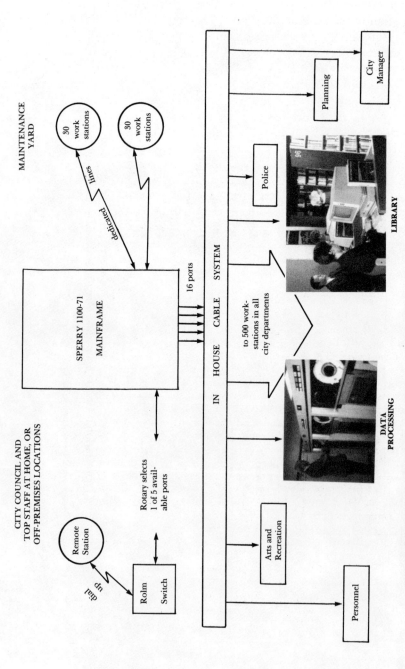

CITY COUNCIL AND TOP STAFF AT HOME, OR OFF-PREMISES LOCATIONS

MAINTENANCE YARD

Remote Station

dial up

Rolm Switch

Rotary selects 1 of 5 available ports

SPERRY 1100-71 MAINFRAME

30 work stations

30 work stations

dedicated lines

16 ports

IN HOUSE CABLE SYSTEM

to 500 work-stations in all city departments

Personnel

Arts and Recreation

DATA PROCESSING

LIBRARY

Police

Planning

City Manager

SCOTTSDALE'S "COMSTAR" SYSTEM: All departments, plus at-home city officials and Maintenance Yard employees, access all city budget data and reports through dedicated lines, Rolm phone system, or in-house cable. Features include electronic mail, meeting bulletin board, personal calendars, and word processing, in addition to access to all city reports. For this installation, Scottsdale won Office Automation Magazine's Gold First Award for 1985.

Source: City of Scottsdale, Office of Management Systems.

Figure 5. Office Automation System (COMSTAR), Scottsdale, Arizona

Pressures for budget increases are everywhere. Unfunded or under-funded state mandates; federal programs that require "just" a 25% share from cities; inflation; pressure from employee organizations in the larger cities; and the sheer growth in population all conspire to push up costs. These pressures are continuous and unremitting. To control them successfully, both citizens and city government must have a tool at their disposal which is equally potent. The most potent tool available is not a technique; it is a policy, such as the one outlined in this chapter.

With a Productivity Policy in place, tailored to the exact needs and political situation of each city, the psychology of the city budget process changes from looking for maximum expenditures to looking for maximum savings. There is no reason why this search cannot be made into a pleasurable activity, and encouraged throughout the ranks. When the desire for innovation, productivity, and cost control becomes a part of the "culture of public employment," just as it has become a part of the culture of Japanese automakers, the battle to control costs, and to tap the hidden wealth of cities, will be closer to victory.

NOTES AND REFERENCES

1. For a complete description of the implementation of Work Management in Scottsdale, see Edward C. Hayes, "In Pursuit of Productivity. Management Innovation in Scottsdale," *National Civil Review*, 73, 6 (June 1984): 273–278.

2. Deloitte, Haskins and Sells, *Fiscal Management Review of the Los Angeles County Contracting Procedures* (Los Angeles: Deloitte, Haskins and Sells, May 1985), pp. 25–26.

3. The Sunnyvale "budget," which includes 10-year plans, capital and operating costs, and performance measures and indicators, all in one document, is titled *Resource Allocation Plan. 1987–88 to 1996–97 Fiscal Years*. The reader is encouraged to obtain a copy as it is the single strongest budget document in local government.

4. Although the phrase "Management By Objectives" seems to have fallen on hard times, parts or all of the system to which the phrase refers are very much in evidence in local government. In addition to the useful works cited in Chapter 6, see also the "how to" book by George L. Morrisey, *Management By Objectives and Results in the Public Sector*, 7th ed. (Reading, MA: Addison-Wesley, 1983); see also Edward C. Hayes, *Performance Measurement and Improvement* (San Diego: Metro Associates, 1986).

5. The City of Crystal Lake, Illinois (population 22,500), located northwest of Chicago, has also had pay-for-performance for hourly employees as well as managers since 1978; see *City and State* (February 1987).

6. See State Government Productivity Research Center, "New Jersey's Productivity Investment Account" (Lexington, KY: Council of State Governments, 1980); see also Theodore Poister *et al.*, "Centralized Productivity improvement Efforts in State Government," *Productivity Review*, 33 (Spring 1985): 5–24. Many of the Productivity ideas used by states are equally applicable to the local level.

APPENDICES

APPENDIX I: PRODUCTIVITY CENTERS
(THE NATIONAL PRODUCTIVITY NETWORK)

The Centers listed below are members of the National Productivity Network. Many are university based; together they serve both public and private sector clients. The Network is a membership organization with bylaws specifying rules for admission and operations. The most recent chairman is Dr. Tom Tuttle (see Maryland Center for Productivity and Quality of Worklife, *infra*). Public agencies should not hesitate to tap the resources of "private sector" Centers.

American Center for the Quality of Work Life
1411 K Street NW
Suite 930
Washington, D.C. 20005
(202–338–2933)

Major orientation: Human Resources Management
Budget: $650,000
Staff: 24 FTPs*

American Productivity and Quality Center
123 North Post Oak Lane
Houston, TX 77024
(713–681–4020)

Major orientation: Human Resources Management
Budget: $4 million
Staff: 40 FTPs*

---

*FTP stands for Full Time Professional. Most centers have additional support staff.

Arkansas Productivity Center
309 Engineering Building
University of Arkansas
Fayetteville, AR 72701
(501–575–3156)

Major orientation: Management, technical
Budget: $40,000

Center for Applied Engineering/Small Business Development Center
University of Missouri-Rolla
206 Harris Hall
Rolla, MO 65402
(314–341–4559)

Major orientation: technical
Size: medium

Center for the Productive Use of Technology
George Mason University
Professional Center, Suite 322
3401 North Fairfax Drive
Arlington, VA 22201
(703–841–2675)

Major orientation: Human resources management
Budget: $200,000

Corporate Productivity Research Group
167 Brycemoor Road
Scarborough, Ontario M1C 24R
Canada
(416–281–4141)

Major orientation: Productivity management, measurement
Size: small

Georgia Productivity Center
Georgia Institute of Technology
219 O'Keefe Building
Atlanta, GA 30332
(404–894–6101)

Major orientation: Management, technical, and human resources
Staff: 40 FTPs, 20 support

Georgia State University Productivity Center
Georgia State University
University Plaza

Atlanta, GA 30303–3083
(404–658–4105)
Major orientation: human resources management
Size: small

Indiana Labor and Management Council Inc.
2780 Waterfront Parkway
Suite 140
Indianapolis, IN 46224
(317–267–8827)
Major orientation: human resources; work innovation
Budget: $100,000

Industrial Extension Productivity Center
(Formerly Productivity Research and Extension Program)
North Carolina State University
Box 7902
Raleigh, NC 27695–7902
(919–737–2358)
Major orientation: technical
Budget: $1.6 million

Institute for Productivity Inc.
592 Hostos Avenue
Baldrich, Hato Rey, Puerto Rico 00918
(809–764–5145)
Major orientation: human resources management
Size: medium

Manufacturing Productivity Center
IIT Research Institute
10 West 35th Street
Chicago, IL 60616
(312–567–4800)
Major orientation: technical
Budget: $6 million

Maryland Center for Productivity and Quality of Working Life
University of Maryland
College Park, MD 20742
(301–454–6688)
Major orientation: human resources management
Budget: $260,000

National Center for Public Productivity
John Jay College
City University of New York
445 West 59th Street
New York, NY 10019
(212–489–5030)

Major orientation: human resources, technical, and management

National Productivity Exchange (NPX)
P.O. Box 261340
San Diego, CA 92126
(619–566–5887)

Major orientation: public sector management, technical
Size: small

Nebraska Technical Assistance Center
W191 Nebraska Hall
University of Nebraska at Lincoln
Lincoln, NE 68588–0535
(402–472–5600)

Major orientation: technical
Size: small

Oklahoma Productivity Center
Oklahoma State University
School of Industrial Engineering
Stillwater, OK 74078
(405–624–6055)

Major orientation: Management, technical
Size: small

Pennsylvania Technical Assistance Program
The Pennsylvania State University
University Park, PA 16802
(814–865–0427)

Major orientation: technical
Budget: $774,000

Texas Center for Productivity and Quality of Work Life
Texas Tech University
College of Business Administration
Box 4320
Lubbock, TX 79409

(806–742–1530, 1537;
  Telex: 910–896–4398, TTU-CID-LBK)

Major orientation: human resources, technical, and management
Budget: $275,000

Utah Center for Productivity and Quality of Working Life
Utah State University
Logan, UT 84322–3505
(801–750–2283)

Major orientation: human resources management
Budget: $140,000

Virginia Productivity Center
Department of Industrial Engineering
Virginia Polytechnic Institute
Blacksburg, VA 24061
(703–961–4568)

Major orientation: technical, management
Size: small

Work in America Institute
700 White Plains Road
Scarsdale, NY 10583
(914–472–9600)

Major orientation: human resources
Budget: $2 million

Work in Northeast Ohio Council
Suite 216
1440 Snow Road
Cleveland, OH 44134
(216–749–0150)

Major orientation: human resources management
Size: small

APPENDIX 2: OTHER NETWORKS ON PRODUCTIVITY

The American Productivity and Quality Center of Houston, TX maintains an electronic Computer Network on productivity in the public sector. All levels of government are invited to participate; the current topic is "Defense Contracting." White collar productivity is under consideration as a next topic for the Network.

For information: Ms. Anne Marsden, Manager of Administration and Research, American Productivity and Quality Center, 123 North Post Oak Lane, Houston TX 77024. (713–681–4020)

The National Productivity Center at John Jay College is in process of organizing an International Productivity Network, whose stated goals are to facilitate the international transfer of productivity-enhancing knowledge, to build the productive capacities of government organizations and enterprises, and to assist productivity improvement in developing countries.

For information: Dr. Marc Holzer, National Center for Public Productivity, John Jay College/CUNY, 445 West 59th Street, New York, NY 10019.

APPENDIX 3: FEDERAL GOVERNMENT SOURCES ON PRODUCTIVITY

The single largest publisher of information on productivity in this country is the United States Government. The following are the major sources.

U.S. Department of Commerce. National Technical Information Service (NTIS). The NTIS database exceeds 1 million titles, with several thousand on productivity, primarily related to the federal government. A telephone call to NTIS will result in a search of this database. Keywords: productivity, cost control, program evaluation. A nominal fee is charged; the user can obtain either a list of titles, or a complete document.

> U.S. Department of Commerce
> National Technical Information Service (NTIS)
> 5285 Port Royal Road
> Springfield, VA 22161
> (703–427–4660)

U.S. Department of Housing and Urban Development (HUD). HUD USER. The HUD USER database of over one million entries is primarily related to housing and development, but also includes all of the studies of the Capacity Sharing Division of HUD of the late 1970s and early 1980s. The Government Capacity Sharing Division produced numerous studies on alternative service delivery methods (including volunteers, contracting with the private sector and other government units, vouchers, franchises, and service demand limitation). Some of this is contained in the Office of Policy Development and Research, Government Capacity Sharing Division, "Alternative Services Kit." A title search is available upon phone inquiry. Current titles include the sale of public housing units to tenants.

> U.S. Department of Housing and Urban Development (HUD)
> HUD USER
> P.O. Box 280
> Germantown, MD 20874
> (1–800–245–2691)

U.S. Department of Labor, Bureau of Labor-Management Relations and Cooperative Programs. The Department of Labor maintains an updated series on productivity (labor costs) in various departments of the federal government. The Bureau of Labor-Management Relations (BLMR) studies white-collar productivity in the public and private sector. See its *Participative Approaches to White Collar Productivity Improvement* (Washington: BLMR 116, 1987), which includes an annotated bibliography of recent books and articles on white collar productivity, a list of white collar productivity study centers (similar to Appendix 1 of this volume), and Case Studies on white collar productivity.

> U.S. Department of Labor (DOL)
> Bureau of Labor-Management Relations and Cooperative Programs (BLMR)
> Washington, D.C. 20210
> (202–523–6231)

> U.S. Department of Labor (DOL)
> Bureau of Labor Statistics (BLS)
> 200 Constitution Avenue NW
> Washington, D.C. 20210
> (202–523–1327)

U.S. General Accounting Office (GAO). The GAO evaluates the performance of federal agencies and programs, including Value Engineering and other programs related to state and local government. Its evaluations now include "Management Audits," evaluating the efficiency and effectiveness of management systems. Its database is accessible to the public. GAO can provide a current bibliography of over 100 items, consisting of its studies of federal agencies and programs. The first five copies of any document are free; subsequent copies are $2.00. Make checks payable to Superintendent of Documents, and send to:

U.S. General Accounting Office (GAO)
Documents
P.O. Box 6015
Gaithersburg, MD 20877
(202–275–6241)

APPENDIX 4: JOURNALS AND NEWSLETTERS ON PUBLIC SECTOR PRODUCTIVITY AND COST CONTROL

Finance Alert (monthly newsletter). Legislation affecting bonds, grants, privatization. Editorial and business office: Nixon, Hargrave, Devans and Doyle, One Thomas Circle, Washington, D.C. (202–223–7200)

Fiscal Watchdog (monthly newsletter). Projects, training, techniques in contracting/privatization. Editorial and business office: The Local Government Center, 2716 Ocean Park Blvd., Suite 1062, Santa Monica, CA 90405. (213–392–0443)

Government Productivity News (monthly newsletter). News, reviews on government productivity and cost reduction. Editorial and business office: Government Productivity News, P.O. Box 27435, Austin, TX 78755–0403. (512–343–1884).

Guide to Management Improvement Projects in Local Government (quarterly, looseleaf pages). Project summaries of good ideas, half related to productivity, with contact names, numbers. Editorial and business offices: International City Management Association, 1120 G Street NW, Washington, D.C. 20005. (202–626–4600)

National Productivity Review (quarterly journal). Extended articles, reviews on both public and private productivity management. Editorial and business office: 33 West 60th Street, New York, NY 10023. (212–489–5911)

The Privatization Report (monthly newsletter). News, projects, meetings, reviews on privatization. Editorial and business office: Council on Municipal Performance/National Civic League, 55 West 44th Street, 6th Floor, New York, NY 10036. (212–730–7930)

The Privatization Review (quarterly journal). Extended articles, reviews on methods and projects in privatization of services and infrastructure. Editorial and business office: The Privatization Council Inc., 1101 Connecticut Avenue, N.W., Washington, D.C. 20036. (202–857–1142)

The Productivity Letter (quarterly newsletter). Projects, methods in public and private sector productivity, Editorial and business office: American Productivity and Quality Center, 123 North Post Oak Lane, Houston, TX 77024. (713–681–4020)

Public Productivity Review (quarterly journal). Academic, in-depth articles and reviews; co-sponsored by the American Society for Public Administration (ASPA). Editorial office: National Center for Public Productivity, John Jay College, New York City. Business office: Jossey-Bass Publishers, 443 California Street, San Francisco, CA 94104. (415–433–1730)

Public Technology (monthly newsletter). Exclusively on technological developments affecting the public sector. Editorial and business office: Public Technology Inc., 1301 Pennsylvania Avenue NW, Washington, D.C. 20004. (202–626–2400)

APPENDIX 5: INDEXES AND REFERENCE SOURCES ON PUBLIC SECTOR PRODUCTIVITY AND COST CONTROL

Index to Current Urban Documents (New York: Greenwood Press). Quarterly; cumulative volume each two years. Lists budget documents, evaluations, department reports, as issued by all municipalities, counties, special districts, and regional councils. Main subject entry: "Public employees—productivity." Typical entry:

> *Philadelphia PA.* Reducing Philadelphia's high compensation costs: two tiering and other alternatives (1 fiche)

Library of Congress *National Union Catalogue 1987.* All works in all languages catalogued by the Library of Congress in 1987; see also previous years, reported on microfiche. Subject entries: production engineering, production management, productivity accounting, productivity bargaining, management, management science, municipal finance, municipal government, personnel management.

Newsbank Urban Affairs Library Cumulative Index (New Canaan, CT: News-Bank Inc.) An annual Index with references to microfiche abstracts from broad range of academic and trade press. Typical entry (fiche citation omitted):

> *Employee and Employer Relations. Productivity.* Attitudes and opinions, Florida. Conference: Troy, New York. Gainsharing, conference: Michigan

Public Affairs Information Service (New York: Public Affairs Information Service Inc.). Quarterly; cumulative annual. An index of several hundred academic and trade publications, including dozens on local government and administration. Typical entry:

> *Efficiency, Administrative.* Pearce, Neil R. and Robert Guskind, "Fewer federal dollars spurring cities to improve management and trim costs." in *National Journal* 18:504–8, Mar 1, 1986

Sage Public Administration Abstracts (Newbury Park, CA: Sage Publications). Quarterly; cumulative annual. Devoted strictly to public administration, politics, and policy. Typical entry:

> *Administration & Politics.* D. R. Lee, "The tradeoff between equality and efficiency: Short-run politics and long-run realities," in *Public Choice* 53(2):149–165, 1987

Urban Affairs Abstracts (Washington, D.C.: The National League of Cities). Weekly; cumulative volume each six months. Typical entry:

> *"Employment & Labor. Productivity.* "Flexible work schedules, work attitudes, and perceptions of productivity," by Jean B. McGuire and Joseph R. Liro. *Public Personnel Management* 15(1):65–73, Spring 86 bibl 2 notes tables

BIBLIOGRAPHY:
PUBLIC SECTOR PRODUCTIVITY AND
COST CONTROL

This bibliography neither repeats references cited in this volume, nor does it stress organizational development (OD) or human resource management. It concentrates on volumes devoted to management-centered and technical methods for local public sector productivity.

Ammons, David N., *Municipal Productivity. A Comparison of Fourteen High-Quality-Service Cities* (New York: Praeger Special Studies, 1984).

Adam, N.R. and A. Dogramaci, eds., *Productivity Analysis at the Organizational Level* (Boston: Martinus Nijhoff, 1981).

Clark, Terry Nichols, and Lorna Crowley Ferguson, *City Money. Political Processes, Fiscal Strain, and Retrenchment* (New York: Columbia University Press, 1983).

Clark, Terry Nichols, ed., *Coping With Urban Austerity.* Vol. 1, *Research in Urban Policy* (Greenwich, CT: JAI Press Inc., 1984).

Clark, Terry Nichols, *Financial Handbook for Mayors and City Managers* (New York: Van Nostrand, 1985).

Committee for Economic Development, *Improving Productivity in State and Local Government* (New York: Committee for Economic Development, 1976).

Committee for Economic Development, *Improving Management of the Public Work Force: The Challenge to State and Local Government* (New York: Committee for Economic Development, 1978).

Cordry, Burton L. and Thomas C. Tuttle, *Performance Self Improvement Manual for Human Service Agencies* and *Executive Summary* (College Park, MD: Maryland Center for Productivity and Quality of Work Life, 1984).

Downs, G.D. and P.D. Larkey, *The Search for Government Efficiency: From Hubris to Help-lessness* (Philadelphia, PA: Temple University Press, 1986).

Eilon, S. *et al.*, *Applied Productivity Analysis for Industry* (Elmsford, NY: Pergamon Press, 1976).

Greiner, John M. *et al.*, *Productivity and Motivation. A Review of State and Local Government Initiatives* (Washington, D.C.: The Urban Institute Press, 1981).

Goldberg, Joel A. and Marc Holzer, eds., *The Resource Guide to Public Productivity* (New York: The National Center for Public Productivity, 1983).

Harvard University. John F. Kennedy School of Government. State, Local, and Intergovernmental Center. *Profiles In Innovation.* Selected Nominees in the 1986 Ford Foundation/Harvard University "Innovations in State & Local Government" Awards Competition (Cambridge, MA: the Center, 1986).

Herbert, Leo, *Auditing The Performance of Management* (Belmont, CA: Lifetime Learning Publications, 1979).

Heaton, H., *Productivity in Service Organizations: Organizing for People* (New York: McGraw-Hill, 1977).

Holzer, Marc, ed., *Productivity in Public Organizations* (Port Washington, NY: Kennikat Press, 1976).

Holzer, Marc and Stuart Nagel, eds., *Productivity and Public Policy* (Beverly Hills: Sage, 1984).

Holzer, Marc and Arie Halachmie, eds., *Strategic Issues in Public Sector Productivity: The Best of the Public Productivity Review, 1975–86* (San Francisco: Jossey-Bass, 1986).

Illinois State Department of Commerce and Community Affairs, *A Catalogue of Municipal Cost Cutting Techniques* (Springfield: Author, Cost Cutters Project, 1981). By the same project see the following monographs: "Cost Reduction Through Better Work Force Utilization"; "Preventive Management"; "Volunteers in Local Government"; "A Blueprint for Controlling Workers Compensation and Unemployment Insurance Costs"; and "Municipal Cash Management."

International City Management Association (ICMA), *Human Services on a Limited Budget* (Washington, D.C.: ICMA, 1979).

International City Management Association (ICMA), *Handbook. Local Government Productivity Improvement* (Washington, D.C.: ICMA, 1982).

International City Management Association (ICMA), *Managing With Less* (Washington, D.C.: ICMA, 1982).

Kendrick, J.W., *Improving Company Productivity* (Baltimore, MD: American Productivity Center, Johns Hopkins University Press, 1984).

Latham, Gary and Kenneth Wexley, *Increasing Productivity Through Performance Appraisal* (Reading, MA: Addison Wesley, 1981).

League of California Cities, *Alternative Service Delivery Project* (Sacramento: California League of Cities, 1984).

Lehrer, R.N., ed., *White Collar Productivity* (New York: McGraw-Hill, 1983).

Levin, Henry M., *Cost Effectiveness. A Primer*, Vol. 4, *New Perspectives in Evaluation* (Beverly Hills: Sage, 1983).

Matzer, Jack, Jr., ed., *Productivity Improvement Techniques: Creative Approaches for Local Government* (Washington, D.C.: International City Management Association, 1986).

Miller, George, comp., *Budget Balancers* (Chicago: Municipal Finance Officers Association, 1983).

Morley, Elaine, *A Practitioner's Guide to Public Sector Productivity Improvement* (New York: Van Nostrand Reinhold, 1986).

Morrisey, George L., *Management by Objectives and Results in the Public Sector* (Reading, MA: Addison-Wesley, 1983).

Mundel, Marvin E., *Motion and Time Study: Improvement Productivity*, 6th ed. (Englewood Cliffs, NJ: Prentice-Hall, 1985).

Prince George County, Maryland, *101 (Plus) Ways to Squeeze More Out of Your Local Government Dollar* (1983). (Available from: Procurement and Materiel Management Division, Prince George's County Government, County Administration Bldg. L-22, Upper Marlboro, MD 20772.)

Prince Waterhouse, *Value for Money Auditing Manual. The Investigation of Economy, Efficiency, and Effectiveness in Local Government* (London: Prince Waterhouse, 1984).

Rabin, Jack, *Public Budgeting Laboratory*. A Curriculum in Four Volumes (Athens: Carl Vinson Institute of Government, University of Georgia, 1983).

Ridley, Clarence E. and O.F. Nolting, *How Cities Can Cut Costs* (Chicago: International City Managers' Association, 1933).

Riggs, J.L. and G.H. Felix, *Productivity by Objectives* (Englewood Cliffs, NJ: Prentice-Hall, 1983).

Ross, J.P. and J. Burkhead, *Productivity in the Local Government Sector* (Lexington, MA: Lexington Books, 1974).

Scottsdale, City of, *Innovations. Scottsdale's Keynote and Tradition* (Scottsdale, AZ: City Government, c. 1987).

Sink, D. Scott, *Productivity Management: Planning, Measurement, Evaluation, Control, and Improvement* (New York: McGraw-Hill, 1985).

Somers, G. et al., *Collective Bargaining and Productivity* (Madison, WI: Industrial Relations Research Association, 1975).

Stone, Donald C., executive ed., *The County Executive's Management and Productivity Program. How To Do It* (Pittsburgh, PA: Carnegie-Mellon University, and the Coalition to Improve Management in State and Local Government, 1987).

Susskind, Lawrence E., Executive ed., *Proposition 2½: Its Impact on Massachusetts* (Cambridge, MA: Massachusetts Institute of Technology/Oelgeschlager, Gunn and Hain, 1983).

Taylor, Frederick W., *Principles of Scientific Management* (New York: Harper and Row, 1913).

Ullman, J.E., ed., *The Improvement of Productivity: Myths and Realities* (New York: Praeger, 1980).

Washnis, G.J., ed., *Productivity Improvement Handbook for State and Local Government* (New York: Wiley, 1980).

AUTHOR INDEX

SUBJECT INDEX

Value Engineering
   (*See* Value Analysis)
Value Management
   (*See* Value Analysis)

Walnut Creek, California
   and General Revenue Sharing cuts, 44

War on Poverty
   compared to Marshall Plan,
   4, 5; and federal grants
   growth, 11; and transfer payments, 231–232; and housing programs, 232, 233;
   compared to Enterprise
   Zones (EZs), 234